THE GROUP AS AN OBJECT
OF DESIRE

In this original and ground-breaking book, Morris Nitsun argues that desire and sexuality are key components of human experience that have been marginalized in the group psychotherapy literature.

Drawing on theory from psychoanalysis, developmental psychology and sociology, while keeping the group firmly in focus, he creates a picture of the potential in group therapy for the most intimate narrative. Highlighting current concerns about sexual identity, boundary transgression and what constitutes effective psychotherapy, detailed clinical illustrations cover areas such as:

- The erotic connection
- The dissociation of desire
- The group as witness
- Erotic transference and counter-transference

Psychotherapists and all those interested in sexual development and diversity will value the challenging approach to sexuality this book offers.

Morris Nitsun is a consultant clinical psychologist in Camden and Islington NHS Mental Health Trust. He is a training analyst at the Institute of Group Analysis and works privately at the Group Analytic Practice, London. He is a widely published author and has lectured and run workshops in many countries.

THE GROUP AS AN OBJECT OF DESIRE

Exploring sexuality in group therapy

Morris Nitsun

Routledge
Taylor & Francis Group

LONDON AND NEW YORK

First published 2006
by Routledge
27 Church Road, Hove, East Sussex, BN3 2FA

Simultaneously published in the USA and Canada
by Routledge
270 Madison Ave, New York, NY 10016

Routledge is an imprint of the Taylor & Francis Group

© 2006 Morris Nitsun

Typeset in Times by
RefineCatch Limited, Bungay, Suffolk
Printed and bound in Great Britain by
TJ International, Padstow, Cornwall
Cover by Hybert Design

British Library Cataloguing in Publication Data
A catalogue record for this book is available from the British Library

Library of Congress Cataloging in Publication Data
Nitsun, Morris.
The group as an object of desire : exploring sexuality in group
therapy / Morris Nitsun.
p. cm.
Includes bibliographical references and index.
ISBN 1-58391-871-X (hbk)—ISBN 1-58391-872-8 (pbk)
1. Group psychotherapy. 2. Small groups—Psychological aspects.
3. Sex (Psychology) I. Title.
RC488.N584 2006
616.89′152—dc22
2006002461

ISBN10: 1–58391–871–X (hbk)
ISBN10: 1–58391–872–8 (pbk)

ISBN13: 9–78–1–58391–871–X (hbk)
ISBN13: 9–78–1–58391–872–8 (pbk)

FOR JOE, BESSIE, LEON AND SHIRLEY

CONTENTS

PREFACE

This book represents my personal journey as a group psychotherapist since the publication in 1996 of *The Anti-group: Destructive Forces in the Group and their Creative Potential.* It reflects a journey from relative pessimism about groups to greater optimism. In the last decade or so, I have become aware of how much I enjoy running groups and how positive a sense I have about the potential of groups as a major psychotherapeutic medium. That it has taken me this long – almost two decades since I qualified as a group analyst – to feel fully integrated with the approach probably reflects my doubting personality but also the complexity and elusiveness of the group psychotherapeutic approach.

The Anti-group attempted to document and theorize the difficulties I and others encountered in the running of groups, etched against a background of the devaluing of group psychotherapy in the treatment milieu. I still believe this to be a problem. In spite of the growing application of group methods, there exists an underlying vein of mistrust of groups, a perception of group therapy as second-best and a tendency to believe that groups can be destructive. *The Anti-group* took the view that 1) such negative views of the group must be acknowledged and not obscured; 2) the recognition and containment of group antagonistic processes, particularly within the group, is vital; and 3) this could transform the potentially destructive into the creative. If this was always going to be an ambitious project, I have a sense that the transformation of my own feelings about group psychotherapy in some ways confirms the possibility. By confronting my own anti-group, through writing and years of conducting groups, I believe I have found a way through the maze of my own uncertainty and doubt.

The gradual strengthening of my belief in group therapy created a new challenge – how to convey my impressions of what it is that makes group therapy work, why running groups can be among the most stimulating and rewarding experiences a psychotherapist can have. My need to formulate a response coincided with the first significant contact I had with the work of Lacan – significantly, in the context of a workshop applying Lacan's ideas to group psychotherapy (at a two-day event run by Marcario Giraldo at the American Group Psychotherapy Congress in 2003). A seemingly unlikely connection, given Lacan's abstruseness, I nevertheless felt an immediate resonance with the Lacanian emphasis on desire. Desire, in Lacan's thinking, is not only the engine that drives human development and relationships, it is the organizing principle in analytic psychotherapy. It is also a contradictory principle. It expresses the forward movement of all things human and at the same time builds in lack and loss as essential parameters of life. This resonated further with me, because although I wanted to convey a sense of the group's vitality and value, I sought to present a realistic, not idealized, picture of group psychotherapy and to recognize the disappointment of desire as well as to celebrate its fulfilment.

The emphasis on desire immediately tied up for me with the subject of sexuality. I had for years been aware of the underrepresentation of sexuality in the group discourse and I could now begin to see a direction of travel. By linking concepts of desire with sexuality I could address an important and neglected area of group psychotherapy.

This connected with another personal theme. I had for years struggled with complex aspects of my own sexuality, aware of how difficult it was to deal with these fully as a patient in both psychoanalysis and group analysis. Possibly, my difficulties in the group experience were compounded by my status as a trainee group analyst, given the additional anxieties attendant on being a trainee. This in turn impressed upon me the extent to which sexuality is linked to social processes, how it is affected by institutional pressures and constraints and how the individual difficulties people have are to a large degree reflective of these processes. This – the social influences on sexuality – it became clear, would have to be a focus in my treatment of the subject, alongside the other dimension of enormous importance – the personal, private and intensely subjective experience of sexuality. How to link the two would be the particular challenge.

Formulating the anti-group was my initial journey of exploration and discovery on becoming a group analyst. Writing *The Group as an Object of Desire* became the second major journey. Although producing the book has been difficult, because of the absence of a discourse of any substance on the subject, it has been an illuminating and enriching journey. I hope it will be the same for readers of the book.

I particularly want to thank the following, each a colleague and a friend, who travelled with me. Wil Pennycook Greaves, my 'muse', accompanied me all the way, a wise, informed and inspiring presence, her help alternating between discussions of the vicissitudes of desire, walks in the woods and therapy over cups of coffee; John Schlapobersky, whose friendship, encouragement and astute criticism helped greatly to give the book its shape; and Bracha Hadar, who met me briefly, intensely and valuably on the journey.

Looking further afield, I want to thank my IGA peer supervision group 'Nexus' (Geraldine Festenstein, Graham Fuller, Diana Kinder, Carmen O'Leary and Phil Schulte), who are an ongoing source of stimulation and support; the Institute of Group Analysis (London) itself for being a welcoming home; and the Group Analytic Practice (London) which gave me the opportunity for some of the most creative group work I could have done anywhere. I also want to thank my many colleagues in the NHS, specifically in the Psychology Departments of both the Camden and Islington Mental Health Trust and the North-East London Mental Health Trust, where the opportunities I have to develop a group culture are a continuing challenge and reward. I want further to thank my many supervisees, some qualified group analysts and some trainees, who bring refreshment and novelty to my work and who have provided many of the examples which, in disguised fashion, I have included in the book. Among those outside group analysis who gave me permission to use their clinical material I particularly want to acknowledge Sheila Melzack. I would like to thank several people in the USA who have inspired and supported my work: Maria Ross, Scott Conkright and Jerry Garrs. I also wish to thank my secretary, Kathy Reddington, who deals patiently with my many technologically-induced panics, and Lucia Asnaghi, the librarian at IGA, who has been a consistent help. My appreciation goes to my publishers, Routledge, who were welcoming and supportive, and to Malcolm Pines, who, as one of the publisher's readers, gave me valuable feedback.

Last but by no means least, I want to thank my partner of 25 years, Tony Fagin, for standing by me, believing in me and insisting that I stick to the same forms of punctuation throughout the book.

INTRODUCTION

The group as an object of desire refers to the passionate group, a group in which there is a high level of commitment and involvement, in which there are intense experiences of closeness and intimacy, and in which there are deep resonances from heart to heart as well as mind to mind. Sexuality as a theme flows naturally in such a group: acknowledging it, sharing it, exploring it.

Does such a group exist or is this an ideal to which we can only aspire? This question preoccupies group psychotherapists in one form or other, since the desire of the therapist is to create conditions in which the group can flourish and in which the challenge of development can counteract the ravages of psychological trauma and injury. In my previous book, *The Anti-group: Destructive Forces in the Group and their Creative Potential* (Nitsun 1996), I explored the darker, disruptive aspects of the group and the undermining effect these can have on the therapeutic task, yet with the possibility that these processes, recognized and contained, could strengthen the development of the group. The present book approaches the group from a complementary perspective – the elements of the group that make it an alive, intense, exciting experience. If *The Anti-group* dealt with the anti-libidinal group, the group that is saturated with hostility and alienation, the present book deals with the libidinal group – the group that encourages the expression of desire, fantasy, affection, attachment and love.

What the two books have in common is the highly charged nature of their themes. Sexuality, like aggression, is germane to the development of the group, but its expression can create anxiety and discomfort and it is often avoided and dissociated. A striking parallel exists in the group psychotherapy literature, where the relative lack of publications on desire and sexuality reflects an equivalent form of marginalization. In my own field of group analysis, sexuality is

1

virtually an absent discourse. In one of the very few group analytic publications on sexuality, Burman (2002) comments on the silence regarding the erotic. She and a handful of other writers have questioned why a theme that is so integral to subjectivity is so missing in the published literature.

Is the answer that sexuality is socially transgressive? In the urge for sexual expression there is a desire to penetrate the conventional boundaries of intimacy, to flout conservative representations of sexuality, even to transgress against the sexual object itself, which may be experienced as withholding and tantalizing. This predicates a temporary divorce from the social field. In the moment of consummation, in particular, there is a suspension of the self. Kernberg (1995: 24) notes: 'The ecstatic and aggressive features of the effort to transcend the boundaries of the self represent a complex aspect of erotic desire'. He quotes Bataille (1975) as proposing that the most intense experiences of transcendence occur under the 'sign' of love and the 'sign' of aggression. There is a breakdown between self and other in moments of sexual ecstasy. These are moments of intense connection, uniting the individual with their biological and social inheritance, but they also express a form of rebellion, a wish to escape the pressures of wider social being, to transgress the constraining and prohibiting effects of society.

Conceiving the term 'the group as an object of desire', I am aware of introducing a complex and ambiguous construct, particularly in the use of the word 'desire'. How can a group be an object of desire? In order to make sense of this seeming linguistic contradiction, I suggest a way of thinking that draws on Cox and Theilgaard's (1994) notion of 'conceptual triangulation'. They use the concept of triangulation not in the psychoanalytic sense but as a metaphor borrowed from the technical work of the surveyor. It is through the process of triangulation that the surveyor is able to take bearings from two different reference points and thus establish a particular location. My two vantage points are 1) the emergence of desire as the object of the group and 2) the evolution of the group as an object of desire – in the sense of a wanted, valued experience. I suggest an interplay between desire as generated *in* the group and desire as developed in relation *to* the group. Of course, I use 'desire' in two different ways here: desire expressed in the group is largely sexual; desire of, or for, the group reflects the broader quest for an experience of engagement, communication and transformation. The point of location in this construct, unlike in the analogy of the surveyor, is not a precise or fixed one but an unfolding, emerging experience of connection in which desire is an integral theme.

The notion of the group as an object of desire is influenced by Lacan's (1988a) emphasis on desire as both the heart of human experience and the mainspring of the analytic process, in which the analysis becomes an 'object of desire'. It is also linked to the concept of transformation (Bollas 1987), in which the therapeutic process functions as a form of 'transformational object'. I of course use the term 'object' in its figurative rather than literal sense and am not attempting to either reify or deify the group. In a sense, the analogy of the surveyor falls away here, as we are dealing with a complex, ambiguous process of communication and identification rather than any form of static object.

This book opens up the field of sexuality in the group and the reciprocal influence of individual and group in the emergence of the sexual subject. We are more used to thinking about sex, desire and the erotic in the dyadic context. Even there, sexuality is a sensitive subject, often difficult to address openly and honestly. Transfer this to the group and the sensitivities are compounded. We begin to get closer here to the social representation of sexuality, to the cultural and moral influences that are mediated by the group. I aim to cover in this book the full terrain from the individual, subjective experience of desire and sexuality to the social processes that construct sexuality. These domains are often viewed as separate, as polar opposites in the structure of self and society. However, I suggest that a group psychotherapy perspective on sexuality might be forged through recognition that these apparently separate domains are mutually constitutive, that 'sexual self' and 'group self' are closely intertwined.

I present an optimistic view of sexuality in group therapy, and the considerable potential for developing a sexual discourse, but I acknowledge the problematic nature of sexuality for many people and the difficulty of revealing the sexual self. I also recognize that the line between libidinal and anti-libidinal forces is a fragile one. In all sexual relationships, hostility, sadism and masochism play some part and in certain relationships these are fused in such a way that sexuality is split and fragmented. Further, I make no assumptions about the ease with which desire is satisfied. Much of human desire cannot be satisfied and, if satisfied, this tends to be on a fleeting, temporary basis. So, the experience of frustration and disappointment must be recognized and with it a sense of lack or loss (Lacan 1988a). But the experience of longing and disappointment is an essential part of growth and the sharing of this in a group helps to assuage the fantasy

3

of perfect fulfilment, while supporting the areas in which desire can be realized. It is this complementary perspective, embracing the polarities of desire and loss, excitement and frustration, in the immediacy of the group, that gives the experience its depth. Through containing these polarities, the group is imbued with authenticity and value, itself becoming an object of desire.

Another aspect of the group as an object of desire concerns its status as a psychotherapeutic medium. In spite of the widespread practice of group psychotherapy, there is a continuing level of mistrust of the group. Relative to individual psychotherapy, it still tends to be viewed as second-best. This view is shared to some extent by professionals and patients alike, reflected in a study by Bowden (2002) on anti-group attitudes in the NHS in the UK. The perceived lack of safety is frequently given as a reason for devaluing groups. How much this is connected with sexuality is difficult to say. Certainly, the sense conveyed is that groups cannot be trusted with the most vulnerable and intimate aspects of the self – and sexuality is intrinsically a part of this. This touches on the important issue of shame. Sexuality and shame are closely linked (Mollon 2003). The problem about revealing the sexual self is often a problem of revealing shame. Hence, the recognition of shame and its expression in the group is a significant aspect of the much-needed sexual discourse.

The focus on sexuality in group therapy is all the more timely in view of the increasing complexity of gender and sexual differentiation in contemporary society. Whereas at the beginning of group psychotherapy and for some decades afterwards the prevailing ethic was essentially heterosexual, we have seen in recent decades the emergence of a range of alternative sexualities, with homosexuality in particular becoming a more visible and accepted part of the social milieu. Although sexual variations have always been present, the growing adoption and living-out of alternative sexual lifestyles has important implications for the individuals concerned and their groups of belonging. People in these sexual categories may increasingly present for group psychotherapy, making it necessary for the group therapist to recognize the spread of diversity, to consider the impact of sexual diversity in the group and to incorporate such diversity in the unfolding of the therapeutic process. Apart from the increasing acknowledgement of sexual diversity between individuals, there is a similar recognition of diversity within individuals, in line with notions of sexual plasticity (Giddens 1992) and fluidity (Schwartz 1995), reflecting the deconstruction of culturally prescribed norms of sexual identity.

I place a particular emphasis on homosexuality as a theme in group psychotherapy. This is a deliberate decision in line with the observation above about the increased recognition of homosexuality in society and the implications this has for psychotherapeutic practice. This is a particularly neglected area of group psychotherapy, including group analysis, highlighting the very processes of denial, marginalization and prejudice that we seek to address in our groups. There is now a substantial literature on the unsatisfactory psychotherapeutic treatment homosexuals have received in past decades, illustrating at best inconsequential and at worst damaging effects on individuals. How homosexuality is conceptualized, diagnosed or understood, pathologized or recognized, is a strong indication of the underlying value systems that inform clinical practice. I suggest that the subject merits serious attention in the emerging sexual discourse in group psychotherapy.

There is a major emphasis in the book on the group therapist/ analyst and their role in the unfolding of sexual and erotic material in the group. The therapist is situated in their own cultural context and the way they define sexual morality will strongly influence the extent to which they establish a group context in which sexuality can be openly, constructively and non-judgementally addressed. Further, the therapist's use of self in the sexual discourse is a significant influence. As sexual beings, we have our own needs for admiration and love, often mirroring our patients' narcissistic needs and creating subtle interpersonal patterns of attraction, arousal and tantalization. While this is a natural part of group intimacy, problems may arise when the therapist, rather than the group, is the object of desire. This is linked to the potential for erotic transference and counter-transference, a particularly complex development in the therapy group.

The book aims to achieve a balance between the theoretical and the clinical, ideally helping to strengthen the theory-practice link which often seems to be missing in group therapy because of the intricate nature of the group process. The book is 'clinical' in the sense that it gives full weight to the experience of the individual in the group and what they get out of it. In so far as the clinical is about the personal, there can be no more personal, subjective and individual material than in the sexual domain. I emphasize this because of my recognition of the social and group processes that influence – and are influenced by – sexuality. But these should help to understand rather than to obscure the individual. The need to hold in balance the individual and group perspective is a constant challenge in group psychotherapy, no less so in the area of sexuality.

Since much of the book is nevertheless concerned with theory, I need to make some preliminary points about this. The absence of a theoretical discourse of any substance on sexuality in group psychotherapy requires us to go further afield, to other disciplines which have engaged with the sexual. Philosophy, psychology, literature and the visual arts have all explored desire and sexuality in their own terms. Some of these contributions are reviewed later in the book but the main port of call is psychoanalysis. Psychoanalysis has not just explored sexuality: it has made it its province. It is a chosen territory, arising from Freud's universalizing of sexuality as the mainspring of human development and psychological conflict. The result is a very detailed account of sexual development that reaches into the sexual psyche as well as locating sexuality in terms of the clash between the sexual impulse and the restraining social order. The problem is that the construction of sexuality in the psychoanalytic view takes limited account of social influences – the recognition that sexuality is socially constructed and that the biological itself is subject to cultural inscriptions. Society in the psychoanalytic view is there in opposition to the instincts rather than as a moulder, a creator of the sexual narrative. The result is a normative account of sexuality based on the 'discourse of nature' (Dimen 1995) that creates a binary perspective of gender differences and pathologizes practically anything outside of a circumscribed notion of heterosexuality. Denman (2004: 65) refers to 'the long and only partially corrected tendency for psychoanalysis to confuse personal, moral and sexual preferences for sexual pathology'.

Compared to the dense, provocative and controversial contribution of psychoanalysis to the understanding of sexuality, group psychotherapy has hardly touched the subject. A peculiar, avoidant, ambiguous silence prevails. But silence on a subject of such human importance may be the focus of critical enquiry: does the silence mean evasion, a collusion with dominant moral standards or an as yet unspecified problem regarding the nature of group psychotherapy?

The dilemma is highlighted when I consider the field of my own specialist interest, group analysis. Here is a field started by a psychoanalyst, Foulkes, that has developed an impressive body of theory and practice which almost totally excludes sexuality. This may reflect the greater social emphasis of group analysis than most psychotherapeutic approaches, including other group therapies. Although this is not necessarily intended, the social emphasis tends to marginalize the individual and areas of experience, such as sexuality, that have both a highly subjective and strongly biological aspect. There is a risk, I believe, that if taken to an extreme, this approach could seriously compromise, if not alienate, the sense of a sexual self in our conceptual discourse. This would reflect what Webster (1995 cited in Nightingale and Cromby 1999) refers to as 'a cryptotheologistic attitude' which has led to the prioritizing of the rational and the mental over the embodied, the desiring and the carnal. In a critique of social constructionism, Nightingale and Cromby describe this attitude as rooted in the evolutionary origins of the psychological disciplines as secular continuations of Christian doctrine. By elevating the mental, they blind us to evidence concerning both the impact of biology on human action (embodiment) and the interlocking constitution of self and society (personal-social history). The challenge is to link rather than separate these discourses, since sexuality comprises the full spectrum of biological, psychological and social domains.

When it comes to sexuality, psychoanalysis and group analysis find themselves in contradictory positions. With its emphasis on an individual perspective, biologically conceived, psychoanalysis is prone to a restrictively normative and pathologizing approach. Yet, it provides a discourse that is rich in detail and resonance. Group analysis, with its tendency to underplay the individual in favour of the social, marginalizes the sexual and compromises the intimate narrative that is essential to sexuality. But it opens horizons of understanding, via the social, that may illuminate the sexual discourse. Both approaches have strengths and limitations. This book explores the possibility of forging a group psychotherapy perspective on sexuality that bridges the gap.

An outline of the book

The book is divided into four parts. *Part 1, 'The Wider Discourse'*, is mainly theoretical, aiming to establish the framework for a sexual discourse which is largely missing in group psychotherapy. Chapter 1 looks at desire as a theme in western culture. The complexities of desire and its relationship to loss and disappointment are highlighted, as are the links between gender, sexual identity and desire. Chapter 2 provides an overview of sexual development within the biopsychosocial perspective of sexuality. The sexual journey from childhood to adulthood is traced, including the origins of sexual identity and orientation, and processes such as attachment-detachment, sexual fluidity-rigidity and shame. Chapter 3 evaluates the contribution of psychoanalysis to our understanding of sexuality.

The achievement of a detailed account of sexual desire and relationships is diminished by its essentialist-biological leanings, the adherence to orthodox norms and a failure to recognize the social construction of sexuality. Chapter 4 focuses on the politics of sexuality. Cultural analysis reveals the impact of conformity and prejudice on sexual experience. Challenges are presented in the form of feminism, the gay rights movement, queer theory and radical psychoanalysis, all of which have supported the emergence of sexual diversity.

Part 2, 'The Group Discourse', evaluates the extent to which group psychotherapy has addressed the theme of sexuality and the potential for representing sexuality in the group. Chapter 5 is a review of a series of published papers on the related themes of desire, eroticism and sexuality, gender and the Oedipal situation in the group. Only some of these papers specifically concern sexuality but this is a promising beginning. Chapter 6 focuses specifically on group analysis. Beginning with Foulkes' original theories, it traces the evolution of group analysis through a succession of writers I call the 'developers' and 'later contributors' to recent formulations that I describe as 'the sociological turn'. The passage of this thinking reflects a continuing marginalization of sexuality. Chapter 7 is my attempt to forge a group psychotherapy perspective of sexuality in which I take account of social and cultural processes in the conscious and unconscious formation of individual sexuality. It is suggested that the therapy group has the potential to provide a more benign, more empathic authority than is usually encountered in the development of sexuality.

Part 3, 'The Clinical Discourse', moves from theory into the consulting room. A wide range of examples illustrates the manifestations of sexuality in the therapy group, highlighting areas of considerable growth as well as those of difficulty in the expression of desire and sexuality in the group. Chapter 8 considers the erotic or libidinal connection in groups, presented here in positive terms as a generative process in the group. Chapter 9 explores the theme of incest in the group, both as historical data and as sexually related feelings in the group itself. Chapter 10 gives examples of the dissociation of desire, describing in one group the destructive impact of encapsulated desire and in another the work of the group in integrating splits arising from the dissociation. Chapter 11 introduces the notion of the group as witness to describe the function of the group as an observing and reflecting presence in relation to intimacy in the group. Chapter 12 addresses the problem of sexual pairing, referring specifically to couples who enact a sexual relationship outside of the group. Chapter 13 explores erotic transference and counter-transference in group therapy and the particular challenges this presents to the therapist. Chapter 14 illustrates the subject of homo-sexuality in groups with mixed sexes and sexual orientations, the examples showing that this can be productive but also problematic.

Part 4, 'The Linked Discourse', draws the book to a close. Chapter 15 focuses on the group therapist and the personal, moral and sexual aspects of the therapist that influence the approach to sexuality in the group. The question of training is highlighted here, alongside organizational issues in the training institute. Chapter 16 is an overview of the theoretical and clinical discourses in the book, attempting to draw together an overall statement about sexuality in the group. Problems inhering in the realization of the sexual dis-course in group therapy, including ethical concerns, are delineated. However, the conclusion reached is that sexuality is a vital aspect of the therapy group and that there is much potential to develop a substantial sexual discourse within the reconstructive sphere of the group.

Part 1

THE WIDER DISCOURSE

1

DISCOURSES OF DESIRE

Andre Breton, one of the leading figures of the Surrealist movement in the 1930s, described desire as 'the sole motivating principle of the world, the only master that humans must recognize' (1937: 11). The Surrealists dedicated their work to the liberation of desire, passionately influenced by Freud's journey into sexuality and repression and the emerging revolutionary trend that sought to 're-sexualize' society. They saw desire both as the inner voice of the self, an expression of authentic being, and a force that linked self to others in an empowered society. In the century that followed, the psychoanalytic emphasis on desire as the central organizing force in human experience waxed and waned, surfacing strongly in the work of Lacan and the French psychoanalysts, diminishing in the evolution of object relations theory and resurfacing in the writing of some contemporary American relational psychoanalysts.

The subject of desire has hardly been touched on by group psychotherapists, including group analysts. Yet, it represents a major challenge to the vision of the group as a therapeutic medium. Since desire is usually very private, and sexual desire in particular may harbour transgressive wishes, how far can group members go in revealing their desires in the social arena of the group, with its connotations of judgement and censure? If desire is at the core of human experience, in all its intensely personal and subjective forms, how is it represented in the group? Is it possible to give voice to individual desire in the collective of the group? Further, what happens to desire in recent group analytic theory developments which argue against an individual perspective in general, and the notion of individual centres of energy in particular, in favour of a social perspective of the group?

Throughout this book, I suggest that group psychotherapy has marginalized sexuality and desire in the evolution of theory and practice and that a critical reappraisal is needed, with the aim of establishing desire in the group domain or at least understanding the constraints that prevent it from being established. How much is the marginalization of desire a product of a particular therapeutic medium with its own, defined value system and how much is it a defence against the intensity and potential disruptiveness of desire, particularly if given free rein in a group? There is also the question of whether the group itself can evoke desire: not so much desire among the participants but desire of the group as an experience in itself. This chapter aims to provide an overall framework within which these questions can be considered, drawing on traditions that include psychoanalysis, philosophy and arts discourse.

The journey starts with Plato and moves on to Freud, the perspectives of Lacan, philosophers such as Bataille and Dollimore, and contemporary American writers such as Emmanuel Ghent, Jody Davies and Jessica Benjamin. These are mostly writers who view desire as both deeply individual and socially contextualized. Although none of them write about groups in a clinical sense, their work frequently verges on group concerns. In fact, it is interesting to see that many writers who give prominence to desire are also attuned to wider social issues and the role of desire in shaping society (and vice versa). Returning for a moment to the Surrealists, Lomas describes how they extrapolated from the poetics of desire a politics and ethics of surrealist revolt, a 'belief in erotic desire as the agent of a critical transformation in human consciousness. Desire, unquench-able and indomitable, is a *convulsive* force to be pitted against the despised status quo of bourgeois, patriarchal society and religion' (Lomas 2001: 55). This agenda was echoed in the views of a group of radical Freudians, mainly Reich and Marcuse, who advocated a revolutionary sexual programme to revitalize society (see Chapter 3).

The aims of group psychotherapy are more modest than the radicalization of society but they concern change at personal and interpersonal levels, and there is a question about how far change can go in the absence of seeing and knowing desire. In any case, desire is multi-form. Dimen (1995) refers to the sea of desire that envelops us. Le Brun (2001: 305) described desire as 'neither masculine nor feminine' and so wide-ranging that 'we are carried away to the very antipodes of what we are'. But desire is not only about the grand passions. It is also about the wish for small and precious experiences. What is common to all levels of desire is the wish to have, to appropriate for oneself, something of the other, of the external world. Recognizing desire contributes to self-knowledge but with it comes an upsurge of conflicting feelings – a sense of the right to desire and a fear of doing so, feelings of shame and guilt about un-nameable desire, resentment about the thwarting and frustration of desire, envy of those who dare to desire and get what they want. It is not an absolute state but is embedded in the intricacies of the self and the relationship to the other. It is in relationships that desire lives or dies, prospers or withers, enriches or deprives. These are as much the themes of group psychotherapy as they are of individual psychotherapy, perhaps even more so because of the interactional setting of the group. If anything, the group, with its plural membership, pulsates with desire, providing a dense playground for the exploration of desire.

Rather than attempting a comprehensive review, this chapter is a configuration of ideas and perspectives on desire that contribute to our understanding of it as a subject in psychotherapy generally and group psychotherapy in particular. I am not arguing for or against a particular theoretical standpoint or value system, other than the substantiation of desire as a crucial aspect of our lives and a vital part of the therapeutic dialogue.

Plato – the perfect union

Although much of this chapter is devoted to the complexity of desire, it is useful to start with a familiar myth that emphasizes a simple but profound quest – the longing to find a perfect partner. The myth recounted in Plato's *Symposium* concerns the theory that each human being originated as a rounded whole with two faces, two backs, four arms and four legs. When the god Zeus cut these creatures in two (out of fear of their strength and aggression), this unleashed a yearning in each part to find its lost partner and return to its original state. The perfect lovers are those who have been joined together in a complete whole.

Armstrong (2003) comments that this vision of original unity has had a powerful influence on the romantic imagination in suggesting that we live with an abiding lack or longing which we hope will be redeemed in love. Echoes of this vision can be found throughout literature and psychoanalysis and are repeated throughout this chapter: the desire to merge with another is widely regarded as one of the most fundamental desires. Whereas Plato's myth offered no resolution to the problem – the one half was destined forever to search for the other – psychotherapeutic approaches have tended to emphasize resolution through a process of mourning: grieving the loss of the ideal and accepting the unavailability of perfect union.

I have previously referred to the preference for individual over group psychotherapy as an expression of the longing for merging with one other individual (Nitsun 1991, 1996). Whereas individual therapy is believed to provide a relationship that in itself will satisfy this need or provide a route to its satisfaction, group therapy is seen by some as counter to this need: having to share attention in the group and having to share the therapist frustrates and contradicts the fantasy of the one perfect other. The group is then experienced as intrusive or superfluous. In this sense, it cannot become an object of desire. I suspect that this may be more of a problem if the underlying desire for a relationship with one other is unrecognized or minimized in the establishment of a group culture. If the group takes account of this longing and deals with the ensuing disappointment and resentment, the likelihood of therapeutic integration in the group, I suggest, is greater.

Freud and desire

Freudian theory has an ambiguous status in the twenty-first century. Regarded by many as anachronistic, a curiosity, reductive in its broad generalizing sweeps and dominated by outdated biologistic and instinctual thinking, it nevertheless revealed and explored in great detail the complexity of desire in the individual and social context. Its themes remain relevant to the present-day and the centring of desire in the work of Lacan and more contemporary theorists is directly traceable to Freud's unflinching investigation of sexuality in human development.

Freud's theory of infantile sexuality and its consequences is in many ways the epic story of desire: desire that is primal, immediate and demanding, that is an intense combination of bodily urges and primitive imagination. But it is also a story of the frustration and surrender of desire. In his earlier writing, Freud envisaged this as a struggle between the pleasure principle and the reality principle: he regarded these as the two most essential but conflicting tendencies in human behaviour. The pleasure principle impels the individual towards immediate, impulsive action and instant gratification. The reality principle imposes the obstacles towards immediate gratification and the need to delay satisfaction. Between them, the individual finds an uneasy, unsettled, reluctant compromise.

Adam Phillips (1998), strongly aligning his views with those of

Freud, laments the loss of the innocent and passionate desire of the child. He describes the child as 'the beast in the nursery', a creature that is born 'in turbulent love with the world' but that is tamed from early on by the dulling effects of education and social conformity. Dollimore (1999) comments on the Victorians' outrage at the idea of childhood sexuality. In spite of overwhelming evidence that this exists, there remains a fierce resistance to it. Dollimore suggests that in part this is because of the discomfort it causes adults: '. . . the child confronts adults with their own renunciation of instinct; the child *is* what we have lost' (1999: 183). In Freud's vision, the infant is the 'virtuoso of desire' and infantile sexuality is seen as 'a kind of apotheosis of curiosity' (Phillips 1998: 6, 16). It is almost as though the child is lived by, or lives through, its sexual curiosity. This sexual curiosity is intensely bodily and at the same time a quest for understanding one's place in the world, in the chain of life and in the relationship with family, parents and siblings (Nitsun 1994). Desire is therefore linked to questions about existence and purpose in life and these twin lines of interest continue throughout life. But whereas existential questions can be addressed in a variety of contexts, sexual curiosity itself is dampened, repressed, dissociated.

Freud's preoccupation with the repression of sexuality and its social implications deepened in his later years when he shifted his focus to civilization as a whole and suggested that the very existence of civilization depended on the subjugation of sexuality. Dollimore (1999: 183) notes:

> As is well known, for Freud the evolution, not to say the very survival, of civilization depends upon the containment, restriction, repression, sublimation and channeling of sexual desire. The early efflorescence of infantile sexuality is doomed to extinction as we become constrained, organized (fixed/fixated) as subjects in the social order, always haunted by the loss of that original libidinal freedom. Our original instinctual energies remain forever alienated in order that civilization may be, but those energies are never entirely eliminated; there remains an unending conflict between the demands of the original instincts and those of civilization. Even when the processes of repression are as successful as they can be, that conflict remains at the heart of the human individual.

Freud's earlier theories of the libido and the pleasure and reality principles yielded in his late work to the concepts of Eros and Thanatos, the life and the death instincts. Abel-Hirsch (2001) describes Eros as 'the principle of attraction'. It is the idea of a force which 'binds together' the elements of human existence – physically through sex, emotionally through love and mentally through imagination. Thanatos, the death instinct, by contrast, is an unbinding force which destroys the ties of sex, love and imagination.

The concept of Eros has significant analogies to the group process in its positive and optimistic forms. Eros is not just about sex: it is about connection and relationship. Freud saw the life instinct as holding all living things together, as creating increasingly greater unities out of living substances 'so that life may be prolonged and brought to higher development' (Freud 1923: 258) and aiming at 'complicating life and at the same time, of course, preserving it' (1923: 40). Freud also described Eros as a force that creates difference. The unifying process is at the same time a differentiating one. This has a disruptive effect and creates renewal through the collision of differences, while the ultimate aim remains that of integration and cohesion. Kennedy (2001) draws attention to the disruptive, even destructive, potential of Eros, reflected in the destabilization of emotions in the passionate response, the turmoil of falling in love and the intense affects that may follow, such as yearning, jealousy and rage.

The parallel between Eros as desire/sexuality and a collectivizing force that both differentiates and unites is a potent metaphor for group psychotherapy. It is surprising that Foulkes, the originator of group analysis, an avowed Freudian who expressed a strong belief in the dual instinct theory, never made this connection or linked desire with the generative process of the group. Freud's definition of the life instinct highlights very similar processes of differentiation/ integration and cohesion/coherence to those which are commonly referred to as the core processes of group development. I draw attention to this not to make of Freud's theory a group psychology, which it is not, but to begin to explore the function of desire as a connecting and differentiating force within the group.

The major thesis of Freud's dual instinct theory, of course, was not the separate operation of the instincts but the clash between the life and the death instincts, and with this came his pessimism about the fate of desire. In his paper, 'Beyond the pleasure principle', Freud (1920) committed himself to a dark vision of the death instinct: 'The aim of all life is death', he stated, an instinctual movement towards a state in which there is a complete absence of excitation, a state of non-tension characteristic of the inorganic or the inanimate. In his view, this explained not only the conflict in the human psyche but the perpetual cycles of violence that keep not just particular societies but civilization itself on the edge of extinction. His pessimism was reflected at several levels: the destiny of society as a whole, the human struggle to keep desire alive in the face of anxiety and repression, and the outcome of psychoanalysis which he saw as more fragmentary and limited than was usually acknowledged (Thompson 1991).

In spite of the intense criticism that Freud's theories evoked, his ideas have in many ways been inscribed in western thinking. Dollimore (1999) shows how they opened up, in particular, a rich seam of thought about desire and loss in western thought. In some of this thinking, what is emphasized is not so much death and destruction as concrete events but a sense of the inherent mutability of life: the inevitability of loss and change. Dollimore describes this as a narrative of human desire riven by loss. The sense of pervasive, lurking loss animates desire, the wish to re-find the lost object, to replenish and renew the subjective world, but it can also foreclose and dissipate desire. Bataille (1987) argues that the aim of eroticism is to replace a deep sense of discontinuity (we must all die) with a sense of continuity. Bowie (1991: 165), in his fine study of Lacan, describes desire as 'the alpha of experience already overprinted with the omega of death'. Different strategies have been propounded for dealing with this dilemma. Dollimore (1999) suggests playing mutability at its own game: instead of yearning for permanence in the relationship with desire, consider the fleeting, subversive pleasures of flirting, of promiscuity, the chance sexual encounter. This challenges a conventional morality tied to the illusion of permanence.

I have previously noted several attempts to interpret the death instinct in terms that make it more palatable (Nitsun 1996). Various writers advocate a psychological reinterpretation. Segal (1993) argues that it reflects the longed-for state of peace and reconciliation in the face of intolerable frustration that is explicable in psychological and not necessarily instinctive terms. Boothby (1991), writing on Lacan, contends that the drive aims not at the extinction of the organism as a whole but the dissolution of the self, the ego in its defensive and imaginary unity. It has also been suggested that the value of the concept of the death instinct lies not in its (arguable) status as an explanatory theory but in its strength as a critical principle. Thompson (1991) maintains that it usefully challenges conventional assumptions about human development as well as the optimism about psychoanalytic outcomes.

In spite of these reinterpretations, the dual instinct theory, parti-cularly the concept of the death instinct, tends to evoke strong criti-cism. Much of this criticism has come from psychoanalysis itself, a point that is often overlooked, particularly in relation to Freud's mechanistic model of the mind. Increasingly, the Freudian meta-psychology has been revised in relational terms. However, it is unarguable that his insights stimulated a narrative of desire that holds significance until the present time and that his emphasis on the paradoxical nature of desire is as contemporary now as it was in his time.

Lacan

The French psychoanalyst, Jacques Lacan, has presented what is probably the most obscure, complex and elusive of all psycho-analytic theories. However, in one respect Lacan is clear – the central importance of desire in both the individual psyche and the analytic consulting room. Bowie (1991: 158) sums up the enormous relevance of the concept in Lacan's vision as 'a theory of the desiring speech in which all living beings live and die'. For Lacan, desire is irrevocably linked to *lack*. The sense of lack is aligned to a desired other, the desire for and of the other, reflecting an ongoing quest for merging with the other, a quest that is essentially unfulfillable since the moment of satisfaction gives way to a new moment of desire, in an unending chain: 'Desire is desire only if it succeeds in postponing something' (Verhaeghe 1999: 151). For Lacan, 'there is something fundamentally impossible about satisfaction itself' (Mitchell 1982: 6).

While lack is a condition of life, in Lacan's terms, its presence is re-evoked in a number of situations – entry into the symbolic area of language, the fantasy of castration, the subjection to the Law of the Father – but the main source of lack is in the original loss of the mother. This is the loss experienced in weaning and, with it, the surrender of the primary desire for mother to the more 'normal' socially prescribed desire of other objects. Dollimore (1999: 184) notes, 'as desiring subjects, we embark on a restless (because always inadequate) search for a substitute'. The cleavage in the original rela-tionship to mother leaves an irreparable rent in the psyche and, in parallel to Plato's vision, an unending search for the other, for com-pletion. There is always more that is wanted, wishes and impulses unfolding as others dissolve. Unlike the Winnicottian baby who is relatively content with the 'good enough mother', the Lacanian baby is forever in a state of desire.

The main purpose of analytic treatment in the Lacanian model is the naming of desire. In spite of the obsessive nature of the search, the individual is seen as largely out of touch with actual desire, with what is wanted at depth, partly because this has unconscious aspects that make it difficult to reach. In states of psychological distress, desire is expressed as demand, the clamouring for something needed, something which someone else can give, which seldom succeeds in its purpose since the underlying desire remains unknown. The naming of desire then becomes the core function of the analysis. With this goes the analyst's close attention to the patient's desire. It is vital, Lacan asserted, for the analyst to desire the patient's desire. In the following quote, a further aspect – the immanence of desire – is highlighted:

> To bring the subject to recognize and to name his desire, this is the nature of the efficacious action of analysis. But it is not a question of recognizing something that would already have been there – a given – ready to be captured. In naming it, the subject creates, gives rise to something new, makes something new present in the world.
>
> (Lacan 1988b, Book 2: 228–9)

This suggests a process in which desire is discovered in the communicative sphere of the analysis. How this happens varies according to different interpretations of Lacan's method. Mostly, transference is emphasized as the route to the recognition of desire, the analyst – and indeed the analytic setting itself – becoming the symbolic object of desire from which emerges a recognition of the deeper desire: 'In the transference, the legislating and pleasure-denying power of the Other can be unveiled, and an experimental sequence of unveilings and re-veilings can itself become a return route to interpersonal sexual enjoyment' (Bowie 1991: 146).

As is well known, Lacan placed much emphasis on language. The child's entry into the symbolic register is both an opportunity and a loss. The opportunity is the opening up of a whole new world of communication with others; the loss is the severing of ties with earlier non-verbal experience that cannot be communicated in words. This creates a further schism in the experience of the self, a further rupture in the sense of lack. This view of lack accords with that of contemporary developmental researchers such as Daniel Stern (1985) who describes language as 'a double-edged sword', enriching and depriving the child at the same time, precisely because of the loss of early non-verbal experience in all its subjective and idiosyncratic nuance.

Although Lacan did not venture into group work, his theory raises important questions for group psychotherapy, including the main question that underlies this book: to what extent is desire capable of being recognized in the group? Further, if the therapeutic medium, the aesthetic of exploration, is itself equated with the desired object, can the group constitute an object of desire?

The relational school

The field of relational psychoanalysis is a largely American development which emphasizes the reciprocal relationship between analyst and patient, linked to intersubjective and mutually transferential processes. I am not attempting a review of this promising body of theory and practice but instead focus on the theme of desire as it emerges in some of the writing. Emmanuel Ghent (1990) writes about surrender rather than desire as such but the concept has considerable relevance. Ghent uses the term 'surrender' in a very particular way: the positive wish to yield emotionally, to let down the defences and to open the self to the unexpected. 'I imply that there is, however deeply buried or frozen, a longing for something in the environment to make possible the surrender, in the sense of yielding, of false self' (1990: 108). He draws a distinction between surrender and both submission and masochism. Surrender is the spontaneous, intuitive response of letting go. Submission is an act of giving up and masochism the eroticized version of submission in which domination and force are enlisted as means towards subjugation. Ghent regards submission as a substitute for longed-for surrender and masochism as a perversion of this longing. But it is the original wish for surrender that is the opportunity for emotional growth: 'The meaning I will give surrender has nothing to do with hoisting a white flag: in fact, rather than carrying a connotation of defeat, the term will convey a quality of liberation and expansion of the self as a corollary to the letting down of defensive barriers' (1990: 212).

The concept of surrender, used in this way, offers a meaningful perspective of desire. A pervasive problem of desire is the anxiety about acknowledging and expressing it. Although holding back desire may be appropriate in some situations, it is often unnecessarily restrained and repressed through fear of exposure, rejection or injury. Surrendering the self through desire seems an apt way of considering the positive option. Additionally, the meaning Ghent attributes to submission and masochism is a constructive way of approaching the 'perversions'. I use the term perversion with caution because of its over-use in psychoanalytic thinking and its pejorative associations. Ghent's suggestion that masochism conceals a deeply-buried wish for surrender in a growthful sense is a useful, non-pathologizing perspective.

Ghent's notion of surrender highlights a particular process: the openness to experience with another, in which something needed, wanted and of personal significance is discovered in the interactional moment. It may not have been known before: it becomes known in the intersubjective space. This observation is close to the quality of immanence I noted in relation to Lacan's work, where desire is recognized in unexpected ways through the analytic relationship. It is also similar to current group analytic versions of emergence in the group process, highlighting the many possibilities for desire emerging in the interactional sphere of the group.

Jody Meissler Davies is well-known for her work on dissociation as a consequence of early sexual abuse (Davies and Frawley 1991). More recently, she has turned her attention to sexuality and desire as primary foci in emotional development as well as in the analytic relationship.

Above all, Davies (1998a, 1998b) situates sexuality in a relational context, highlighting the interpersonal aspects of desire: 'It is this experience of ourselves as "wanters" that most consistently and systematically challenges an insular and fundamentally solipsistic self-sufficiency and binds us irrevocably to the psychic intricacies and vicissitudes of those with whom we share our deepest internal longings' (1998b: 806). Following on this, she encourages an active invitation to explore sexuality in the analytic relationship, with positive views about the potential to restore sexual desire in the face of trauma and disappointment:

> we often use ourselves and the loving and affirming qualities of the current analytic relationship to suggest to a patient that it is okay, safe, even desirable to once again need, yearn and love – to take from the analytic work a template for relationships that can nourish, empower, and sustain. To revive such hope, we extend ourselves in myriad ways . . .
> (Davies 1998b: 808)

The 'myriad ways' Davies suggests above refer to the analyst's active engagement in the patient's sexual reawakening, including the judicious disclosure of the analyst's own sexual responses and feelings about the patient, at times in the process when this can be viewed as freeing and enabling. Davies argues that the analyst is in the position of a post-Oedipal parent, there to approve, support and facilitate the patient's emerging sexuality. Not surprisingly, this view has triggered controversy in analytic circles in the USA.

Davies' approach is in various ways refreshingly direct and transparent when compared with most other analytic writers on sexuality. The pessimism of Freud and Lacan and their followers is nowhere present in her vision. At the same time, this is not a naïve approach. She is aware of the risks, the potential for destructive enactments, for disappointment. However, she remains optimistic about the potential of the analytic couple to manage these risks and she presents a positive notion of their shared responsibility in doing so:

> From a purely relational perspective, I suggest that the psychoanalytic situation is one in which each participant – patient and analyst – becomes responsible for holding, containing and responsibly managing the unconscious desires of the other until such time that those desires can be reclaimed, experienced, and symbolically represented . . . As such, it is not the specific quality of desire, the bodily zone or developmental period from which it emanates, that marks developmental/therapeutic accomplishment. Rather, it is the degree to which the patient (and the analyst) comes to know, feel, and own his desirous states – those that have the potential to be satisfied and those that can only be sustained unmet – without the crushing blows of despair, humiliation, and impotent rage.
>
> (Davies 1998b: 810)

There is much in Davies' account that seems to me relevant to group psychotherapy. Although her work is very much positioned in individual analysis, with no reference at all to groups, her relational emphasis is transferable to the group, except, of course, that the dyad would have to be extended to take in all the members of the group, including the therapist. The intensity of her focus on a single patient's emergent sexuality – and the corresponding responses of the analyst – raise questions about whether and how this could ever be achieved in a group. Or could it be achieved in the group in a different way, through an interaction of members, including the therapist, that facilitates an openness about desire in ways that are generative not only for an individual but for all the members of the group?

Identity and desire

Much of the foregoing review of theories of desire has been written from a non-specific gender perspective. However, issues concerning gender and sexual identity profoundly influence the experience of desire, its individual and social representation, its realization and repression. It is necessary to make a brief detour here in order to acknowledge these issues, with a view to their fuller consideration later in this book.

One aspect concerns gender differences in the experience and expression of desire. Writers coming from different psychosexual perspectives have noted the well-known distinction: active desire in men and passive desire in women. Recent research (see Chapter 2) seems to confirm that desire in men is spontaneous and proactive and that this sets in motion the sexual search, whereas desire in women emerges during sexual intimacy, dependent more on contact and stimulation. The implication is that this is a biological difference. However, other writers have suggested that it is socially constructed rather than biologically based. Jessica Benjamin (1990) links the difference to childhood identifications with parents in a way that reflects cultural role stereotyping. The girl identifies with 'the mother of reproduction' who adopts a nurturing, attaching and merging role, the boy with a father who is active, independent and exploratory. The girl's and boy's later sexual relationships then reflect these identifications as part of a continuing cycle of gender representations. Although children also make opposite-sex identifications with their parents, these are more likely to be problematic because of the pressure of social conformity.

A further aspect concerns the assumptions linking sexual identity and desire. O'Connor and Ryan (1993) attribute this to conventional notions of complementarity deriving from a biological perspective: men and women are made for each other. They quote the psychoanalyst John Sklar's (1989) assertion that this difference constitutes 'a baseline for being human' as reflecting a particular emphasis on complementarity in orthodox psychoanalysis. The implication is that only heterosexuality is normal sexuality: men love women and women love men in a complementary way. In such a view, homosexuality can only be viewed as an aberration, a distortion of biological givens, a defensive reaction to failed heterosexuality. O'Connor and Ryan see this perspective as enshrined in the institutionalization of the Oedipus complex. They link much of psychoanalytic theorizing to the formulation of the Oedipus complex and its 'normal' resolution, which embodies the dualism of being and having in relation to the objects of desire. The polarity at the core of the Oedipus complex is: 'You cannot be what you desire, you cannot desire what you wish to be' (O'Connor and Ryan 1993: 239).

These writers quote the work of Judith Butler (1990) who criticizes psychoanalysis and similar approaches for reinforcing a masculine/feminine binary frame through assumptions that are outside language and social discourse. This is in line with Lacan's questioning of the 'fiction' of fixed, unified and unchanging identities and his interpretation that this fiction obscures hidden dimensions of social categories.

The convention of fixed identities creates problems for the recognition and realization of sexual diversity, including homosexuality. This affects a large number of players: homosexuals who, in spite of the greater social acceptance of sexual diversity, may be struggling to come to terms with their own sexual preference, probably as a result of internalized homophobia; heterosexuals who feel threatened by the presence of homosexual desire; and the sizeable and seemingly growing number of 'in-betweens' – people who are unsure of their sexual orientation and are struggling to find a moral and aesthetic basis on which to decide who they are and how they want to live their sexual lives. Friedman and Downey (2002) contend that the nature of sexual fantasy is the key to sexual orientation, but whatever the defining issues, reconciling homosexual preference with other aspects of life, such as work, family and social role, is often fraught with difficulty.

In a psychotherapy group of mixed sexes, and indeed in single-sex groups, there are likely to be several people at any one time who are struggling with these issues. The extent to which they are voiced in the group and the degree of openness in the discourse will vary considerably from group to group, depending on the composition of members, the developmental stage of the group, the level of trust, and – very importantly – the sensitivity and openness of the therapist. The therapist's awareness of the diverse nature of sexuality is absolutely crucial in any consideration of sexuality in psychotherapy.

While in group psychotherapy there is great potential for these issues to emerge in the interactional sphere, there is equally great potential for concealment and obfuscation. Desire, sexual fantasy and the erotic imagination are often kept separate from the group.

This may parallel the social paradox whereby the wider public tolerance of sexual diversity actually conceals deep-rooted conservatism and anxiety about sexual difference.

A third aspect of identity and sexuality, I suggest, is the question of who the subject of desire is and who the object of desire. Who desires whom? In an ideal world, there would be symmetry here: people mutually desire each other. But this is seldom the case. Instead, there are usually disparities in the flow of desire from one to the other. These disparities often touch on deep narcissistic sensitivities: am I attractive, desirable, desired by the other? The engagement through desire, whether mutual or divided, is often fraught, with subtle interpersonal manoeuvring: flirting, testing, tantalizing, taking control, power playing. It is likely that in a psychotherapy group these processes are operating outside the field of immediate vision. Even if they do become visible, it may be difficult for therapists to know how to deal with them. There is often a sense of the dangerous about sex in the group. Erotic feelings, as noted many times in this book, can be intrusive and disruptive in the group and therapists may be tempted to leave well alone. This may be why sexuality is so often neglected in group therapy. However, non-recognition may encourage acting-out outside the group. It may also derail the therapeutic task, without it being clear why this is happening.

All of the above points to the hidden sexual life of the group, in which issues of desire and attraction, acceptance and rejection, have a major but elusive influence on group development. Within this, tensions, both spoken and unspoken, about gender and sexual identity figure prominently.

Culture and desire

The predominant focus of this chapter has so far been on the individual as the source of desire, a necessary emphasis given the very personal nature of desire. However, reference has been made to social and cultural influences on desire and I will elaborate briefly on this theme, to be extended in Chapter 4.

Here, I wish to select just two relevant themes. The first concerns the publicizing of desire through the media, the internet and pornography. Although we think of desire as very personal and subjective, it is at another level common property, as reflected in the externalization and commodification of sexuality and desire. This is not a new idea. Craib (2001) points out that Kant referred to it in his time, as did Karl Marx in his treatise on commodity fetishism.

However, the externalization of desire has obviously been boosted by the intense spread of communication in the late twentieth century, particularly the far greater availability of sex through the internet. It is now possible to satisfy, with relative ease, a wide range of sexual desires, including some bizarre sexual preferences. It is difficult to know exactly what effect this has had on the imagination of the majority of the population. It could be argued that it is a hugely liberating trend, that the propulsion of sexual diversity into the public arena and the easier route to gratification must dissolve some of the secrecy and orthodoxy surrounding sexuality. It could be just what the Surrealists, cited at the beginning of the chapter, and the Sexual Revolutionaries (Reich, Marcuse, etc.) would have wanted. But the overall impression is not particularly of a more liberated sexual universe. The internet has spawned a restless, obsessive search for sexual stimulation, countless hours spent in repetitive sex talk in chat rooms, while communication about sex is often cryptic, coded and under the guise of fictitious and fugitive identities. All this may diminish rather than augment the actual capacity for sexual relationships. The sexual gesture becomes increasingly facile and dissociated.

The second, linked, aspect concerns the mobilization and exploitation of sexual desire in consumer culture. Sexual imagery, ever more brazen and seductive, is the favoured motif of advertising – 'sex sells' – and with it is peddled the lure of youth and beauty, bodily perfection, sexual prowess, erotic glamour and romantic fulfilment. All of this makes ordinary life, the immediate self and other, seem banal and irretrievably dull. This is akin to the culture of narcissism described by Lasch (1979), a culture that breeds dissatisfaction and alienation through the cultivation of illusion, through the insinuation of unattainable perfection into the sexual lives of imperfect people.

This perspective challenges the assumption that the individual is solely the generator of desire. Perhaps they are also the repository of desire. A paradox emerges: sexual desire is so often tainted by secrecy and shame, so private, so concealed – yet it is also public property. The lack that Lacan elaborates so insistently in his theory of desire is both individually and culturally configured.

Which desire?

Desire is not a unitary phenomenon. We tend to associate it with sexual desire but that is not its only meaning. It occurs in many forms and each of these has different subjective and intersubjective representations.

Bowie (1991) gives a vivid account of Lacan's perception of desire. Although Lacan was of course concerned with sexual desire, he envisaged desire as a more general process. Bowie refers to his approach as an 'eroticized science of meaning' rather than a detailed exploration of sexuality in its diverse forms. Compared to the 'leaden instinctualism' of much analytic thinking, Lacan's desire was meant to be 'the purest quicksilver' (p. 122), a force that moves life along. To quote Bowie more fully:

> Lacan's Eros finds its primary expression neither in physical sensations nor in desirous mental states, nor yet in the organs and erotogenic zones that, for other theorists of sexuality, allow the pursuit of pleasure to be mapped and logged on the surface of the human body. Indeed the attributes of Eros are often negative ones: it is not an instinct, nor a quasi-biological libido, not a variable flow of neural energy or excitation, not an appetite, not the concealed source from which appetites derive and not, as it had been for the later Freud, the life-principle itself. The sole positive attribute that Lacan sets against all these negative ones seems at first fragile and empty: desire, as he came to call it in preference to all other terms, is what keeps the signifiers moving. It is the dynamo, everywhere in motion and nowhere at rest, that propels all acts of speech, all refusals to speak and all conscious and unconscious representations.
>
> (Bowie 1991: 122)

Lacan, we know, was influenced by an earlier 'master', Hegel, who also gave central importance to desire. In his socially conceived understanding of the universe, Hegel emphasized the desire for recognition and what is described as 'the desire for the desire of the other'. Desire and recognition are understood here as the desire for affirmation of the self, its aspirations and ambitions, rather than sexual desire as such. However, the desire for recognition is complicated by the operation of power and competition, in which one self seeks to assert its desire, its right to recognition, over another self. This leads to a master-slave type relationship in which recognition may be achieved through submission of the other. However, this is a fragile relationship as the dominance-submission arrangement can be denied, exposed or reversed. A more mature solution is the movement towards mutual rather than self-recognition. Social identities are formed through this process of mutuality, interdependence and the pursuit of a shared communal goal – the basis, as Hegel sees it, of an ethical society.

Hegel's analysis inspired the psychoanalyst Jessica Benjamin's theory of recognition and negation. The question Benjamin (1998) asks is 'how is it possible to recognize another?' She sees the process of recognition as an ongoing tension between recognition and negation. When confronted by an external other, the self realizes the threat that the other poses. Not only is it difficult to accept that the other does not desire what we desire, but the self may seek to deposit its undesirable parts into the other, using it to represent what is despised or repudiated. Through recognition of the other as a subject with their feelings and thoughts, the self can begin to own the rejected aspects it has projected onto the other, and bear the differences within. This requires balancing one's need for fantasied objects of desire with the need for real others and entails a suspension of omnipotence.

We can see the relevance to the therapy group, which comprises various selves, all with their desire for recognition and their potential to negate the other. This operates continuously in groups, in both obvious and subtle ways, and although there are the risks of negation, the group provides opportunities to confront the dilemma of self and other and move closer to mutual recognition. This is also a useful framework within which to view sexuality, in which the tensions of recognition and negation can be particularly marked.

Conclusion

Desire in some ways defines the human condition. It is the subjective, personal aspect of being, a motivating force that reaches into all aspects of human life, sexual and otherwise. Bowie (1991: 163) describes it as 'the inner theatre of individual passion and affectivity'. The way it is represented in the individual narrative, its successes and failures, is the essential texture of a life. As Adam Phillips states (1998), all our stories concern our desires and their destiny.

The unbound potential of desire, as envisaged by the Surrealists, is contradicted by its many restraining influences: through life's impermanence, through the experience of inevitable incompleteness, through the dependence on the other for uncertain gratification, through the gap between fantasy and reality. Culture and society also represent desire in paradoxical ways: on the one hand, glorifying sexual and romantic desire, apparently setting it free; on the other, demanding conformity to prescribed patterns of relating and restraint in the name of decency and morality. Gender identity and sexual orientation are constantly challenged by social paradox, particularly at present where freedom and prejudice exist side by side.

Desire presents a significant challenge to all psychotherapy. It demands to be seen and heard, but how to contextualize it in therapy raises many questions. The possibilities vary from total absorption in desire to the marginalization and even eradication of desire from the therapeutic agenda. If group psychotherapy has to some extent veered towards the latter option, it could reflect anxiety that the intensity of desire would overwhelm the group, that there might be uncontrolled acting-out. The group is very close to the social domain with its ambivalence and double standards, so that shame and guilt about sexuality must be constant deterrents. These are all real possibilities, not to be taken lightly. But the minimization of desire, sexual and otherwise, in the group is a denial, a loss in the depth and resonance of the personal narrative. It is necessary to reconfigure our understanding of groups in order to give fuller substance to desire, to name desire in its many forms.

2

SEXUAL DEVELOPMENT

The striking gap in publications on sexuality in group psychotherapy, including group analysis, means that there is very little
that can be derived directly from this field. Attempting to close the
gap opens the door to a vast, complex and often elusive literature.
The body of writing is also constantly changing as sexual orthodoxy
is challenged, sexual definitions become more diverse and researches
on all aspects of sexuality, from neuroscience to cultural studies,
undergo revision and expansion.

This chapter considers sexual development from the contemporary 'biopsychosocial' perspective of the complex origins of sexual
behaviour (Denman 2004). In line with recent challenges to the lin-
earity of conventional developmental models (Galatzer-Levy 2004),
the view of development I present here is not of fixed stages leading
in an orderly sequence to a state of resolution, but a series of developmental tasks or foci that are accomplished in differing ways with
variable end points of maturity and oscillating criteria of functional-
ity. I also attempt to highlight the main points of tension and debate
in the developmental discourse and I begin with some continuing
controversies.

Controversies concerning sexuality

Sexuality is riven by controversy: few fields of discourse are as subject to debate and disagreement. I wish to highlight three particular
areas of controversy and to sketch out my position on each.

Nature-nurture

One controversy concerns the origins of sexuality. Here the debate,
put simply, concerns the nature-nurture dichotomy. Are we born

with a particular sexual disposition and future trajectory or do we learn this through our developmental pathways? The contemporary viewpoint that has gained most ground in recent years is summed up in the term 'biopsychosocial'. As described by Denman (2004), this is a paradigm which integrates biological, psychological and cultural domains. The assumption is that in the study of human sexuality all three domains contribute to the origin and development of sexuality: throughout life, there is an interaction between these domains. This is the perspective to which I subscribe and that informs my understanding of sexuality. In this book I will to a large extent assume the biological and focus on the psychological and social/cultural because these are closer to my agenda. But I wish to make clear that biology is taken as a given and that any attempt to eradicate the significance of the biological in relation to sexuality is misguided, indeed illusory.

Since I will be taking the biological for granted in most of the book, I wish to highlight here some of the findings of the current research on the neuroanatomical and neurophysiological substrates of gender identity and sexual response, as highlighted by Hiller (2005). In particular, research into brain differentiation and hormonal functioning in the womb tends to show that human sexuality and gender potential are laid down during foetal development (Panksepp 1998; Friedman and Downey 2002). Brain differentiation appears to be linked to the span of female to male sexuality, creating a range of potentials from same sex to opposite sex choice which are actively manifested at puberty. These potentials continue to develop and influence sexual behaviour throughout life, mediated by hormonal and physiological processes.

Some of these findings can be interpreted as indicating that sexuality is powerfully determined – and constrained – by its biological origins in foetal and early childhood development. To some, this is welcome evidence that sexual diversity is natural and inborn as opposed to psychologically deviant. For example, the gay discourse points to genetic studies of homosexuality as evidence that homosexuality is a constitutional variant and not to be pathologized as dysfunctional (Hamer and Copeland 1999). To others, the entrenchment of the biological view of sexuality is regarded as an oppressive practice that reinforces essentialist notions of gender and sexual orientation (Dimen 1995). Between these extremes lies the biopsychosocial perspective which accepts the relevance of neuroscientific and neurochemical research but sees sexuality as operating within complex life narratives in which psychological, social and cultural factors constantly interact with the biological.

Normality-pathology

The second controversy concerns the question of normality and pathology in the sexual area. Since the beginning of psychoanalysis there has been a preoccupation with drawing the line between so-called mature adult sexuality, commonly defined as genital heterosexuality, and a range of alternative sexualities. The term 'perversion' has been used liberally to categorize practically any sexual fantasies and practices that did not fit with the preconceptions about what constituted 'normal' sexuality. Much of this has been challenged and re-evaluated in recent decades, with the complexification of heterosexuality itself and the emergence of a variety of alternative lifestyles. In many ways, psychotherapeutic culture lags behind these social changes and part of the purpose of this book is to draw attention to the more diverse sexual landscape that exists in contemporary society. With this goes an attempt to argue the potentials of adopting a non-pathologizing attitude in the clinical setting. This excludes sexual practices which are harmful to self and others and that transgress agreed boundaries, such as those of age. But it includes a wide range of manifestations of the erotic imagination and the possibility of embracing the different and the unusual in our understanding of sexuality. This is especially relevant to group psychotherapy, given its valuing of diversity and dialogue.

Sexual choice

A third controversy concerns the question of individual choice. In contrast to the biological perspective which mainly sees sexuality as the living out of inherited potential, there are approaches which emphasize the variability of sexuality and the potential for choice. The sociologist Giddens (1992) considers the social implications of contemporary sexual relationships and how these both reflect and mould modern society. His vantage point is that of 'self-creation', a process of individualized self-development which he sees as characteristic of the modern age and opposed to traditionalist approaches which perpetuate conventional normative behaviour. To this, Giddens adds the notion of 'plastic sexualities'. This refers to sexuality as freed from its original association with propagation and available as a medium of personal identity and development. Giddens views this change as the outcome of several social developments – the reduction in family size starting in the eighteenth century, the introduction of contraception in the 1960s and the ascendance of women in the sexual sphere, producing a greater social and sexual egalitarianism. In this era, sexuality emerges more as a lifestyle, a matter of personal choice about a 'sexual aesthetic' than as the outcome of purely biological or even psychological influences. As Denman (2004) notes, this legitimates a wider range of sexualities and reflects the greater tolerance of diversity in our current culture.

This viewpoint differs markedly from both biological and evolutionary psychology (Buss 1999) perspectives, the latter regarding sexual behaviour as driven by a universal aim of maximizing the successful propagation of genes and hence perpetuating the species. Sexuality in the alternative view is no longer a given at the start of life or the condition of an evolutionary agenda but an individual choice that helps to transform society as well as being transformed by it. This creates a more liberal and open agenda for psychotherapy, particularly group psychotherapy, in which issues of social identity, conformity and non-conformity are very much to the fore. At the same time, there are always constraints of one sort or another, be they biological or psychological, or indeed social, and part of the challenge to any psychotherapy is the potential for change in the light of constraints and the way these are negotiated in the interests of creative individual choice.

The controversies delineated above all highlight the value of the biopsychosocial approach to sexuality and the frame of reference it provides for a realistic but potentially liberating view of sexuality.

The developmental journey

Having established the biopsychosocial frame, it is possible to look more closely at the journey of sexual development, considering what this might mean for males and females at different stages of life. In order for sexuality to become a tangible force in group psychotherapy, it is necessary to have a view of normal sexual development that at the same time takes account of the plasticity of sexuality and the diverse sexualities that may emerge in the process. Although I use the word 'normal' at several points in this chapter, it is in very broad terms and with the recognition not only that what constitutes normal is open to debate but that the very idea of normality is questionable – hence my reference to diverse pathways of development.

Is there a purpose, a direction of travel that unites the spectrum of sexualities? It seems useful to postulate that for most human beings the desirable outcome is the acquisition of a relatively cohesive sexual self which generates pleasure and satisfaction and is consistent with a given individual's values within a framework of interpersonal attachment and group belonging. This usually entails a striving towards the formation of intimate relationships, in which sex and emotional involvement come together. For many, there is a fantasy of an idealized love relationship which is sustainable and enduring over time. However, within this normative account, we know that sexuality and desire are often complex and fragmentary and that there may be significant discrepancies between what is wished for, what is possible and what actually exists in an individual life. How frustration and disappointment are dealt with is as much a part of sexuality as excitement and satisfaction. Sexual development for many people ends up in less than ideal ways, with confusions about the role of self and other, problems in intimate relationships, disjunctions between mind and body in sexual expression and difficulties in integrating sexuality with other aspects of identity and day-to-day social being. How this is linked to earlier periods of development is the subject of the remaining chapter.

Childhood

Sexual development starts in early childhood, many writers agreeing that the infant-mother relationship is a precursor of the capacity for sexual intimacy in later life. This does not assume that infantile sexuality is a given but that the physical experience of a bonded relationship with the primary caregiver instils the early sense of a bodily self in sensual contact with a loved other. Scharff and Scharff (1991) describe this as the first psychosomatic partnership. An important part of this relationship is the regulation of excitement without either understimulation or overstimulation, which could constitute an intrusion or impingement. With this early experience of a bodily and sensual self intact, the child is amenable to the entry into its life of the wider family, father and siblings, and the potential sexual excitements and challenges that arise in these relationships. Father is obviously crucial here, both as the first major representative of male sexuality and as mother's actual sexual and emotional partner. The parental pair represents the child's first example of a sexual couple and the nature of their relationship and the complex sexual identifications embedded therein are likely to influence the child's own sexuality in significant conscious and unconscious ways (Nitsun 1994). Further, father's attitude to the child as mother's infant 'partner' is likely to communicate itself to the child and to influence its growing sense of its own sexual entitlement.

The influence of siblings on the child's sexuality has hardly been explored in the literature. It is only in recent years that the full impact of sibling relationships on emotional development has been recognized (Volkan and Ast 1997). But it is likely that the configuration of siblings in a family, with its particular birth order, gender distribution and patterns of attachment, attraction and rivalry, will arouse same-sex and opposite-sex identifications and desires that are closely woven into sexual development.

Beyond this, there is the sexual atmosphere of the family as a unit, largely under the influence of the parents, and the way the family represents the prevailing sexual morality in terms of processes of openness vs. concealment, idealization vs. denigration and conformity vs. non-conformity. Much of this will influence the 'mentalization' (Fonagy *et al.* 2002) of sexuality in the family, the way that sex is understood and communicated between members. Sexuality, whether in individual relationships or the family as a whole, does not exist separately from the wider and deeper current of interpersonal and social communication. I mention this specifically because of its obvious relevance to the psychotherapy group. The group symbolizes a family group in which unresolved aspects of the original family sexual configuration may find expression but in which there are new opportunities for sexual discovery and development.

Moving beyond the family, the child's relationship to peers becomes the next major context for the formation of sexual identity. This is mediated largely through play. Friedman and Downey (2002) note that childhood play is the predominant psychosocial influence beyond the family and that this is crucial for the development of gender-based identity and self-regard. Hiller (2005) reports observational studies which tend to confirm fairly stereotyped normative pictures of male and female preferences in childhood play. While girls and boys both show a preference for same-sex social groupings, boys typically engaging in physically energetic behaviours, such as rough-and-tumble play, with an emphasis on dominance and competition, girls show a propensity for conversation and symbolic nurturance, with greater attempts to maintain group cohesion. Maccoby (1998) views such same-sex play activities as precursors of gender-specific styles in later sexual interactions, such as men's emphasis on sexual conquest and performance and women's greater need for intimacy. Hiller (2005) comments that the child's sense of group belonging at this stage, and its identification with gender-based activities, is important in aiding the emergence of a valued gendered and sexual self. Friedman and Downey (2002) note that children on a developmental course of same-sex sexual orientation, and who tend towards gender non-conformity, can experience pronounced discomfort at this stage, with a consequent lowering of self-esteem. Boys, in particular, have difficulty since male groups tend to condemn and ridicule other boys who show an interest in feminine activities. The feelings evoked in children who feel different through not belonging to the 'right' gendered group can create a painful sense of insecurity and isolation from others.

These themes are resonant in the group psychotherapy context. Group therapists composing mixed-sex groups are usually intuitively aware of these differences which, although originating in childhood, tend to have a continuing effect on sexual identity and self-worth. But therapists may not always be aware of the impact these experiences have on current group process; how, for example, they affect the gender balance in the group, or how they impact on a new member, male or female, entering the group. This is one area in which the lack of a sexual discourse of any substance in the group psychotherapy literature is problematic. The greater present openness to sexual diversity in social groups is an important advance but this does not eliminate the lingering effects of childhood histories of difference and discrimination. We need to understand more about how this may be manifested in therapy groups.

Adolescence

The onset of puberty plunges the child into a heightened awareness of sexuality. Bodily changes and psychoendocrinal activity trigger a surge of desires and impulses. While intensely private experiences arise, there are continuing and vital links to the peer group. Adolescence is marked by an oscillation between absorption in the self, including autoerotic activity, pair formation of a potentially sexual and romantic kind, and attachment to the group. All of this assists the adolescent in their struggle to gain independence from the family nexus and begin to forge a separate adult identity. However, this process is also subject to oscillation: forceful rejection of the family alternating with dependent, if resentful, clinging.

Adolescence is also a time of secrets. For most young people, the first form of sexual activity is masturbation. The linking of sexual desire and fantasy with bodily release in masturbation is an intensely private experience that becomes the precursor, in most cases, of actual sexual relationships. Scharff (1982) views masturbation in adolescence as a self-gratifying activity that weakens early mother-infant and family bonds and connects the inner object world with mature forms of relatedness. The continuing preference for masturbation in some people, however, may reflect difficulty in making the break from the symbolic mother-infant constellation, compounded by fears of vulnerability and failure in adult sexual relationships. But for many people, including those with active sexual relations, masturbation remains an important sexual outlet. More than almost any other behaviour, it reflects the individual's suspension between a private world of fantasy and sensual gratification and a public world of relationships and the negotiation of self and other.

In the context of the therapy group, masturbation and accompanying sexual fantasy probably represent that part of the individual that is most difficult to share with others in a group. Mollon (2003) describes masturbation as inherently asocial. The extent to which it is necessary to talk about it in the group is debatable, but if we regard sexuality as a core concern for most people in therapy, then this aspect can be seen as a vital expression of the individual's sexuality. Trust would have to be high in any group in which it is possible to talk about masturbation and sexual fantasy. It is more likely to happen if there is generally an openness and honesty about sexual matters in the group. It is also worth considering the social meaning of masturbation. It can be seen as a statement of social intent – to isolate oneself, possibly as a needed temporary withdrawal from others. Further, the story embedded in sexual fantasy is usually a narrative concerning people in some form of relationship. Interpersonal themes of power, control and dependency, as well as cultural expressions of the sexually idealized and desirable, are all part of the narrative. The unravelling of the story may yield important insights, but can the story, this intimate sexual narrative, be risked on the group stage? And as therapists, what is our responsibility in influencing this process?

Adult sexuality

The intense sexual longings of adolescence usually find expression in exploratory sexual relationships in early to later teens and tend to culminate in the more enduring sexual partnerships of adulthood. The path of exploration is often fraught with anxiety, frustration and disappointment, and adult sexuality, in the view of many writers, is seldom if ever complete or resolved. There is usually a longing for sexual fusion in an intimate engagement with an idealized other.

But part of the excitement – and difficulty – of achieving this lies in difference – the attraction of difference constituted by the other. Let us look briefly at some sources of difference.

Male and female differences

Hiller (2005) describes some of the consistent and normative male-female differences reported in the literature, such as men's more active exploratory sexual orientation, their attraction to novelty and variety and their difficulty with sexual and emotional commitment. This is contrasted with women's tendency to experience themselves more as the object of desire than the desiring subject. Female desire and arousal are commonly described as arising in an actual sexual relationship, rather than being generated from within. Women's sexual problems are often characterized in terms of passivity, a lack of sexual agency and a lack of enjoyment of coitus, with associated anxiety and guilt.

Whereas women's problems in sexuality have for some time been a focus of attention, there has been a tendency more recently to highlight the considerable problems men have in the realization of their sexuality. Denman (2004) describes male sexuality as 'profoundly troubled'. She comments that therapeutic work with men in relation to sexual problems is usually more difficult than comparable work with women. Much of this is seen in relation to rigid and sometimes contradictory prescriptions for men's gender and sexual roles – being expected to be active and aggressive but at the same time criticized and policed for their aggression; being expected to be dominant and confident but also sensitive and vulnerable; being expected to perform penetrative sex but also to be receptive and allowing. Denman highlights the internal conflicts heterosexual men typically experience in relation to definitions of masculinity – the deep-rooted sense that in spite of 'new man' philosophies (being more sensitive and owning their feminine selves), they have to be strong, powerful and fully 'male'. With this goes a dread of passivity and a repudiation of femininity that can create contempt and hatred for women. There are repressed, though sometimes conscious, longings for passivity, sometimes in relation to women but also towards other men, with lurking fears of homosexuality.

Stoller (1975) suggests that male identities are both more rigid and fragile than female ones. He links this to the earliest emotional bonds, women having the advantage of their original female identification with mother: this establishes the sense of femaleness in women more firmly than the sense of maleness in men. According to Stoller, this renders men more vulnerable in their bisexuality and more prone to the development of perversions.

This account makes clear the interaction of physical and social processes in the sexuality of men and women. The way these influences are embodied in sexual relationships is a measure of the unique solutions found by men and women to the complex challenges of sexuality. From a clinical point of view, when these processes arouse more than the usual levels of anxiety and hostility in sexual relationships, they can impair the underlying physiology of the sexual response cycle, creating problems of sexual function that may present in the consulting room. The therapy group in its plural membership is faced with many possibilities of sexual function and dysfunction. The extent to which these problems are openly revealed and discussed in groups is variable, but there is probably greater concealment of sexual concerns than of any other subject.

Sex and parenting

A further source of tension for men and women in early adulthood is the question of reproduction and the extent to which this represents a priority in their sexual relationships. While sexuality has become uncoupled from procreation owing to contraceptive methods, the choice of having children and creating a family remains an important issue for many if not most adults. The field of evolutionary psychology assumes that reproduction is the ultimate human motivation and explains much of human behaviour as shaped by the need to ensure reproductive success in the service of propagating the species. This approach has influenced other disciplines – Fonagy *et al.* (2002), for example, suggesting that attachment theory is highly compatible with an evolutionary perspective. Their argument is that attachment serves a variety of evolutionary needs, ranging from heterosexual bonding to reciprocal altruism and the facilitation of care for children. Much of the theorizing of evolutionary psychology is mechanical and distal, however, conveying a version of human development that is based on phylogenetic assumptions, and is the subject of considerable criticism by non-evolutionary theorists. However, at the level of contemporary adult choice, these concerns cannot easily be dismissed.

In spite of the diminished emphasis on marriage and the family in current western society, much of adult heterosexual development still concerns the search for a long-term partner, with marriage at least an option and having children a serious consideration. Hiller (2005) addresses the question of how adults make choices about combining sexual urges with attachment and bonding on the one hand and procreation on the other. She notes that these options are often linked but frequently also operate independently. Individuals can sexually desire someone they do not love and be attached to another without any sexual attraction or desire. People vary considerably in their configuration of sex drive, attachment proclivity and reproductive desire, these differences themselves being linked in some research to neurological brain differentiation (Fisher 1998). Variations on these dimensions between two partners in a couple, whatever their basis, can account for considerable problems in intimate relationships – many of which present in the clinical setting.

While these are obvious sources of tension in heterosexual couples, they may also be concerns for homosexual individuals, whether in couples or not. The likelihood of never having children because of one's sexual orientation, while being able to conceive biologically, can be disappointing for gay men and women. There is an increasing tendency for gay couples, or individuals for that matter, to have children through IVF or to adopt, so as to overcome the problem. Straight or gay, there is often a wish to feel part of a reproductive line, to contribute to biological and social continuity, while also having the comforts of a family. The failure to conceive children is not uncommonly a source of regret and pain.

Attachment and detachment in sexual relationships

Attachment

The strength of sexual bonds is influenced by the nature of the original attraction. Hiller (2005) notes that partner choice, involving conscious and unconscious attraction, the quality of the emotional bond and the physiology of sexuality as reflected in the sexual fit, are inextricably interwoven in the durability of the couple. She cites the psychoanalytic interpretation of unconscious partner choice (Ruszcynski 1993) as providing insight into how couples form an emotional commitment. This is understood as a mutual transference relationship that creates an unconscious contract for development or defence. The 'contract' relates to aspects of the self of each partner that are projected onto the other partner, creating an unconscious conduit for attraction. 'Developmental' attraction allows for rejected parts of the self to be externalized in the other: through the ongoing relationship, regular contact enables reintrojection of that part of the personality in a more tolerable form. 'Defensive' attraction involves a collusion to retain splits and projections in a way that provides a mutual defence against acknowledging disowned parts of the self. Where projections become rigid and irretrievable, flexibility in the relationship diminishes and the couple veers between impasse and unravelling.

These processes have a bearing on groups, in so far as coupling often occurs in groups, while more generally projection and splitting occur between members, accounting for both affectionate and hostile attachments. Some of this may be sexually tinged in ways that are not immediately apparent.

Detachment

Regarding detachment as opposed to attachment, Kernberg (1995) introduces the useful notion of discontinuity in sexual relationships. By this he means not a significant or untoward disruption in the relationship but breaks and withdrawals that occur naturally in the rhythm of intimacy. Whereas sexual desire is associated with the longing for intimacy and fusion, this is counterbalanced by the wish to withdraw from intimacy and to return to the non-erotic world. Kernberg quotes Andre Green (1986) as commenting that discontinuity is a basic characteristic of human functioning in both normality and pathology.

Difficulties arise when the individual is torn between the wish for erotic engagement and the wish for disengagement, especially where this is compounded by fears of intimacy. This presents problems in both establishing and sustaining relationships. It also presents problems for established couples in working out a *modus vivendi* in which the needs for both attachment and separation can be met. Glasser's (1979) concept of the core complex pinpoints this dilemma, highlighting fears about engulfment in sexual relationships on the one hand and fears of painful isolation on the other. The individual is trapped in an ongoing cycle of wanting closeness, which evokes fears of engulfment, and seeking withdrawal, which triggers emotional isolation.

The issue of discontinuity seems very relevant to groups. Group members not uncommonly show confusing patterns of engagement and disengagement that can disrupt and undermine the group process. Dealing with this may be helped by recognition that absence and inconsistent attendance could express fears of intimacy and engulfment in the group, paralleled by similar fears in relationships outside the group. Particularly where groups are delving into areas of sexual and emotional intimacy, some members may become anxious and want to retreat.

Gay and lesbian development

Considerable confusion and controversy surrounds the genesis of homosexuality. The whole biopsychosocial discourse is more split and polarized around this subject than usual, some writers arguing strenuously for genetic and neuroanatomical causality and others arguing strongly against it, with conflicting interpretations of 'evidence', both on the genetic and environmental side. No doubt, the controversy is fuelled by the deviation homosexuality constitutes from the dominant heterosexual norm. Psychoanalysis, as will be seen in the next chapter, was marked in the mid-twentieth century by highly pathologizing accounts of homosexuality, viewed as a regressive response to Oedipal anxieties that had to be subjected to psychoanalytic revision. That this view has shifted, particularly in the last decade or so, is a reflection of the greater normalization of homosexuality, the increasingly open acknowledgement of homosexuality in society and the sustained criticism of oppressive discourses concerning homosexuality (see Chapter 4).

There are inconsistencies in this progress, however, with a recent wave of 'sexual reorientation therapies' emerging in the USA. Also known as reparative therapy and conversion therapy, these approaches mainly target homosexual men seeking change to heterosexuality but also make assumptions about the undesirability of homosexuality (Nicolosi 1991; Throckmorton 1998; Spitzer 2003). Whereas these approaches are now being criticized and deconstructed by other writers (Riggs 2004), the advent of these therapies highlights the continuing complexity and ambivalence about homosexual identity. Some of this originates in earlier experiences of growing up gay – and it is here that I return to the developmental journey.

There are many accounts of the anxiety and pain attendant on the emergence and recognition of being homosexual (Crespi 1995; Frommer 1995; Rutkin 1995). Denman (2004) notes that homosexually-inclined boys often undergo threatening and humiliating experiences in the playground. This usually emanates from contempt and hatred of the un-masculine, intensely located in particular boys who are seen as sissies. This tends to lead to homophobic bullying and the social and emotional isolation of the identified boy. Denman describes the anxious concealment of sexual orientation and delay in coming out, often approached with great trepidation and tending to reflect the individual's own internalized homophobia. There is also a degree of hypocrisy among adolescent boys, leading to projection and scapegoating. Homosexual experimentation between boys is common, but this is often concealed and denied while the identified 'poof' is denigrated and marginalized. This is not unusually repeated in adult circles, in which straight men are able to disown homosexual wishes by projecting them onto gay men.

Literature on the problems of coming out as gay describes the build-up of anxious anticipation and fear of rejection and ridicule. A large part of the difficulty is the phenomenon of internalized homophobia (Frommer 2005). In spite of the increasing assertiveness of the gay population, gay individuals frequently struggle with feelings of self-hatred and a deep sense of inadequacy, so that coming out involves the dual achievement of a social and a personal statement. Also, Denman makes the important point that gay men (and women) do not come out just once, since they encounter a variety of different social contexts through their lives (school, work, social group etc.) and each time are faced with the decision of whether to come out or not. This creates considerable tension for the individual in holding together the different renderings of self and predisposes homosexuals to an uncomfortable schism between true and false social selves.

There is considerable commentary on the sexual lifestyles of gay men, particularly their apparent greater promiscuity and attraction to casual sex. These accounts can be highly pejorative and Denman (2004) cites the well-known paper by Christopher Bollas (1992) on cruising, which starts with a fairly open account of all male sexuality and ends up with an interpretation of casual homosexual sex as a pathologically alienated expression of loss and hatred. As noted in Chapter 4, there are much more positive and affirming accounts, such as that of Mohr (1992), who sees in gay casual sex the potential for friendship, for a brief but meaningful sharing of intimacy and for the building up of social networks that cross the social divide and create a sense of camaraderie and identification.

What is missing from these accounts are some critical social perspectives on the problems of gay relationships. The first is sociohistorical in that it emphasizes the difficulties gay men traditionally have had in making sexual contacts, given society's rejection of homosexuality, necessitating clandestine and fleeting encounters.

The second emphasizes the relative lack of social support for sustained homosexual partnerships. Whereas in the heterosexual world relationships are often celebrated in engagements and marriages, usually with strong family and peer support, and continually reinforced culturally, long-term gay relationships are often conducted in isolation from the family, unsupported, unmarked in the sphere of public ritual and approbation. It is not surprising that gay men have resorted to secret and casual relationships, which then breed an underworld of their own. Currently, there are important changes in the recognition of gay couples, their conjugal and legal rights, and this may gradually remove the shadow that for so long has hung over homosexual coupling.

Turning briefly to lesbian sexuality, this has been even more shrouded by confusion and mystery than male homosexuality. Possibly there is greater social ambiguity in relation to female same-sex attraction than male-male attraction since it is easier in western society for women to openly express affection, admiration and love for each other than it is for men, and so the line between sexual and non-sexual female attraction is more blurred. At the same time, this may have led to a greater denial of lesbian sexuality and a failure to elaborate the lesbian erotic imagination. Lesbians seem to 'pass' more easily in all walks of life – fashion, the arts, even psychoanalysis – where there are well-known examples of distinguished homosexual women who have not officially come out but are known to be gay. Although the social concealment of lesbian sexuality has been more successful than that of male homosexuality, this is part of a picture of oppression and self-oppression in the lesbian community.

Denman (2004) notes that lesbian women are more heterogeneous than gay men in the development of their emerging sexuality. She suggests that one of two stories is usually told. The first reflects lifelong awareness of difference and an early attraction to females. The second describes initial heterosexual adjustment followed by later change to lesbian relationships. In the latter case, initial choice of a male partner may have been influenced by economic and social considerations. Particularly in times when women were more dependent financially, coupled with social pressures to conform, there was recourse to conventional marriage. The marriage then unravels at some later point, when the woman can no longer deny her sexuality, and there follows a difficult period of adjustment as the woman leaves, often both husband and children, to embark on a new life. This is not an uncommon situation in a world of greater sexual freedom, but the increased opportunity for change does not mitigate the pain of separation and anxiety about an uncertain future.

There are serious implications for psychotherapeutic practice in the above accounts of both male and female homosexuality. An increasing number of writers are now commenting on the failure for many years of the psychotherapeutic establishment to meet the emotional and therapeutic needs of homosexual patients. O'Connor and Ryan (1993) give a variety of almost heart-stopping accounts of the insensitivity, brutality and sheer ignorance of the treatment received by lesbians, particularly in the psychoanalytic setting. Friedman and Downey (2002) give similar accounts of the psycho-therapy of gay men. Most of the examples are of homosexual patients in therapy with straight psychotherapists but there are also examples of difficulties with homosexual therapists, since the presence of a therapist with the same sexual orientation is no guarantee that prejudice, anxiety and confusion will be absent, or that transferences and counter-transferences in a gay therapeutic partnership will be understood and worked with constructively. The field is crying out for more information, training and supervision.

All this applies in equal measure to group psychotherapy. The problem is lessened in same-sex homosexual groups, usually run by gay therapists, where the high degree of commonality tends to facilitate open sharing, identification and cohesiveness. A greater challenge exists to the typical long-term psychotherapeutic group where the mixed-sex membership includes homosexual men and women. Much as this is an advance, there is a risk that the greater acknowledgement of gayness in contemporary society could produce facile assumptions about sexual difference and acceptance, as if the fears and prejudices of the past have simply been wiped out. For one thing, there continue to be many people who are struggling to define their sexuality and are anxious about revealing homosexual attraction in a group. Even 'out' gay people may have difficulty revealing the nature of their sexual desires and practices in an otherwise straight group. Political correctness may make it difficult for straight people to express negative feelings or anxieties towards gays. An attitude of easy tolerance may conceal disquiet, prejudice and a sense of threat. And gay members may have problems about straights, about their easier sexual path, about their mainstream acceptance. A lot will depend on both the gender and the sexual orientation of the therapist and the extent to which they represent an open and enquiring approach to *all* sexuality, which includes recognition of their sexual preferences, anxieties and blind spots. There is an enormous amount in this area for the therapist to absorb and understand and much of this is highly loaded and value-driven. The further implications of the therapist's role are explored more fully in Chapter 15.

Having sounded a word of caution about homosexuality in the psychotherapy group, there is of course huge potential in a mixed group for the opening up and deepening of the erotic imagination, in which, ideally, both gay and straight, male and female sexuality can locate their desires.

Can sexuality change?

The question of change, its potentials and its limits, is uppermost in psychotherapy. Most people come to psychotherapy seeking some form of change, from small but intensely important change to dramatic change. There is often a longing for sexual change of one sort or another – to find release from sexual inhibition, to have better sex and greater sexual enjoyment, to have more sexual partners, to have fewer sexual partners, to contain sexual impulses, to express sexual impulses, to understand one's sexuality better, and so on, in great variety. This raises the question of sexual flexibility, of what the possibilities are for significant change in sexuality.

Money's concept of 'lovemaps' (1986) is an important contribution to the debate. The lovemap refers to a template or script for sexual activity established at an early age and determining the nature of the sexual object and sexual relationships. It is biopsychosocially constructed, with biological, social and personal influences which produce an idiosyncratic outcome – referred to by Denman (2004) as a kind of sexual fingerprint. While having some explanatory power, the concept holds out limited hope for transformation in sexuality: the lovemap has deep-rooted and enduring features. This contrasts with Giddens' notion of plastic sexuality, reviewed earlier in this chapter, which sees individual sexual choice as a feature of contemporary society. Giddens' concept, however, is etched against a broad social canvas, not necessarily implying the possibility of sexual change in the lifespan of a particular individual. Denman takes strength in the idea of the erotic imagination and the possibility that through this, its opening up and elaboration, the individual can discover the potential to be a sexual agent who takes risks and makes something different of the influences that define their sexuality. It is tempting to wonder whether this could be achieved more readily in group than in individual therapy, on the assumption that the sharing of differences, particularly in a group that is working openly and creatively with sexuality, can liberate the erotic imagination and the choices it offers.

The quest for psychotherapeutic change in sexuality is different from situations in which individuals go through natural changes in their sexual make-up. This touches on the issue of intra-individual variation in sexual identity and desire, in other words, diversity within the individual rather than between individuals. Most of this chapter has focused on the two main categories of sexuality, hetero-sexuality and homosexuality, as if this is how the world is divided. But, in reality, many people's sexual make-up is a complex and shifting amalgam of preferences and inclinations: perhaps a series of lovemaps rather than one exclusive lovemap. In his early pioneering research, Kinsey posited a continuum from 'complete' heterosexual-ity to 'complete' homosexuality (his famous six-point scale), with the majority somewhere between the two extremes (Kinsey and Pomeroy 1949). This suggests that most people have a degree of bisexuality and a personal configuration of opposite-sex and same-sex attrac-tions. Part of the challenge of sexual development is finding a relatively cohesive sexual self within this range of potentials, while managing the confusion that arises from different and seemingly contradictory tendencies as well as the practical and moral implica-tions of sexual choice.

Such internally-generated sexual choice ties in with Giddens' notion of sexuality as a form of self-creation in a more fluid society. Welcome as this change is, it also brings the inevitable problems of a new freedom. For many people, it engenders confusion as they struggle with uncertain and ambiguous opportunities, wanting con-sistency, craving difference, torn between conservative leanings and radical impulses. Perhaps the most common example of this is the bisexual dilemma (Angelides 2001; Hemmings 2002). Some writers argue that true bisexuality does not exist, that one sphere of sexual preference is always dominant. However, many men and women struggle with a subjective sense of bisexuality and the disturbing pulls of opposite desires. This is aggravated by the possible need for lifestyle decisions, particularly in the case of married people who are faced with the painful choice of living a double life or disrupting family life for the uncertainties of an alternative sexual life.

A further source of individual variation is the process of change through the lifespan. Sexuality is seldom a static phenomenon that is fixed at a given age but rather a fluctuating process in which the nature of sexual desire, interest, orientation and capacity are all subject to change from one life stage to another. To pick up on the example immediately above, many married people who have assumed a heterosexual identity discover, either earlier or later in their lives, that they have a stronger homosexual orientation and face the question of how to live their lives. But this is just one example of many, from adolescence to old age, of sexual plasticity in the individual. Even within an established and enduring sexual orientation, there may be significant variations over time in the nature of desire, fantasy and the sexual impulse. For example: a heterosexual woman in mid-life discovers a wish to be more active in sexual intercourse; a homosexual man who has always played an active sexual role gets in touch with passive yearnings. Some changes can be exciting and accommodated without too much difficulty but others have complex implications for self-regard, for the sense of personal continuity and for negotiating change within existing relationships.

Many problems of the above sort are presented in psychotherapy. Whereas individual and couple therapy have an obvious relevance, group psychotherapy offers assistance in an alternative way. The group usually represents a spectrum of sexualities, in gender, age and sexual preference: a kaleidoscope of the sexual universe. This presents active opportunities for learning, comparison and support from others in a way that is very different from other forms of psychotherapy: the group holds a pool of experience from which the individual may derive knowledge and insight, as well as support in the search for sexual fulfilment.

Sexuality and shame

Sexuality tends to evoke a range of affects that can be intense and discomforting: jealousy, envy, guilt, resentment and shame. Whereas the other affects will be dealt with in different parts of this book, I wish to focus here on shame, since it is so closely linked to the development of a sexual self and so intertwined with the struggle to establish satisfying sexual relationships.

Mollon (2003) emphasizes the intimate association between shame and sexuality. Much of this has to do with the privacy of sexuality and the tension between the sense of a public self, which is often made up of what are felt to be false representations of self, and a private self, which may be experienced as very different. This discrepancy is the source of potential shame: the feared exposure of inadequate, humiliated and injured aspects of the self. The private self involves the body to a significant degree and with it the subjective experiences of bodily imperfection and ineptitude, as well as intense sexual need. Andre Green (1982), cited by Mollon, suggests that for some people, hell is not other people but the body, with its incorrigible appetites and impulses. Sex is very much of the body, the body in its nakedness and vulnerability. Some of the shame associated with sexuality is bodily shame but there are other sources of shame:

- behaviours that are thought to be immature and signs of weakness, such as masturbation;
- sexual inadequacy and lack of experience, often associated with difficulties in negotiating adult sexual relationships;
- transgressive sexual wishes, that cross conventional boundaries of age and the sexual rights of others;
- sexual fantasies that are thought to be perverse, often involving sado-masochistic and fetishistic wishes;
- failure and rejection in sexual relationships;
- compulsive sexual activities such as visiting prostitutes and addiction to internet pornography.

These areas of shame account for the difficulty many people have in seeking psychotherapeutic help, as well as the anxiety about talking openly about their sexuality. As Mollon points out, just seeking psychotherapeutic help can be experienced as shameful. He describes the psychotherapeutic situation as 'saturated with the potential for shame' (2003, p xii) and postulates two main reasons for this: 1) the information to be communicated is inherently of a private and latently shameful nature; and 2) the possibilities of failures in communication and empathy are manifold. Seidler (2000) observes that shameful situations are always 'envisaged': they involve exposure to the gaze of others. Since the sense of self is formed in relation to others, through envisaging oneself in the eyes of the other (Mead 1934 based his theory of self on this), it suggests that shame is inherent in the genesis of the self. Psychotherapy presents a major challenge to this constellation: potentially helping to deal with shame and its undermining effects but at the risk of exposing the patient to further shame.

If all of this applies to individual therapy, how much more so does it to group therapy? The problem with envisaged shame is multiplied in the group by the number of people present and anxiety about this is an important condition for anti-group developments, for fear and resistance to joining a group in the first place and for continuing sensitivity to the possibility of re-shaming. There is now, after a long period of neglect of this topic, a substantial and useful body of literature on shame in group psychotherapy (Alonso and Rutan 1988; Hahn 1994). Gans and Weber (2000), in particular, draw attention to the shame-inducing potential of the group and, more so, to the difficulty of detecting shame when it is by nature hidden from others. It is interesting to note, however, that very little attention is paid to sexuality as a source of shame in group psychotherapy. Even Gans and Weber, listing a number of differences that can generate feelings of shame, do not mention sexuality. There is clearly a need to develop and document this aspect of groups. As Pines (1995) points out, shame has an important regulating function in group membership, since it sensitizes the individual to the ethical and moral standards of the group and so reinforces the potential for group belonging. But, in my view, groups should not have to depend to more than a certain degree on the binding effect of shame, nor should groups have only a regulating function. They can also provide the stimulus for challenging conventional morality, as well as the empathy needed to counteract and modify shame. Mollon notes that empathic sensitivity and openness are the major correctives of shame and offers a useful description of how this might operate on a social and interpersonal level:

> It is through a sensitivity to shame in others that we can show social kindness, minimizing the potential for our fellow human beings to feel embarrassed, inadequate, awkward, left out, and so on. Social intercourse always hovers on the edge of potential shame and embarrassment, since the possibilities of misunderstandings, misperceptions, and misjudgements are ever-present. The absence of feelings of shame can be taken as a signal of being 'at home', amongst friends, and of *belonging to the group* . . .
>
> (Mollon 2003: 48, emphasis added)

Conclusion

This chapter has explored some of the major influences on sexual development, describing the child's emergence from the intimacy of the infant-mother relationship through a relationship with the parents as a couple, to the affiliation with siblings, the identification with peers and the formation of adult sexual relationships. Each of these contexts has an influence on the child's developing sexuality in a matrix of emotional bonding, sensual desire, jealousy and rivalry. Gender identification and sexual orientation are discovered and tested in peer group affiliation through childhood and adolescence. The excitement of sexual development is often tinged with emotional pain, anxiety, difference and shame. Through this process, and based on an individual's particular biological propensities, the qualities of a unique sexuality are formed. Although sexuality is intensely personal and individual, it is at the same time deeply social, since it is about relationships and the attempt to define a sexual identity in a cultural context. It is likely that much of this will be transferred to the psychotherapy group. Here, the tensions between the individual and the social are bound to recur. But the therapy group offers new opportunities, new challenges to conventional morality, new possibilities of dealing with the fear, guilt and shame that so frequently beset sexual development.

3

SEX AND PSYCHOANALYSIS

Of all psychotherapeutic approaches, psychoanalysis has produced by far the most detailed account of sexuality in the development of the individual as well as its representation in the consulting room. Sexuality seeps through the entire vision of psychoanalysis. Although the prevalence of the psychoanalytic model of treatment, along with its theoretical foundations, has been challenged in the last few decades, its approach to sexuality remains influential, if controversial. In their introduction to a collection of papers on contemporary approaches to sexuality, Hiller *et al.* (2005) comment that the theoretical model to which practitioners return over and over again is the psychoanalytic one. Notwithstanding problems with its empirical framework, they maintain, psychoanalysis has a richness and breadth of explanation of sexual functioning and development which remains unrivalled.

In this chapter, rather than attempting to review the entire psychoanalytic *oeuvre* of sexuality, which is vast and much more complex and contradictory than first meets the eye, I intend to take a particular perspective. Apart from offering a considered view on a controversial subject, I intend this to provide a departure point for a consideration of sexuality in group analysis. I begin this here and pursue it further in later chapters. The perspective is this: the psychoanalytic discourse on sexuality is riven by a paradox concerning liberation and restraint. On the one hand, it is a liberalizing discourse, opening up sexuality in its diverse forms, highlighting the anxieties and denials that inhibit sexual expression, and encouraging the potential for living fuller sexual lives. On the other hand, by adhering to a 'naturalist', mainly biological view of sexuality and by reflecting dominant social prescriptions for sexuality, it serves to protect conventional sexual repression. With this goes a strong tendency to pathologize almost anything outside of a narrow conception of heterosexuality, leading to categorical and pejorative judgements of sexual diversity in its many forms.

This contradictory situation, I suggest, has to a large extent been absorbed by the group psychotherapy culture, partly by default, because of not having a sexual discourse of its own, partly by the ease of submission to a dominant discourse. But because group psychotherapy has not yet developed its own discourse, there are opportunities to evolve a different one, more reflective and critical of the conventionalizing processes that link society and psychotherapy. In order to do this, it is useful to have some understanding of the dilemmas and double-binds which have constrained psychoanalysis – and by which psychoanalysis has in turn constrained the representation of sexuality. In order to achieve this, I focus on several dominant themes in psychoanalysis, starting with Freud's contribution (a wider perspective than in Chapter 1), moving on to the Oedipus complex, the mother-infant relationship, erotic transference and counter-transference and the psychoanalytic approach to sexual orientation. Within each of these spheres, I attempt to consider processes of restraint and counter-restraint and the emerging implications for a sexual discourse in group psychotherapy. In line with my reference to homosexuality as a pivotal concern in contemporary sexual discourse, there is some emphasis on this subject as a reflection of prevailing attitudes in psychoanalysis.

Freud

Freud's views on desire, particularly within the framework of the life and death instincts, were reviewed in Chapter 1. Here, Freud is revisited, with the focus more on sexuality.

It is important to situate Freud's original researches on sexuality in time and place. That he first started writing about the subject more than a century ago in Vienna meant that he was opening a window to Victorian society with its sexual hypocrisy, in which strict social controls concealed a feverish sexual *demi-monde*. His first theory, the seduction theory, presented as a lecture to the local psychiatric society in 1896, generated a conflict of interests that was to mark the progression of his views on sexuality through his life's work. Arguing that hysteria was the outcome of the trauma of childhood seduction, he retracted the theory in the face of disquiet about what it implied about Viennese society. Instead of actual seduction, he now proposed that the hysteric's recall of sexual abuse was the product of wishful fantasies. Although he subsequently gave convincing reasons for abandoning the theory, various commentators have suggested this was self-protective and motivated by professional/ political considerations (Masson 1984). Freud's conflict of interests concerned a view of sexual disorder as generated by external events in a social milieu – the original hypothesis – contrasted with a view of it as internally generated, that is, through intra-psychic fantasy. Freud's change of mind suggests not only how sexuality itself, but the theoretical discourse on sexuality, is constructed by social processes, including the politics of convention and belonging.

At the same time, as Peter Gay (1988) points out, Freud's renunciation opened a new chapter in the history of psychoanalysis. From now on, childhood sexuality becomes the mainspring of his theory. His own dream analysis and that of patients (Freud 1900) propelled the vision of sexual development back into early infancy and widened the notion of sexual to a complex range of bodily experiences. It was during this period that Freud also formulated the theory of the Oedipus complex – which, given its importance for the subject at hand, is treated in greater detail below. Continuing the progression of his theory, however, Freud's three essays on the theory of sexuality (1905) are his next major statement. They particularly reveal the paradox of an expanding and contracting erotic imagination, of the potential for sexual liberation and the actuality of restraint. Denman (2004) notes how the initial basis of sexual development in Freud's theory is the polymorphously perverse, bisexual infant. Sexuality in origin is diverse, multi-faceted, ambiguous. However, through a single universal path of development – the sequence of oral, anal and genital stages – the final 'normal' sexual resolution is achieved in genital heterosexuality. Freud saw adult sexuality as a compromise between the sexual instinct and the demands of society, as vested particularly in parental prohibition, but the outcome of sexual development is nonetheless highly normative.

Dimen (1995) links the theoretical underpinnings of Freud's theories of sexuality to what she terms the 'Discourse of Nature'. In spite of his appreciation of the ambiguity and mutability of sexual desire, Freud was himself constrained by the pull towards notions of biological and reproductive necessity, the power of Darwinian evolutionary thought and its blueprint for social normativity. It is not surprising therefore that sexuality begins in polymorphousness but that: 'By the end, cultural stricture, psychic integrity, and reproductive survival speak in one voice' (Dimen 1995: 133).

This notion of a complex bisexual potential that is progressively (and of necessity) constrained within adult heterosexual adjustment informs a significant body of further psychoanalytic writing on sexuality. Kernberg (1995), for example, in a major treatise on sexual development, endorses the notion of polymorphous perversity as integral to all sexuality, and is at pains to elaborate on our bisexual constitution in particular, but insists on the possibility of all this being contained – and expressed – in a single heterosexual relationship. He goes to great lengths, for example, in showing how bisexuality is experienced in the lover's identification with the sexual experience of the opposite-sex partner. Although some of this has the air of possibility, there is a sense of strain in having to force all sexual variations into the one relationship. The following gives a flavour of this effort:

> The body of the beloved becomes a geography of personal meanings, so that the fantasied early polymorphous per-verse relations to the parental objects are condensed with the admiring and invasive relation to the lover's body parts . . . All of this is expressed in the perverse components of intercourse and sexual play – in fellatio, cunnilingus, and anal penetration, and in exhibitionistic, voyeuristic, and sadistic sexual play.
>
> (Kernberg 1995: 26)

There are further sections in which Kernberg describes the enact-ment of sado-masochistic desire and elaborates the details of oral and anal pleasures in the same relationship. This depicts either a very free and rich sexual liaison or the pressure to incorporate all sexual diversity within the one heterosexual relationship. The corollary is that diversity does not have a life of its own. Diverse desire has no path, no outlet, other than in one prescribed direction.

McDougall (1979, 1989), who has written extensively and in great depth about sexuality, similarly starts from an assumption about the profound bisexuality that is common to men and women. This she sees as predicating a deep longing in each sex to be both sexes and to possess both sets of parents, precipitating an ongoing struggle to surrender these unrealistic claims. However, mature sexual develop-ment once again involves the renunciation of bisexuality in favour of heterosexuality, with homosexuality seen as a defensive and illusory solution to the problem.

A further outcome of Freud's formulation was the increasing categorization and pathologization of the 'perversions'. Although there is clearly a difference between a 'perverse' sexual fantasy or impulse that is part of a wider repertoire of sexual activity, on the one hand, and a rigid adherence to a narrowly 'perverse' practice, on the other, the further development of psychoanalysis saw an increasing emphasis on the labelling, stratification and denigration of the perversions. Once the biological imperative is established, there must be a way of dealing with that which exists outside it, even defies it. Often, there was a lumping together of lifestyle choices and 'sexual deviations', a conflation of the notions of sexual difference and psychic immaturity.

O'Connor and Ryan (1993) comment on how far psychoanalysis drifted from Freud's notion of the mutability and variety of sexuality and how his original formulation became subsumed in a culture of pathologization. Dissenting voices have included those of Waddell and Williams (1991), who suggest that the category of perverse be dropped from considerations of object choice and limited specifically to sexual preferences expressing states of mind that are marked by destructive and life-denying motives. In relation to the common psychoanalytic notion that homosexuals envy and deny the creativity of parental intercourse, Cunningham (1991) argues that homosexuals are as capable as anyone else of appreciating heterosexual procreativity. Although she agrees that unconscious conflicts about parental intercourse may be an important aspect of an individual's sexual make-up, 'this is very different from the Kleinian postulate, which fetishes a certain version of parental intercourse by giving it a foundational and mythological status in the psychic lives of individuals' (O'Connor and Ryan 1993: 204–5).

The pathologization of homosexuality and the 'perversions' had the effect not only of creating a psychoanalytic environment that was hostile to patients who fell into these categories – as will be seen further in the section on homosexuality below – but of supporting the dominant social prescriptions for sexuality and contributing to the repression of all sexuality through the reinforcement of a restrictive morality. That this has to some extent changed in contemporary society through the emergence of a more diverse sexual landscape is in spite – rather than because – of psychoanalysis. Psychoanalysis has struggled, and by no means entirely succeeded, in keeping pace with these changes. This is one reason why a group analytic discourse on sexuality, with its potential for a more radical and contemporary social vision, is timely.

But this is no reason to deny the positive aspects of Freud's creation. Returning to his three essays on sexuality, one important contribution was his unswerving attention to the embodiment of sexuality. Although this may seem tautological – how can sex not be embodied? – Freud's detailed tracing of states of bodily arousal, excitement, inhibition and release encouraged a long line of continuing work on the bodily aspects of sexuality. This point is made to highlight the tendency in some discourses – including psychotherapy itself – to deliteralize and disembody the sexual subject through interpretation and theory, quite apart from the more fundamental denial of sexuality. This tends to happen also in more sociologically inspired accounts of sexuality – a point highlighted in the next chapter. When the biologistic stance inherent in Freud's theory is criticized, therefore, it tends to obscure the illuminating aspects of his emphasis on the body, his detailed elaboration of the body as the site of sexuality. Part of Freud's achievement in the three essays is his insistence on the importance of desire. Sexuality is not just a response to an object or a stimulus but a subjective experience of desire in its complex manifestations that interacts with sex as a behavioural act. Through this is developed the erotic imagination and the intricate web of desire that weaves through embodied sexuality.

The Oedipus complex

The Oedipus complex is possibly the most widely theorized and controversial of all psychoanalytic concepts. 'Discovered' by Freud in 1900, the complex has been taken up by successive generations of psychoanalysts and represents one of the defining features of psychoanalysis. I suggest that it has important implications for group psychotherapy – and, if anything, has been under-utilized in my opinion – but at the same time is prone to a rigidity of interpretation and application that has supported the psychoanalytic narrative of the human condition, with its prejudices and blind-spots.

The Oedipus complex describes the love for one parent and rivalry towards the other: a simple configuration but one that brings in train a host of affects. These include jealousy that may harbour destructive wishes towards the rival, guilt about the desire for one parent and destructive wishes towards the other, fear of retaliation, and shame and anger consequent to a deep sense of exclusion from the parental union. The concept in the 'positive' heterosexual form also has an equivalent 'negative' homosexual form with love for the same-sex parent and rivalry towards the opposite-sexed parent. Surprisingly, this version of the Oedipus complex is seldom referred to, in spite of its potential usefulness, particularly in relation to homosexual development.

The psychoanalytic assumption is that the way the complex is resolved – or not – underlies sexual development through life and is enacted in some form in adult sexual relationships. Kernberg (1995: 53) agrees with David (1971) that 'the quality of longing for the unavailable and forbidden oedipal object, which energizes sexual development, is a crucial component of sexual passion and love relations. In this regard, the Oedipal constellation may be considered a permanent feature of human relations . . .'. The spectre of the excluded third party is forever present, whether identified as oneself or the rival. Every man and woman, says Kernberg, consciously or unconsciously fears the existence of someone who would be loved more by the sexual partner. In this sense, the nature of the Oedipal configuration touches on narcissistic concerns, self-esteem, the requirement to deal with rivalry and competition, and the capacity to endure the vicissitudes of sexual coupling.

The Oedipus complex is a generative concept that has extended the psychoanalytic focus beyond the two-person relationship. Foulkes (1972) reinterpreted it in group terms, describing the Oedipal situation as one that draws in the entire family in its various alliances and rivalries. Blackwell (personal communication) comments that, in a sense, Freud begat a group psychology by formulating the Oedipus complex. Halton (1998) suggests that the concept is indispensable in understanding the group psychotherapy process in so far as it predicates rivalry in the group for the attention of the therapist. The therapy is seen as incomplete without interpretation of the way the Oedipal situation is configured in the group. Whether we agree or not with this view, it seems to me undeniable that the issues of inclusion, exclusion, jealousy, rivalry and shame, which are so much part of group process, make sense in the light of an Oedipal explanation, particularly if sexuality and desire are at play. Whereas some of these dynamics are explicable in a non-desire based social theory, such as that of Elias, this is very limited if we look into the 'heart' of human relationships (see Chapters 6 and 7 for a further discussion of this point).

Kernberg (1995) has looked more broadly at the social representation of the Oedipal couple and makes pertinent points about the social implications of sexual and love relations. He suggests that the exclusivity and intensity of the sexual couple is socially transgressive. The couple is always, in his view, deeply asocial, private, rebelling against conventionally tolerated sexuality. He describes social groups as prone to fostering a restrictive sense of conventional morality, hewn from the collective urge to establish a shared consensus on basic values. But this morality often conflicts with the more personal morality of the individual and the couple. Romantic love and sexuality reflect a desire for liberation from the surrounding group and its oppressive morality. These reflections raise important questions about psychotherapy groups and the extent to which they mirror the same conventional morality of society or a different and more expansive morality, an issue which surfaces strongly in the clinical examples in Part 3 of this book. Similarly, the place of the sexual couple in the therapy group comes under scrutiny in Part 3, touching on similar issues about the group's tolerance and support – or otherwise – for sexual coupling.

Kernberg suggests that the group both admires the couple for its Oedipal triumph and envies the couple's success. A well-functioning couple is seen as potentially evoking intense envy in groups, eliciting in others the uncomfortable sense of being the excluded Oedipal third. This contrasts with Bion's (1961) pairing assumption which hypothesizes a group that is fascinated by the sexual couple, hoping for a solution through their pairing. However, admiration and envy can of course exist side by side.

Apart from the interpersonal and group implications of the sexual pair, the Oedipus complex has stimulated ideas about the cognitive capacities required to deal with the desires and subjectivities of the three people involved in the Oedipal configuration – father, mother and child. Britton (1989) derives from the Oedipus complex the notion of triangular space. The links between parents and child are hypothesized as forming an internal triangle that unites the child's inner world. By identifying with each position on the triangle, the child constructs the capacity both for observing a relationship between two people and for being observed while participating in their own relationships. The acquisition of this observing capacity facilitates the individual's understanding of relationships in the wider interpersonal sphere. Britton's thesis is very relevant to group psychotherapy, where being observed in one's relationships as well as observing the relationships of others are ongoing aspects of group participation. This is close to what Foulkes (1964) described as 'ego training in action', the development of skills of observation and judgement through group participation.

Generative as the concept of the Oedipus complex has been, its achievements are strongly countered by criticism of the orthodoxies it propounds, specifically in the 'positive' Oedipal version that holds sway over sexual discourse. Feminist writers, in particular, highlight the assumptions about gender and desire that are part of this formulation. Benjamin (1986, 1990) criticizes the 'deep structure of complementarity', which she sees as inherent in the Oedipal model and its implied theory of difference. Through its sharp division between the roles of the sexes, the Oedipus complex defines masculinity and femininity in opposition to each other and gender organized as polarity. For both sexes the Oedipal prescription is the same: identification with the same-sex parent and desire for the opposite-sex parent. O'Connor and Ryan (1993: 240) refer to this as 'a theory of desire based on a total and prohibitive disjunction between the objects of desire and identification'. Concerned about the negative construction of homosexuality this implies, these authors note the uncritical tendency 'to tie desire and identification so tightly together in opposition to each other that other sources of desire and other forms of identification other than gender-based ones recede into oblivion' (1993: 239). This affects not only homosexuals but all those struggling to hold together in creative balance the male and female components of their gender identities within the spontaneous flow of desire. It has major implications for group psychotherapy, where men and women come together in a search of their authentic gendered selves and sexual desires. As both Elliott (1986) and Rose (2002) point out, the work of the group requires the deconstruction of gender stereotypes so that participants are freer to relate within a spectrum of identifications. That this work is often so difficult is an expression of culturally entrenched gender attributions that, notwithstanding a degree of social change, tend to be inscribed in conventional family relations and individual development.

The Oedipus complex, then, paradoxically opens up a significant seam of the sexual discourse, illuminating a common though elusive aspect of sexual relations, helping to bridge the gap between individual, couple and group, but at the same time consigning gender and desire to a binary framework that reflects and reinforces social orthodoxies.

The mother-infant relationship

Following Freud, decreasing importance was attributed in psychoanalysis to sexuality as the mainspring of development, sexual and otherwise. This de-emphasis was particularly advocated by object relationship theory which highlighted the object-seeking aspect of relationships in contrast to drive and desire. Another change was the increasing regard for the early mother-child relationship as the foundation of emotional development. By focusing so intensely on the earliest dyad, this change seemingly set the psychoanalytic version of development further back from an appreciation of wider social influences. However, it served to strengthen understanding of the intimate nature of relationships and became absorbed into further psychoanalytic narratives of the sexual encounter.

Kernberg's (1995) account of the genesis of erotic desire starts with the mother-infant relationship. Based on the work of Braunschweig and Fain (1971), he regards the mother's physical stimulation and enjoyment of the infant as essential in engendering the infant's 'body-surface erotism' and, later, the full experience of sexual desire. Hiller *et al.* (2005) agree that this early bond, which includes both physical and psychological stimulation in a sufficiently secure and sensitive relationship, without undue impingements and discontinuities, is a vital precursor of the capacity for sexual relationships. Where early levels of anxiety are prolonged and maternal rejection a feature, the pleasurable link between bodily sensations and intimate contact may be disrupted and sex becomes imbued with anxious and possibly destructive meanings.

Various writers have emphasized the maternal relationship as a paradigm for loving intimacy in all its nuances, arguing for its positive and progressive effect in terms of both tender, sensual longings as well as the intensity of aggressive, possessive connection (Meltzer 1973; Irigaray 1991; Wrye and Welles 1994). These writers have also encouraged the use of the maternal transference and counter-transference in psychoanalytic treatment, including the patient's experience of the analyst's body, aiming to deepen the experience of intimacy in the encounter. Other writers have criticized the emphasis on the maternal as regressive and avoidant of the impact of the Oedipus complex with its competitive challenges and mobilization of jealousy, guilt and rage. Here, the mother-infant emphasis is seen as constraining development and creating the illusion of a dyad separate from the tensions of interpersonal and social contexts. Schaverien (1995) is particularly challenging, suggesting that analysts who concentrate on the mother-infant relationship, and neglect to take up more adult sexual feelings, are abusing their power. By vesting all in the infantile relationship, they discourage growth towards independence and more mature sexuality.

The mother-infant paradigm, with its parallel in the two-person relationship of individual therapy, would seem to be in contradiction to group psychotherapy, with its emphasis on the wider group, both inside and outside the consulting room. However, it may paradoxically define the 'missing' element in group therapy in so far as exclusive two-person contact is minimized, even prohibited, in the group, with patients often complaining that what they want is individual rather than group therapy. The longed-for intimate closeness between two people, for merger with the other, for the fantasy of total togetherness, is unavailable. As I have previously suggested (Nitsun 1996), this is one of the determinants of the anti-group, patients resenting the absence of the 'special' relationship and seeing the group as inimical to their desires. This leads me, in several parts of this book, to suggest that the tendency to minimize two-person relationships in group therapy can go too far and that there may be ways of recognizing and supporting pairing within the group as constructive and not simply pathological or group destructive. At the same time, it is useful that the group with its plural membership can, in theory at least, provide checks and balances which discourage symbiotic dependencies and which bring the couple back into the shared space of the group.

It is interesting also that both Foulkes and Bion, group theorists who in other ways differed radically in their conception of groups, agreed that the group represents in symbolic terms the mother's body. Foulkes' concept of the group matrix is interpreted in the literature as a maternal entity, the womb, or the mother's body more generally (Roberts 1983). This, however, rather like the environmental mother described below, is seen as having a broad, containing function rather than offering provision for more intimate encounters.

Winnicott's (1963) distinction between the environmental mother and the object mother seems to me a useful way of reconciling these disparate aspects of a maternal perspective of the group. In Winnicott's thinking, the environmental mother has – as in Foulkes' concept of the group matrix – a holding or containing function, providing a safe, environmental backcloth. The object mother is the mother full on, the mother who engages intensely with the child, arousing feelings of desire, passion, love, frustration and hate. My own view of group analysts as therapists is that they are usually excellent at creating the environmental mother function of the group but tentative about allowing the object mother its full presence in the group. Partly, I think, this is out of anxiety about the unleashing of powerful feelings, generating a fear that the group will be overwhelmed and the containing function of the group damaged or destroyed. This is also why, I believe, sexuality appears to have no acknowledged place in group psychotherapy – a denial born of the fear that responding to the object mother, in the symbolic sense of passionate engagement, will be uncontrollable and uncontainable.

My view is that there is considerable potential here, potential for finding ways of facilitating both the environmental mother and the object mother, perhaps trusting that the strengthening of the former can facilitate in less defended ways the latter. In an approach which so highly values and utilizes the social process, there must at the same time be room for the expression of the most intimate desires and longings. But the safety of the group, the level of trust, is essential in making this possible.

Erotic transference and counter-transference

Much of the psychoanalytic discourse on sexuality is vested in the subject of erotic transference and counter-transference. This is also one of the most tendentious and controversial aspects of psycho-analysis, at least partly because it touches on the highly charged issue of sexual enactment between therapist and patient.

As presented by Mann (2003), the controversy centres on the ques-tion of whether erotic transference is regressive or progressive. The regressive view is that erotic transference is backward-looking in that it derives from the patient's infantile experience, creating resistance to analysis through a compulsion to repeat the past and avoid the challenge of emotional development. The progressive narrative sees erotic transference as seeking a different outcome to previously unsatisfactory sexual development. In this view, the patient is in search of a transformational object through whom they can give up infantile relationships in favour of more mature erotic attachments. The analyst is potentially the patient's transformational object and the constructive handling of the transference the route through which sexual transformation may be achieved.

The recognition and utilization of erotic *counter*-transference is, if anything, more controversial than erotic transference. In so far as the analyst is usually anything but a neutral participant in the relation-ship, the arousal of sexual feelings at some point in the analysis, and possibly even on a continuing basis, is inevitable (Britton 2003) – how to manage these feelings is the question. The classical psycho-analytic view, strongly derived from Freud, is that there is no place for the analyst's erotic feelings in the analysis: they are potentially disruptive, dangerous and must be repressed. As against this view-point is the belief, which has grown stronger with the development of psychoanalysis, that these feelings not only cannot be ignored or repressed but that they are valuable, if not indispensable, in the progression of the sexual narrative.

Mann cites a number of protagonists on either side of the argument. On the critical side, which regards the expression of the erotic in analysis as regressive and counter-therapeutic, Sandler *et al.* (1970) see the eroticized transference as entailing a psychotic loss of reality-testing and potentially damaging to the analysis. Stoller (1979, 1985), who emphasizes hatred and hostility in sexuality, suggests that the desire to harm that is contained within erotic excitement may overwhelm the patient and the analysis. Kumin (1985) talks about 'erotic horror' accompanying patients' awareness of an upsurge of sexual feelings in the analysis: the experience of anxiety and aversion to the feelings aroused is counter-productive to the aims of the treatment. Other writers see erotic transference as a form of resistance but also suggest ways in which it can be usefully managed. Blum (1973), for example, regards strong erotic transference as a sign of a sexualized family history, including abuse, and considers the therapist's role not to mirror but to distinguish past from present, fantasy from reality, in this way counteracting the regressive potential of the sexual transference.

In contrast to the above viewpoints there are a large number of writers who unambiguously state the value of the erotic in the transferential relationship. Writers such as Wrye and Wells (1994), Covington (1996) and Mann himself (2003) all emphasize the erotic as the defining point in emotional development generally and psychoanalysis specifically. The importance of both the patient's erotic strivings and the analyst's erotic counter-transference are underlined. Samuels (1995) talks about the importance of 'erotic play-back', both in childhood development and the analytic process. The analyst's sensitivity and responsiveness to the patient's sexuality is seen not so much as a choice as a responsibility. Wrye and Welles (1994) contend that the greatest danger to the therapeutic process is the therapist defending him- or herself from participation with the patient at the most intimate levels, which include the erotic. The therapist needs to 'tolerate the heat without fanning the flames' of the erotic transference (Wrye and Welles 1994: 87, quoted in Mann 2003: 11). There is some unanimity of opinion that the analyst's awareness of their own erotic response in the therapeutic encounter is vital.

Mann expresses concern about the number of writers who regard sexuality in psychotherapy as dangerous and regressive, seeing this as a reflection of 'the encapsulated erotic narrative'. Based on the work of the group analyst, Hopper (1991), he defines encapsulation as a defence against the fear of annihilation. Attempting to ward off annihilation anxiety, the individual secretes intense feelings within a buried part of the self. Linking this to the erotic, Mann suggests that sexuality can arouse annihilatory anxiety and hence is dissociated and divorced from the body of discourse. In the same way that patients encapsulate their sexual selves, so analysts/therapists encapsulate sexuality in a buried discourse.

While supporting the value of the sexual in the analytic dialogue, Mann nevertheless ends up on a realistic note about the progressive and regressive aspects of the erotic transference. He suggests that both apply: the erotic can be regressive, overwhelming, creating resistance *and* it can be liberating and growthful, creating connection and intimacy. Rather than constituting a duality, it is 'both things simultaneously, though one or the other may be stronger at any one time' (Mann 2003: 4). Also, the nature of erotic expression in therapy depends very much on the two people involved and what sort of relationship they develop: 'there are as many narratives as there are analytic couples' (2003: 5).

How does the concept of erotic transference and counter-transference apply to group psychotherapy? The fact that so little is written about it is deceptive, suggesting that this is a non-subject. However, not only do the same issues as in individual analysis apply, but more so, since the potential for sexual transferences in the group is multiplied by the number of participants. Denman (2004) produces an interesting statistic about the complexity of erotic transference and counter-transference in individual therapy, assuming we take account of variations in gender and sexual orientation. Looking at a grid comprising male, female, heterosexual and homosexual, she suggests that there could be 32 different forms of erotic transference and counter-transference in dyadic therapy. If we multiply this by eight, the number we might expect in a group, we come up with a figure of 256 possible types of erotic transference and counter-transference in group therapy! This includes transference and counter-transference relations between the therapist and patients, as well as potential transferences between the patients themselves. In group analytic terms, this is referred to as the *horizontal transference* as opposed to the *vertical transference* of psychoanalysis. Horizontal transferences may require alternative understandings from vertical ones, for example they may be more sibling than child-parent based and because they operate in the generally freer interpersonal environment of the group, they may be expressed more openly and more directly.

But there is a more fundamental question about erotic transference and counter-transference when considering the group. The question is: is it always transference? Can you not have sexual feelings that are precisely that and nothing else? Erotic transference and counter-transference are schematic accounts of what might be entirely spontaneous responses. It could be argued that these accounts force sexuality in psychotherapy into a conceptual paradigm and in this way constitute another form of defence, even encapsulation. To consistently categorize sexual behaviour as transferential may be an attempt to intellectualize a process which is potentially intense, arousing and uncontrollable. I mention this specifically in relation to group therapy where, because of the greater immediacy of interaction in a setting with significantly more people, there is an ongoing likelihood of sexual attraction and desire, with the potential for sudden eruption and intense expression. This immediacy creates both a different set of potentials and problems from individual therapy and requires a perspective on how to handle the spontaneous sexuality that arises in the natural flow of a group.

This is not meant to suggest that erotic transference and counter-transference do not exist in a group therapy or that similar questions about what is progressive and what is regressive do not apply. Dealing with erotic transference and counter-transference in a group is obviously more complex than in individual therapy but this should not be the basis for denial and neglect. It presents a different and potentially difficult challenge in so far as transference in a group cannot be seen in isolation but in relation to the overall group process. As Moeller (2002) points out, sexual transference and counter-transference in group therapy are group events.

Finally, there is the ever-present and problematic aspect of sexual enactment in the group – or rather outside the group. Here, too, the possibilities are manifold, including sexual relations between the conductor and group members in addition to the more likely possibility of enactments between members. Most group therapists espouse a notion of sexual abstinence between members which is usually implicit in the discouragement of extra-group contact but, in my experience, the fact that this is not necessarily explicit leaves open the temptation to act out sexually away from the group. At the same time, the explicit prohibition of sexuality, we intuitively know, puts ideas in people's minds and at the same time potentially increases desire and the transgressive impulse. What is forbidden is often all the more desirable.

In line with my thesis about the paradoxically freeing and constraining aspects of the psychoanalytic discourse on sexuality, erotic transference and counter-transference emerge in the same contra-dictory light. Some of this has to do with actual social constraints which mitigate against a freer sexual culture, some with the con-ventional morality inscribed in much of psychoanalysis, and some with realistic anxiety about sexual enactment, even though several writers decry the tendency to de-sexualize psychoanalysis and opt instead for 'safe analysis' (Samuels 1999). However, as Denman (2004: 281) points out, no psychotherapeutic discipline other than psychoanalysis has generated such an 'extended meditation' on sexuality in the consulting room.

Sexual orientation

Within the mix of liberalizing and constraining influences in psycho-analysis, the most sustained area of prejudice is probably that concerning sexual orientation. There is now an increasing literature challenging psychoanalytic assumptions about homosexuality and the impact this has had not only on clinical practice but on the cultural representation of homosexuality. O'Connor and Ryan (1993: 9) say of psychoanalysis that 'it provides no articulated conception within its own terms of an integrated, non-perverse, mature and manifest homosexuality, or what is required to achieve this'.

An initial point of controversy concerns Freud's view of homo-sexuality, since there are differing interpretations of what he said in his writings and what this revealed about his attitude. The customary view is that Freud took a liberal view of homosexuality. This is epitomized in his famous 'Letter to an American mother', in which he responds to her concern about her homosexual son. Countering prevailing opinion at the time, Freud (1935: 786) says 'homosexuality . . . is nothing to be ashamed of, no vice, no degradation, it cannot be classified as an illness . . .'. This letter has frequently been held up as an illustration of Freud's mature, compassionate and non-judgemental view of homosexuality. He appeared to regard sexual orientation as constitutional and not subject to the 'cure' which later analysts sought to impose on 'sexual inversion'.

Weegmann (forthcoming), however, has questioned this conclu-sion on the basis of Freud's (1920) documented response to the presentation of a female homosexual, in which he claims to under-stand the psychogenesis of her orientation with 'complete certainty' and invokes concepts such as fixation, embittered retreat from her father and other rivals, 'changing into a man' and taking her mother's place. Weegmann highlights Freud's 'complete certainty' as a case of narrative prejudice. He refers also to a subsequent paper by Freud (1922) in which he links homosexuality to the regressive, the narcissistic and the defensive. When linked further to the binary framework of desire and gender identification constructed by the Oedipus complex, the extent of Freud's liberal views and his influence on the later psychoanalytic construction of homosexuality now come under scrutiny. This goes back to the discourse of nature noted above and its parallel in the heterosexist discourse of the Judeo-Christian tradition which upholds the sanctity of marriage and the procreative heterosexual couple, repudiating any sexuality that exists outside the narrow margins of this conception.

In the decades following Freud, there was a hardening of the psychoanalytic approach to homosexuality, reflected in a stream of psychoanalysts, usually male, who not only pathologized homosexuals but advocated treatment actively geared to heterosexual conversion. Mitchell (1996) describes this period as a stain on American psychoanalysis. The consensus was that homosexuality represented the failed development of heterosexuality through fear and inhibition, a defensive solution to the Oedipus complex in which there were unresolved anxieties about castration. The mission of psychoanalysis was the uncovering of these dynamics as part of the programmatic conversion of homosexuals.

The pathologization of homosexuality in the USA reached a head in the work of Socarides, which May (1995: 155) describes as 'a particularly troubling example of vilification in the guise of diagnosis'. He quotes the following extract from a publication by Socarides:

> The 'solution' of homosexuality is always doomed to failure and even when used for utilitarian purposes, e.g., prestige, power, protection by a more powerful male, the accomplishment is short-lived. Homosexuality is based on the fear of the mother, the aggressive attack against the father, and is filled with aggression, destruction, and self-deceit. It is a masquerade of life . . . However, the unconscious manifestations of hate, destructiveness, incest and fear are always threatening to break through. Instead of union, cooperation, solace, stimulation, enrichment, healthy challenge and fulfilment, there are only destruction, mutual defeat, exploitation of the partner and the self, oral-sadistic incorporation, aggressive onslaughts, attempts to alleviate anxiety

and a pseudo-solution to the aggressive and libidinal urges
which dominate and torment the individual.

(Socarides 1968: 8, quoted in May 1995: 155).

Interestingly, by the 1990s, when Socarides was invited by the
Portman Clinic in London to give a public lecture, the tide of counter-
criticism had grown so great that a massive protest led to the cancel-
lation of the lecture.

May (1995) has attributed the virulent psychoanalytic injunctions
against homosexuality in the USA at that time to what he describes
as 'American moralism masquerading as medicine'. But in the UK,
in the somewhat less aggressively moralistic culture of the English,
there are numerous parallels. Perhaps the best-known and most disturbing of these is that of Fairbairn. The disturbing aspect arises
from the fact that by introducing object relations theory, Fairbairn
advocated the social construction of human relationships, getting
away from the biologistic and deterministic aspects of drive theory. In
principle, this could have facilitated a more tolerant, enquiring view
of homosexuality, but Fairbairn concurred with a highly pathologizing and pejorative view. Influenced by the binary construction of the
Oedipus complex, he regarded homosexuality as a profound failure
of the Oedipal drama. In 'normal' development, the argument went,
the child relates to the opposite-sex parent as the exciting 'libidinal
object' and the same-sex parent as the hated 'anti-libidinal object'.
Through the resolution of the 'complex', the child comes to identify
more deeply with the same-sex parent and at the same time adopts
the 'moral defence', internalizing the good and the just that is associated with this parent. In homosexual development, the child fails
both to achieve identification with the same-sex parent and to
adopt the moral defence. This led Fairbairn (1946) to write that
homosexual behaviour is an expression of one of the most severe
pathologies and that rather than being neurotic, the homosexual is a
psychopath. His recommendation to the Scottish Advisory Council
was to remove homosexuals from society and put them into settle-
ment camps. Not psychotherapy but rehabilitation was advised:
'They should be put in controlled environments with a view toward
a gradual approximation of the life of the community at large.
Fairbairn also saw these settlements as a unique opportunity for
social experimentation and a scientific study of social relations'
(Domenici 1995: 42).

The protest that greeted Socarides' planned lecture in London
in the 1990s was part of the growing challenge to psychoanalytic

prejudice concerning homosexuality. This reflected the increasing liberalization in western society of attitudes towards sexual diversity generally and homosexuality in particular. There had in the intervening years also been dissenting voices within psychoanalysis itself. The most notable of these was Stoller (1979, 1985), who argued strongly against the notion of the unitary 'homosexual' and at one point suggested eliminating the term altogether. Stoller was also one of the few psychoanalytic writers to recognize the dread of homosexuality in the straight population. Drawing on the work of Greenson (1964), he documents how heterosexual men react with panic to homosexual fantasies or impulses. From this comes the observation that heterosexual gender identity may depend on a disavowal of homosexual feelings. Stoller not only helped to de-pathologize homosexuality but to draw attention to the homophobia that characterized conventional society and which Domenici (1995), interestingly, attributes in part to psychoanalytic prejudice.

One of the major shifts in the last decade or two has been the acceptance of homosexual men and women for psychoanalytic training – truer of the USA but also beginning in the UK. A product of this is the writing of homosexual analysts themselves which has begun to fashion alternative psychoanalytic perspectives of sexual development. Some of this, interestingly, harks back to Freud in an affirmative way. Isay (1991) and Lewis (1988), for example, embrace Freud's notions of constitutional bisexuality and the negative Oedipus complex in their explication of male homosexuality. By arguing that the young boy's erotic attraction to his father represents as valid and formative an impact on his development as that of a boy to his mother, they embody Freud's theories in a positive homosexual discourse. Corbett (1993) takes this further by challenging the traditional view that the passive, receptive aspects of homosexuality are based on a feminine identification. He argues that gay men inhabit a gender difference which is neither feminine nor a culturally defined masculine, but a different *kind* of masculine. Schwartz (1995: 120) comments 'for these gay writers there is more than one healthy sexual orientation. Homosexuality is no less natural, basic, or enduringly real a sexual orientation than is heterosexuality. It emerges in psychological development on a par with heterosexuality'.

The intense debate about homosexuality in psychoanalysis contrasts with the near absence of a debate in group psychotherapy, including group analysis. As Burman (2002) says, there is a particular silence about the homoerotic. Mixed psychotherapy groups now undoubtedly attract more gay and lesbian patients than before but, in the absence of a discourse or observational studies, what do we know about how this impacts on the group? The loss is not only of a guiding discourse but of the opportunity to use the rich resources of the group to generate its own perspectives on homosexual identity and its interrelationship with heterosexual identity. Looked at positively, the absence becomes a potential, an opportunity. Within this potential is the need to avoid the prejudicial excesses of psychoanalysis while drawing from it some points of reference that can facilitate understanding.

That the battle to legitimate homosexuality as a valid sexual choice has been fought with and through psychoanalysis – and to some extent, won – benefits group analysis in so far as the same battle need not be fought all over again. However, the battle to embody these new meanings in the work of the group – and to take them further – is just beginning.

Conclusion

Dimen (1995) refers to the 'sea of desire' that envelops human experience and the problems of managing this in our individual lives and our theories of development. It seems fair to say – and this chapter largely substantiates this view – that more than any other psychotherapeutic approach, psychoanalysis has confronted the sea of desire. That it has responded categorically and judgementally in ways that vary from the trivial to the profound may, paradoxically, have been part of its hold on the psychotherapeutic imagination. Dimen (1995: 144) observes:

> One of the accomplishments of a normalizing theory of sexuality is that it provides landmarks in an otherwise open and seemingly endless sea of desire. Even its inherent pathologizing serves as a guide of sorts: if it pathologizes you, well, at least you know where you are, you've been wronged or you are wrong, but you do have an identity.

But Dimen is at the same time deeply critical of the approach, particularly its embeddedness in the discourse of nature. Her solution is simple: to sever the tie between psychoanalysis and the discourse of nature: 'We should forgo not only the classical grounding of sexuality in the requirements of evolutionary survival, but also the relatively recent idea that what's natural is not sex but attachment' (Dimen 1995: 142).

This chapter has revealed, in line with the above, the extent to which the psychoanalytic discourse on sexuality is confined by its biological and heterosexist inheritance, its limited recognition of the power of social construction and the uncritical absorption of social norms in shaping a vision of development and maturity. All of this reflects the constraints both inherent in psychoanalysis and imposed on the sexual subject. However, this does not obscure its major contribution in providing a language for understanding the erotic imagination and, within this, the uniqueness of individual sexuality. Its essentializing and universalizing tendencies notwithstanding, the drift of psychoanalysis is towards what O'Connor and Ryan (1993: 148) refer to as 'the singularity of the speaking sexed body'. Psychoanalysis, in its theory at any rate, does not flinch from the encounter with the body and while its presumptions are too often informed by its prejudices, it offers us an embodied sexuality which stands in dramatic contrast to the disembodied discourse of so much psychotherapy, including group therapy.

If there is a plan, a programme, required to update the psychoanalytic study of sexuality, it must be in the deconstruction of its many categories and judgements of sexual experience. In line with the critical commentaries of Judith Butler (1995), what is needed is a vision which sees hetero-, homo- and other- sexuality as mutually constitutive rather than the prongs of a categorical and hierarchical binary.

That group psychotherapy has lagged so far behind psychoanalysis in generating a sexual discourse of its own and, if anything, has taken the easy path of assimilating some psychoanalytic 'givens', is a matter for recognition and regret. The regret, in part, is that by not identifying its own position it runs the risk of association with some of the prejudices that inform psychoanalysis, inscribing these unwittingly in the theory and practice of the group. But the absence of a discourse is also an advantage and an opportunity: to take from psychoanalysis, in so far as this link remains pertinent, the fruits of its journey and to leave behind the spoils.

4

SEX AND POLITICS

The last few decades of the twentieth century saw an explosion of change not only in the opening up and living out of sexual difference but also in the accompanying literature that supported these choices and challenged the dominant sexual discourse from every conceivable angle – political, social, cultural, philosophical, literary. These dissenting voices varied considerably in their focus – from the very intimate to the widely social, from reflections on the erotic handling of genitalia to the sexual underpinnings of entire societies. But what they had in common was the production of new, radical ways of thinking to subvert the old. This literature, it appears, is largely unknown to many psychotherapists, judging from the absence of reference to this work, either in publications or in the clinical discourse. Yet, it is at least as important as psychoanalysis, for example, because of the implications it has for the therapeutic stance in relation to the increased sexual diversity which is encountered in current clinical practice.

The theme is particularly relevant to group psychotherapy, not only because of the emphasis on diversity but because social and cultural influences on the sexual subject gain sharp prominence in this debate. An overriding theme is the social control of sexuality in its various guises. This is seen most obviously in the legal regulation of sex in some cultures, the dominance of religion in prescribing a sexual morality, and the circumscribed notions of conventional sexuality as appropriated by institutions such as marriage and the family in their support of western society. But there are also subtler forms of control. Therapy itself may be seen as a political activity. It seeks to influence, change or take control over a personal condition and even though this usually operates on an individual level, this process immediately sets it within the sphere of social judgement and intervention (Samuels 2001). Group therapy could be seen as even closer to the political domain because of the influence it exerts over larger numbers of people and the potential for a widened impact through group processes of amplification and mirroring. But because the discourse on sexuality is as yet so undeveloped in group therapy, there are no parameters or guidelines within which to address the subject in the clinical sphere, leaving the field open to practically everything from repression and marginalization of the sexual subject to sexual enactment of a destructive sort.

Much of the literature reviewed in previous chapters has political significance in the sense that it concerns relationships of power, control and exclusion. These themes are implicit in much of the previous discourse, whether stated openly or covertly suggested. The present chapter takes this perspective a step further. The theories and movements highlighted here are not simply oppositional views that argue their case within the parameters of the familiar or mainstream discourse. They reflect a deep dissatisfaction with orthodox ways of acquiring and evaluating knowledge, including the entire body of psychotherapeutic knowledge and practice. Their argument is against the uncritical acceptance of social structures, language as an organizer of values and bodies of information that hold sway in the contemporary world. Not only by maintaining a dominant discourse, but by presenting the discourse as natural and unquestionable, are conventional power groups seen as rendering dissent unacceptable, daring and dangerous. The opposing voices outlined here come mainly from feminism, gay liberation, sociology and activist psychoanalysis and are set within a contemporary historical framework concerning the sexual subject. I also consider how institutional processes in the psychotherapies have reinforced the transmission of conformist views about sexual difference.

Foucault and the history of sexuality

The work of Foucault (1981) probably represents the single most substantial treatise on the historical relativity of sexual practice and the 'deployment' of sexuality – a translation of Foucault's own term – within the social order. Foucault's overall agenda was to expose how prevailing social discourses powerfully regulate social practices and constitute individual selves. Sexuality is one such institutional site where power operates through the 'government of individualization', creating the very nature of sexual identity and subjectivity. Some of its operation appears paradoxical. The Victorian social discourse, for example, is revealed as having been overtly sexually repressive but covertly obsessed with sexuality, and this was in turn categorized and medicalised for the purposes of social control. As a result, Foucault argues, sexuality became an inscribed identity, with heterosexuality as the dominant normative identity and divergent sexual natures as distinct non-normative identities. Once these identities were established, sexual variations acquired essentialist attributions that ruled out flexibility and representation in a common pool of human diversity.

Foucault sees the sexual discourse in the West as having its roots in the type of power relations that emanated from Christian culture. A major feature of this is the Christian practice of confession, in which individuals are required to reveal their sins to a priest. This predicates a science of sexuality, such as psychoanalysis, in which in the relationship between analyst and patient the latter is expected to share intimate details with the former. The analyst is trained to comprehend and decipher this material and through it to establish the 'truth' of the patient's sexuality. O'Connor and Ryan (1993) have highlighted how Foucault demonstrated psychoanalysis' alliance with the search for truth in terms of challenging taboos, particularly the incest taboo. By focusing on sexuality in terms of repression, psychoanalysis assumes an essentialist notion of human identities, particularly the notion of a 'true' underlying sexuality. This is associated with the assumption that sexuality is inherently fixed and constant in its nature, oversimplifying its complexity and fluidity.

These points are important not only in terms of the sexual subject generally but also in the context of this book, which seeks to develop a greater consciousness about sexuality in group therapy. Its purpose is to embolden the sexual discourse in the group, but Foucault's points also alert us to the possible problems inhering in the project. His observation that the implementation of the sexual discourse always sets up relations of power, even in the very telling of a sexual narrative to another, is important to consider in evolving a group therapy perspective of sexuality.

The sexual revolutionaries

The term 'Freudiomarxists' has been given to a group of theorist/activists who advocated a form of sexual revolution to replace social repression (Denman 2004). Influenced by Freud and the perceived opposition between repressive civilization and sexuality, they opted for a radical programme of sexual liberation. The Marxist influence was expressed in a critique of the capitalist work ethic and the authoritarianism of an exploitative social system seen as subjugating sexual freedom.

Reich saw the family as the most powerful medium of sexual repression. Marcuse linked sexual repression directly to work and the rigid order imposed by production on human spontaneity. Both evolved ambitious programmes to re-sexualize society. Denman (2004) has pointed out, though, that for all the revolutionary fervour of the Freudiomarxists, their vision of sexuality was entirely normative. Reich regarded genital heterosexuality as paramount and Marcuse saw perversions and homosexuality as by-products of a destructive social regime. Both believed that homosexuality and the perversions would evaporate in a culture of progressive sexual liberation. Both Reich and Marcuse have been criticized for their oversimplified and ultimately conservative views of sexual difference but this should not obscure the strength of their vision of sexuality not only as a driver of social change but as a statement of the value of the collective as opposed to the individualism of other versions of sexual liberation.

The spirit of the collective is of course part and parcel of the value system underlying group psychotherapy. While we are no longer in an age of revolutionary idealism about sexuality, this vision of a collective sexual consciousness with radical intent invites speculation about the potential in group psychotherapy to generate a discursive erotic imagination and a freer sexual morality. Burkitt (1998) refers to the reconstructive potential of social discourse. How far group therapy can go in making wider social claims of this sort is debatable but a point worthy of debate.

Feminism

Feminism is a political movement that gained considerable momentum as the twentieth century progressed, resulting in significant changes in both women's role in society and the recognition and celebration of female sexuality. It was also generative of a powerful theoretical discourse that looked at the human condition from a female perspective, in particular challenging prevailing maledominated assumptions. As Denman (2004) points out, though, feminism is not a single theory. The movement went through a complex process of evolution from about the late 1960s onwards. Giddens (1992) attributes its vigorous growth to the introduction and widespread usage of the contraceptive pill, freeing women to consider their sexuality as unfettered by sexist and procreative restraints. However, there was discord about what constituted the proper agenda of feminism and in time this covered areas as wide-ranging as male dominance, pornography, racial issues, gender identity and homosexuality. Much of the attack was directed at assumptions and practices arising from conformist and reactionary interpretations of biological difference, many of which elevated male identity and sexuality and denigrated the female.

Within the vast literature produced in the feminist frame, there is an important subsection coming from female psychoanalysts who culled their views from a wide range of clinical experience. There are a number of impressive contributors here, of whom Jessica Benjamin in the USA and Luce Irigaray in France are two important examples.

Jessica Benjamin (1986, 1990) focuses on the marginalization of women's desire in contemporary society. She links this to conformist interpretations of the roles of mother and father, some of which are reflected in psychoanalytic theories about parental role. Mother's passion, desire, subjectivity and agency are suppressed in relation to feminine dependency, symbiotic union and desexualized regression – 'the mother of attachment' – while fathers are viewed in terms of active desire and independence – 'the father of liberation'. In families in which parental identity is constituted in this way, fathers are seen as offering the missing excitement of the mother-child relationship. Boys then have an immediate point of identification in their fathers. Girls, however, struggle to find points of identification for their own sexual agency. They may achieve this not through mother but through a vicarious identification with father and idealization of him, accompanied by a sense of yearning for him and a submission of their own potency. But the consequences apply not only to the female sex: with mother's potency so compromised, she cannot constitute a figure of separation for either boys or girls.

Not surprisingly, in this schema, gender differences are drawn along rigid lines. In spite of cultural attempts at breaking down the differences, male and female are typically seen as opposites. As previously noted, Benjamin criticizes what she refers to as the 'deep structure of complementarity' in relation to gender and sees this as intrinsic to the Oedipal model and its assumptions about difference. Further, as part of the institutionalization of these differences, there is a repudiation of the gender of the other sex. This is seen particularly in the male rejection of femininity, from childhood onwards. Benjamin argues that repudiation does not allow for differentiation. A gender identity based on repudiation requires collusive reinforcement.

Instead of a true appreciation of difference, there is difference based on exclusion and denigration.

Irigaray (1985, 1991) is a contemporary French psychoanalyst who has made one of the most original feminist contributions to the sexual discourse, with a particular emphasis on female homosexuality and lesbian desire. She positions her views in opposition to those of Lacan. Whereas feminist writers have generally been drawn to Lacan's work because of his recognition of culture and language as creating subjectivities, Irigaray is severely critical of his patriarchal emphasis, his inscription of all gender and sexual development within the Law of the Father and the pre-eminence he ascribes to the phallus as the chief signifier of male and female identities. She emphasizes instead the child's earliest connection to the mother's body, arguing that a fuller recognition of this relationship would engender freer and more creative bodily and sexual expression for both men and women. For women specifically, it would augment the capacity to love, create and work.

Irigaray explores the qualities of female intimacy embraced within an image of women's primary homosexual desire. In contrast to Lacan's view of women as embodiments of lack – the objects of desire of the male sex – she envisions intimacy of great depth and delicacy between women. Although Irigaray's contribution has been strongly affirmed by feminist and lesbian writers, she has also been criticized for substituting an exclusivist model of female sexuality for the dogma of heterosexism. Denman (2004) takes issue with Irigaray's seemingly idealized and romanticized rendition of the female body and relationships between women, as if there is no room for the doubt, conflict and divisions of self-experience that tend to occur in all sexual relationships.

Irigaray gives a sensitive account of the transferential process. This is linked to the notion of the mother's body, with an emphasis on the rhythms of closeness and distance in a way that applies to both women and men analysands. O'Connor and Ryan (1993: 156) comment that Irigaray saw beyond transference to a conception of analysis as providing 'a space for birth and growth, a space for gestation . . .' – for eventual calm.

This description of analysis as linked to a space for gestation and birth, conceived within a maternal framework, is highly reminiscent in group analysis of Foulkes' (1948, 1964) concept of the group matrix. This has the symbolic properties of a womb or mother, able to nurture its members through a process of gestation and growth (Roberts 1983). However, the link also highlights the differences between the intensely individual focus of writers such as Irigaray and the plural emphasis of group psychotherapy. Further, the matrix in group analysis is an abstract symbol of containment rather than a facilitator of intimacy. A question then arises about whether the group can provide anything like the kind of attention and intimacy that is associated with the psychoanalytic transference and what bearing this has on the development of the sexual subject. It seems evident that the group cannot provide a comparable level of individual attention. However, there is an argument that through the shared properties of the matrix, in which all group members can give and receive, the group provides a different form of intimacy, possibly one that is more real because of the immediacy and directness of feedback and response that is characteristic of therapy groups.

The homosexual discourse

As previously noted, homosexuality merits close consideration as its treatment in the psychotherapeutic discourse epitomizes the problem of how sexual diversity is understood and handled. There are strongly political implications in the tendency to categorize and marginalize large tracts of sexuality that do not fit the conventional picture. Recent changes towards a more tolerant approach in the psychotherapies cannot obscure the fact that just a few decades ago aversion therapy using electric shock was considered an appropriate treatment, that homosexuality was described as an illness by the American Psychiatric Association and that psychoanalysts such as Socarides (1968, 1995) led a campaign to drive home the belief that homosexuality was severely pathological and that analysis should aim at a 'cure' (see Chapter 3).

Mitchell (1996) gives a vivid account of the atmosphere surrounding these issues in the USA in the period between about the 1950s and the 1980s. Reflecting a strong vein of biological determinism, the overriding position in the American psychoanalytic literature in the early part of this period was that everyone is constitutionally heterosexual and that homosexuality is a pathological and defensive retreat from castration anxiety. This led to what Mitchell calls a 'directive-suggestive' approach in which homosexual patients were urged to renounce their sexual orientation and undertake an unswerving process of conversion to heterosexuality. Mitchell refers to this as a 'dark period' in American psychoanalysis in which many patients were subjected to 'considerable pain and massive interference in the pursuit of their own personal meaning and satisfaction' (p. 66). In

Chapter 3, I described a parallel situation in the UK, epitomized by Fairbairn, who, while making an important overall contribution to psychoanalysis, recommended that homosexuals be interned in rehabilitation camps.

Mitchell contrasts this with the contemporary view which tends to regard sexual orientation and gender identity as complex constructions rather than direct extensions of anatomical reproductive differences. This includes heterosexuality, which can no longer be understood as the natural unfolding of biological givens but a human condition that is constructed through a variety of biological and social processes. Mitchell quotes Chodorow (1992: 273) as saying: 'Biology cannot explain the content either of cultural fantasy or private erotism. We need a story to account for the development of any particular person's particular heterosexuality'.

Within the period of emergence of the contemporary perspective, the gay rights movement took root and became an active force in reshaping social perceptions. Gay liberation generated a literature and theoretical discourse of its own, including a body of thought known as 'queer theory'. As the name suggests, this appropriated a once widely-used pejorative term to underline the point about subjugated identities, while seeking at the same time to substantiate and celebrate these identities. Influenced by poststructuralism, including Foucault's writings, queer theory is a critique of the dominant sexual discourse, showing how heterosexuality creates a variety of sexualities at the margins of the discourse, simultaneously necessitating and disavowing them. Stein and Plummer (1996) outline the purposes of queer theory – to problematize all sexual and gender categories, to reveal the power dynamics contained within them, to produce strategies for political subversion and to accept the value of alternative and even extreme forms of sexual expression.

Among the radical perspectives of female identity emerging from this theory, Halberstam (1998) addresses the issue of 'masculinity' in women. She argues that masculinity is not the sole property of men: female masculinity has a distinct identity and is not just a poor imitation of male masculinity. Further, she suggests, there is transformative potential in a revolutionary subversion of mainstream sexuality through the recasting of gender identities.

On the male homosexual side, queer theory has given voice to similarly subversive strategies. Much of this centres on opposition to the aggressive policing of male sexuality in our society. Gay sex is characterized by Bersani (1995) as explosive and revolutionary, rather than placatory and conforming to the mainstream. Gay men who merge with the heterosexual world by becoming invisible come in for strong criticism. There is an emphasis on the validation of sexual relationships that deviate from the idealized norm of long-term intimacy: casual sex is condoned and encouraged, seen as forging a society that is playful and open as opposed to formal and hierarchical (Hocquenghem 1978; Mohr 1992).

These challenges raise consciousness about the familiar and comfortable assumptions concerning sexual nature and sexual practice that underlie most psychotherapeutic approaches. Denman (2004) suggests that the agenda for political action generated by queer theory is relevant to psychotherapy in raising questions about the politics of therapeutic action and the potential to rethink and revise this agenda. This has led to the emergence of 'queer therapy', forging a new form of psychotherapy by giving substance to what occurs at the margins and challenging the orthodoxies at the centre. How this applies to group psychotherapy raises intriguing questions. Does the group conform to the dominant social morality or not? Further, is there the potential in the group to cultivate a morality of its own and then to require, either explicitly or implicitly, conformity to its morality? We know from small group research as well as group psychotherapy that groups quickly establish their own norms and that these can have a powerful influence. This can lead in the direction of conformity to wider society or to the subversion of prevailing orthodoxies. While most therapy groups probably exist in an in-between space, trying to balance the wish to conform with the impulse to challenge, the therapy group probably comes much closer than any other form of psychotherapy to the social processes that govern people's lives.

There are significant aspects of the interaction between group and therapist that contribute to the formation of a group morality. Unlike individual therapy, where the therapist as expert holds the authority, group therapy provides checks and balances – via the group itself – for any biases or excesses on the therapist's part. This applies to sexual morality as much as to any other norms since therapists, like everyone else, are subject to their own inevitable blind spots, prejudices and limitations. Conversely, the group therapist can provide a challenge to the group, so that any oppressive norms or constraints on the part of one or more group members can be held up to scrutiny and debate. This reinforces the point, quite often made about group psychotherapy, that it provides a more democratic setting than individual therapy and that it has an inherent and realizable system of checks and balances. In a field as highly charged politically as sexuality, this is a significant advantage.

Institutional processes

Why did psychotherapy, particularly of the psychoanalytic variety, maintain for such a long time an oppressively conservative position regarding sexuality? Why did these schools of thought resist, so resolutely, the impact of social change on the patterns of sexual behaviour? To refer to this in the past tense is also not entirely accurate – many of these schools maintain their conservatism until the present day and do not necessarily show encouraging signs of shifting their position. The answer must have something to do with institutionalization, with the fact that the psychotherapies became absorbed into training institutes and that these institutes subjected their bodies of knowledge to reification and idealization. This was reinforced by the hierarchical operation of the institutes, replete with processes of grace and favour, inclusion and exclusion, loyalty and disloyalty. A case in point is the way Freud's original theories of sexuality, daring and potentially liberating in some respects, were objectified and conventionalized. The consequence is that generations of psychoanalysts were spawned who inherited and transmitted the party line, discouraging, with few exceptions, dissent against any of the fundamental premises.

It is noteworthy that such dissenting voices as there were (Stoller is a good example), came largely from the USA and that the British psychoanalytic world was particularly closed to divergent opinion. The exclusion of homosexuals from training institutes is a striking example. A review by Cunningham (1991) examined the criteria by which homosexuals were considered as unsuitable for psychoanalytic training and concluded not only that these criteria were unwarranted but that the decisions made took no account of the positive contributions that many homosexuals could make to the psychoanalytic/ psychotherapeutic field. In a comparable study, Mary Lynne Ellis (1994) approached several psychoanalytically-orientated organizations requesting interviews to discuss their attitude to intending homosexual applicants. While wanting to encourage a debate, she instead found overriding attitudes of defensiveness, evasiveness and prejudiced thinking, confirming the impressions of Cunningham's review.

The poignancy in all this is the loss to the institutions of the strength of the divergent voice and the loss to succeeding lines of clinicians of a culture of openness and receptivity. Although the situation, some 10 to 20 years after the above studies were published, has undoubtedly improved, with a greater freedom in attitudes all round, there are still significant pockets of orthodoxy and resistance. There is still a long way to go. As O'Connor and Ryan (1993) point out, the only way through this is via dialogue. Where silence and concealment prevail, there is no hope of change. The problem of institutional conformity in relation to sex is to a large extent a group issue – denial and splitting within a defensive process of group identification. The same defences operate in psychotherapy groups and can result in a similar foreclosing of the sexual subject. It is hoped that the present study will stimulate the dialogue in a way that facilitates the creativity of group psychotherapy – its theory, practice and institutional representation – in dealing with sexual diversity.

Part 2

THE GROUP
DISCOURSE

5

SEX IN GROUP
PSYCHOTHERAPY – A REVIEW

In Part 2 of the book, attention shifts from the wider focus of Part 1, which embraced philosophy, psychoanalysis, developmental theory and political perspectives, to a specific focus on group psychotherapy and how sexuality has been represented in this field. This is itself a wide-ranging area, covering a variety of different approaches and value systems. What is common to the field, however, is the under-emphasis, if not silence, on sexuality – a silence which is striking for any contemporary discourse, let alone a widely practised psycho-therapeutic approach. I have chosen to cover the field in three dis-tinct chapters. The first is a review of existing journal publications on the subject, since this is virtually the only area in which there is a discourse of any sort. The second considers the position within Foulkesian group analysis and the third represents my attempt to formulate a group psychotherapy perspective of sexuality.

In the first of these chapters, I review the existing publications on desire and sexuality in group psychotherapy: what has already been written, what it reveals and what directions of travel emerge. These are all papers: there is no single book on the subject. The quantity of publications is sparse. However, there is value in the way these papers open up the field of enquiry. The fact that they have not generally been absorbed into the group psychotherapy literature is a product of the slowness of the profession to respond to this subject rather than any inherent weakness in the papers themselves. Singly, and in com-bination, these papers highlight the importance of sexuality in group psychotherapy and begin to create a framework for understanding this neglected subject.

Several of the papers start by highlighting the dearth of relevant literature. Courville and Keeper (1984: 35) describe sexuality as an 'often unspoken and ignored issue in group psychotherapy'. Moeller (2002: 484) comments that 'Amazingly, no literature exists on love in the group ... yet the group is a highly charged libidinal network'. Burman (2002: 540) refers to the absence of discussion of the erotic (including the homoerotic) within groups. There tends also to be little cross-referencing between the papers, giving the impression of a small, fragmented body of literature.

Here I present a broad review, with a leaning towards group analytic papers, as this is my particular area of interest. The papers overlap in some respects but I have grouped them under several predominating themes: desire; eroticism and sexuality; gender; and the Oedipal situation in the group.

Desire

This is perhaps the most loosely constructed theme in the papers under consideration, but I begin here because of its broad relevance to my subject.

It is noteworthy that the papers which ascribe a particular significance to desire in group psychotherapy mainly do so in its general, non-erotic sense (Nitzgen 1999; Giraldo 2001). Their approach is strongly linked to Lacan's perspectives on desire, which are usefully transferred from individual analysis to group psychotherapy. Although the erotic aspect of desire is generally missing, the papers provide a meaningful framework for the consideration of the sexual subject.

Desire, as reflected in these papers, highlights the individual speaking voice and the extent to which it reveals the self in its seeking, wanting, desiring form. The expression of desire is a communicative act, linked to the presence of the other through whose recognition desire can be named. This is what in the Lacanian view gives desire its centrality in analysis. It is vital, according to Lacan, that the analyst desires the patient's desire. Nitzgen (1999) describes how in group psychotherapy this is transposed from the analytic dyad to the group context in which it also becomes a core, organizing motif: 'It is only by mutual recognition within the symbolic matrix of the group that desire can be brought into existence' (1999: 234).

Giving desire such prominence in the therapy group suggests a new motivational perspective in a field in which belonging, cohesion and commitment are more commonly emphasized. While the latter are undoubtedly important aspects of the group process, desire offers a different although complementary perspective. It is a perspective which emphasizes individuality and subjectivity within a relational frame.

The papers also highlight the transition from *demand* to *desire* as an essential part of the psychotherapeutic process. Demand is seen as the pressure for recognition and gratification, usually in an inchoate, unformulated way, a product of the Lacanian 'imaginary', whereas desire is seen as that which can be named in symbolic verbal language. It is the expression of desire in speech which is seen as the principal action of analysis. The discovery and naming of desire is seen as an emergent process. It is not necessarily there at the outset, waiting to be said, but a creation in the sphere of relationship: a 'new presence' in the world (Lacan 1988a, b). 'This marks the surprising, unforeseeable, creative moment in psychoanalysis as well as in group analysis' (Nitzgen 1999: 234).

The emphasis on emergence is consistent with a group analytic perspective, such as that outlined by Stacey (2003), as well as current relational psychoanalytic perspectives, such as represented by Ghent (1990) and Davies (1998a, b). The discovery of the self, its hidden and elusive bits, is seen as occurring in interactive moments in surprising, spontaneous, unpremeditated ways.

Tylim (2003), who focuses more specifically on erotic desire, distinguishes desire from agony and ecstasy, highlighting the distinction as an important parameter of group therapy. Agony and ecstasy are similar to demand and are linked to the Lacanian concept of *'jouissance'*. This term refers in essence to orgasm but also to the intense pleasure of fulfilled desire in a general sense. Tylim considers neither agony nor ecstasy as appropriate to group therapy: they are excesses that 'overflow' the group. Desire, by contrast, is 'other directed' and promotes differentiation and awareness of boundaries between the desiring subject and the desired object. The aim of group therapy is the recognition and naming of desire and the encouragement of neither agony nor ecstasy. In other words, the group is there to help members to articulate their desires but not to gratify them.

These writers usefully argue for the recognition of desire not just as an issue in a particular therapy group but as a principle in the overall group psychotherapy discourse. That their argument tends to be general and rather abstract, without a strong sense of embodiment in the group, may reflect the elusiveness of desire itself. Verhaeghe (1999: 151) notes: 'Desire is desire only if it succeeds in postponing something'. Yet, there is the potential to anchor desire more substantially, more physically, in the communicative sphere, a potential that becomes crucially relevant to sexuality and desire.

Eroticism and sexuality

Several papers deal directly with eroticism and sexuality in group psychotherapy. They emphasize how important but also how difficult the expression and understanding of sexuality in groups can be. The papers describe problems about trust, boundaries, confidentiality, acting-out and the erotic aspects of transference and counter-transference. They also highlight the role of the therapist in facilitating the sexual subject in the group and the ways in which the therapist's own sexuality influences this process: 'How effectively therapists can diagnose and intervene in group situations that deal with sexual issues is dependent not only on the therapist's ability to use their awareness of who the client is and how he/she relates and reacts as a sexual being, but to a large measure on their self-awareness and comfort with their own sexuality' (Courville and Keeper 1984: 35). However, rewards are promised: 'therapists who can allow their own and their clients' sexuality to be included among the other legitimate concerns of the group will practice psychotherapy in a more competent, integrated and successful manner' (Courville and Keeper 1984: 42).

The above-quoted paper by Courville and Keeper is in fact the first publication specifically focused on sexuality that I can identify in the entire group therapy literature. By the time of its publication, group psychotherapy had already been established for decades. That it took until the mid-1980s for a paper on sexuality to appear in the literature is an indication of the particular reticence regarding this subject.

Courville and Keeper are especially interested in the link between sexuality and the development of lasting intimate relationships, and how this process is reflected in mixed psychotherapy groups. They highlight the potential for sexual pairing in the group. This can take different forms – an intimate bonding in the group or a liaison outside the group which can vary in the degree of sexual enactment and the extent to which it is revealed in the group. The authors note the problematic relation between the prohibition of actual sex and the acting-out of sexuality outside the group. They emphasize the importance of bringing this into the open and exploring its meaning in the group.

Courville and Keeper also consider the potentials and problems of erotic transference and counter-transference feelings. Patients who have sexual needs in relation to therapists are frequently in conflict: wanting greater intimacy with the therapist but also afraid of the feelings arising and the possibility of being shamed. The attraction, however, may not be one-way: therapists have their own powerful attractions and desires and have to find ways of containing them in the group, whether in relation to patients who desire them or others who do not. The authors highlight the danger of possible seduction by either party and the difficulty therapists have in knowing whether and how they may be encouraging reactions of this sort.

Because of the intense pressure that can be generated by sexuality in group psychotherapy, Courville and Keeper recommend that the group is run by a co-therapy pair. This provides the opportunity to share and process emergent sexual issues, particularly those along transferential lines. They also recognize the potential for eroticization and other complexities of sexual feeling within the co-therapy couple itself. However, these authors believe that working on these aspects of the relationship is well worth the effort. They say of co-therapy: 'The reward for developing an open relationship that confronts intimacy and attraction issues is a powerful, complementary partnership in group work' (1984: 41). This contrasts with the particular challenges a single therapist working on their own may experience in the presence of desire and sexuality as they emerge in the group.

Jumping to the late 1990s (some 15 years after Courville and Keeper's paper), a paper by Moss (1999) explores a subject he refers to as 'the hysterical group'. This describes group resistance in which there is an avoidance of sexual material that is close to group awareness but not openly acknowledged. Moss suggests that this is masked by group processes that deflect attention from the underlying sexuality, particularly through a form of active, mesmerizing story-telling that captures everyone's attention, turning members into an audience. The result is that the group, including the therapist, avoids the real task of the group, which Moss suggests is 'to acknowledge the sexuality in the moment and reflect upon it' (p. 561). The therapist is liable to become lulled into 'the hysterical state' and colludes with the group in missing the significance of the moment. However, with self-monitoring and supervision, the therapist becomes able to address the group resistance. This helps to bring the dissociated sexual material into consciousness. Moss believes this will affect a significant change in the group – 'from dramatic though superficial story-telling to a richer, more authentic vitality among members' (p. 568).

This article is useful in drawing attention to the propensity of groups to avoid sexual material and the defences that are erected against its acknowledgement and expression. Whether this is appropriately or best described as 'hysterical' and whether it necessarily takes the form of dramatic story-telling are moot points. However, the paper succeeds in making the point that the recognition of dissociative processes can help to embody sexuality in the group.

Einhorn (1999), in a commentary on this paper, highlights the omission of any discussion of gender, particularly the therapist's, as well as any reference to erotic transference and counter-transference. Is it possible that Moss, in line with his own thesis, is himself dissociating some important aspects of sexuality in the group?

The first published paper on the subject in the new millennium (that I can locate) is Stone's (2001) treatment of the cultural and political influences on the expression of sexuality in group psychotherapy. Now that a discourse on sexuality in the group has tentatively been established, it is possible to delve into the wider territory of social influences. Here, the cultural phenomenon is highly specific: the widely publicized scandal of President Clinton's sexual liaison with Monica Lewinsky. The author highlights the cultural voyeurism that was stimulated by the scandal and the way this penetrated into the consulting room. The themes that generated heat concerned not only sexuality but power and the abuse of power, as well as insistent questions about morality and judgement.

Stone describes how group members became obsessed with the scandal, taking positions on the main political and sexual issues that reflected their own wishes, fears and guilts concerning sexual transgression, as well as their moral prejudices. Among the group processes generated by these themes was a scapegoating dynamic that seemed to mirror the pressure of judgement inherent in the case. Moreover, Stone believes that the group's preoccupation with the external sexual drama concealed sexual attractions experienced in the group itself. The author reflects that through her own preoccupation with the Clinton-Lewinsky affair, she unconsciously colluded with the denial of current sexual tensions in the group itself.

Stone sees this as a missed opportunity in relation to the sexual dynamic of the group. She emphasizes the denial of the here-and-now sexuality of the group in relation to the preoccupation with external social events. It is an interesting illustration of how, while the significance of external events is easily marginalized in psychotherapy, the reverse also applies: absorption in the social can be used as a way of avoiding current and immediate sexual tensions in the group. Hence, the social can be a defence against the subjective and not just the other way round.

This illustration is reminiscent of Moss' description (above) of the hysterical group consumed with interest in a dramatic story that conceals actual sexual awareness in the group itself. The same dissociative elements and the mesmerizing story-telling noted by Moss are present in Stone's group in the absorption with the Clinton-Lewinsky affair. However, I suggest another interpretation that is linked to my own paper on the primal scene in group analysis (Nitsun 1994), which I review below. The preoccupation with a powerful sexual couple could be interpreted as the symbolization of the primal scene in the group. That public exposure and shaming was such an important part of the narrative highlights the overall anxiety about sexuality as well as group members' displaced guilt about their own prurient wishes and transgressive impulses onto the parental or sibling couple.

A paper by Moeller (2002), practically bursting with libidinal energy, strongly challenges the reticence about sexuality in group psychotherapy. Moeller describes the sexual paradox of the group: a highly charged libidinal network that at the same time mobilizes the incest taboo. He argues: 'incestuous and other erotic impulses are far more strongly mobilized in the group than in individual treatment' (p. 493). But Moeller is committed to following through: to dealing with the fears and tensions surrounding sexuality so as to liberate sexual expression. He notes some important cultural differences in attitudes towards sexual intimacy. Citing a study by the psychoanalysts Parin and Morgenthaler (1963), he describes the practice of the Dogon, an African tribe, in encouraging a love relationship between two people to become more rather than less public as the intimacy develops: 'In Europe, two lovers tend to withdraw, whereas in Africa they integrate themselves in to the community of the group' (Moeller 2002: 486).

Following this line of thinking, Moeller describes several aspects of what he calls the 'multi-person matrix' of sexuality:

- sexuality is socially created through the influence of the parents and the family group, as well as the peer group;
- in its reproductive origins, sexuality concerns the creation of the next generation, so perpetuating the group;
- our inherent bisexuality engenders a form of internal group sexuality: a combination of heterosexual and homosexual identifications with the parents and their own complementary bisexual identifications.

Moeller's paper places particular emphasis on the group conductor, not just as a mediator of sexuality but as the source of the erotic impulse and longing in the group. He is very open about his own erotic involvement: 'I can give a precise ranking of my libidinal cathexis of every single group' (2002: 491). Further, a member of the group may seem like an ideal partner to the conductor: 'someone, in other words, whom one could happily marry on the spot' (p. 491). Although some of this is transference and counter-transference based, Moeller believes that group members may have an intrinsic attractiveness to the therapist for several reasons: they are psychologically reflective; an intimate understanding develops between them and the therapist over time; and, added to this, the group situation is 'so suffused with libido' (p. 491).

Moeller is very aware of the risks of the therapist acting-out a sexual relationship with a group member and the likely destructive consequences of this. He points to the need for supervision. However, he appears at the same time to encourage as open a contact with sexual feelings as possible in both the group therapist and members, arguing that this is so central to our lives that it cannot be ignored.

The paper by Tylim (2003), mentioned in an earlier section on desire in group psychotherapy, is very much about sexuality in the group.

Tylim describes a paradoxical situation in the group. He sees it as pulsating with sexual desire. However, the morality of the group is both regressive and repressive. Its regressiveness, in his view, is linked to Freud's original thesis about the immediate and sweeping intimacy which can be established in a group, largely through a shared idealization of the leader and the libidinal charge this precipitates. The counterpart in group psychotherapy, the author suggests, is the transference to the conductor and the mobilization of desire through this process. The repressiveness of the group is reflected in the imposition of a restrictive conventional morality. This is instituted and reinforced by the usually tight boundaries put around sexuality in the group, linked to the rule of non-socialization outside the group. Paradoxically, this stimulates 'incestuous' erotic longings among members. The group must come to terms with the imposed frustration of gratification by strengthening the capacity to transform desire into symbolic language.

Tylim describes ways in which group members deal with the tension of conflicting pulls. One way is through sexual teasing, described by Kernberg (1995) as having both exhibitionistic and sadistic aspects. This could be seen as a form of tantalization, reflecting the tantalizing aspect of the group itself. Tylim also describes an oscillation in the group between the wish for sexual secrecy and the impulse to reveal all in the open forum of the group: another source of tension that has to be managed.

The paper also usefully emphasizes the visual element in the expression of erotic tensions in the group. Looking at and being looked at, seeing and being seen, are important means of conveying sexual information: 'The eye has the capacity to penetrate and be penetrated by the subjectivity of the other' (p. 450). This applies generally and in a specific sexual sense. Tylim believes that the visual is a neglected area in group work. The therapist needs to be very attentive to visual clues in the group and their possible sexual meanings: this includes those directed to the therapist and *initiated* by them, since the therapist is subject to the same processes of attraction that are inherent in the group.

Tylim makes clear his view that the therapist is as much a player in the sexual currents that run through the group as anyone else. He suggests that there is a constant possibility of either enactment (in the group) or acting-out of sexuality (outside the group). Enactment is seen as the better option: the expression of desire within, rather than outside, the group. There is a variable risk that the therapist could be implicated, as either a direct or indirect participant. The author gives an extended example of a patient couple's meetings outside the group that became sexual. He describes the group's highly ambivalent reaction and he also questions, very honestly, whether his own erotic longings may have been stirred up, preventing him from dealing effectively with the situation.

Gender

A series of papers on gender in the journal *Group Analysis* in the period 1986–2002 represents a serious attempt to grapple with this important issue in group psychotherapy. As indicated throughout this book, gender is intimately related to sexuality since it directly concerns the expression of masculinity and femininity. Given contemporary deconstructions, it is especially important to gather differing perspectives on gender and consider their implications for group relationships. Hence, gender forms an important background – and at times foreground – to the exploration of sexuality and desire in the group.

A significant gender issue arises at the outset in that all four papers published in the designated period, and reviewed here, are by women. This contrasts not only with most of the papers considered in this chapter but with the group-analytic literature as a whole, which, if anything, tends to be male dominated. One of the authors of these papers, Burman (2002), comments herself on the preponderance of writing on gender by women. There may be differing interpretations of this: one is that women have greater experience of oppression within their gender and so are moved to write about it; another is that women are more attuned to the nuances of gender and hence more open to its exploration.

I propose to consider these papers in chronological order, starting with Elliott's (1986) rendering of gender identity in group analysis. She distinguishes gender from sex in so far as sex is generally a physiological given, whereas gender is an interpretation of that physiological given, a point originally highlighted by Stoller (1968). This includes a wide range of positive and negative identifications with one's biological sex, reflecting our inherent bisexuality. It also includes conscious and unconscious gender identifications.

Elliott's treatment of gender derives from clinical observations of male and female sub-grouping in psychotherapy groups, sometimes creating unhelpful splits in the group. She suggests that group psychotherapy, of an analytic variety in particular, is viewed by both men and women as a feminine activity. Its exploration of the emotional, the hidden and the unseen is more naturally associated with the feminine. This gives female participants an apparent advantage, creating a power differential between them and males that subverts conventional assumptions about male dominance. The nurturant, breast-like qualities of women are then perceived not as breast-like but penis-like. In parallel, men feel inadequate, disempowered, impotent. The difficulty of negotiating and working through this paradox is compounded by the threatening nature of bisexual identifications, so that the opposite sex identifications of men and women arouse intense anxiety. A process of splitting ensues whereby group members act out perceptions of the destructive attributes of the opposite sex: the women potentially become more penetrating and penis-like, the men more submissive and withdrawn. However, if these elements can be recognized and understood, patients may begin to explore their bisexual wishes and identifications more openly:

> Men can begin to enjoy their femininity as an expression of receiving and containing rather than withholding. Women can begin to enjoy their masculinity as an expression of potency and creative force rather than of sadistic power.

> When envy and fear of the opposite sex is eased, less energy
> will be required to defend against these elements and both
> men and women can begin to give and receive of each other
> in a more flexible way.
>
> (Elliott 1986: 203)

Elliott suggests not only that the gender of the group therapist influences the group process but that the particular *way* the therapist deals with their masculine and feminine identifications influences the degree of gender flexibility in the group.

Since the publication of Elliott's paper, there has been a further intellectual deconstruction of gender stereotypes in the wider body of writers such as Judith Butler (1990), as well as a shift in the social representation of gender. These changes to some extent challenge the conventional assumptions about gender attribution made by Elliott, so that the gender baseline may well be looser now than in 1986 and her rendering of gender differences in the group slightly outdated. However, the difficulties inevitably continue and her paper remains a valuable statement not only of the complexities of gender identity in group psychotherapy but of the potential of the group to affect change in this area.

Conlon (1991) focuses specifically on gender-related issues concerning the female group therapist, particularly her perceived power and authority as a conductor. This is examined in the specific context of all-female groups. Given the mix of responsibilities of the conductor, which include functions which may be seen as either more feminine (such as understanding, attuning and responding empathically) or more masculine (such as holding the authority, affirming boundaries and making challenging interventions), there arises a tension within and between the therapist and the female participants. One set of reactions in group members may be doubt and resentment about the conductor's assumed 'masculine' authority and a tendency to denigrate and attack her authority. The therapist in parallel may feel anxious about assuming this role, struggling with her own difficulty in owning her power. There may then develop a split between the 'paternal' and 'maternal' functions of the conductor and a tendency to suppress one in favour of the other. This is similar to the 'dissociative splitting' of gender identifications described by Elliott (1986) in the paper reviewed above.

While delineating the tensions that arise from the gendered functions of the therapist, Conlon also sees the opportunity in the group to confront and explore the whole issue of gender identity and the defences against doing so. She extrapolates some of this to male conductors, suggesting, in parallel, that it may be difficult for males to integrate or have their feminine, maternal attributes recognized. However, she argues that it is less threatening for the group to experience a male conductor behaving maternally than for a female conductor not to do so.

Conlon notes that group-analytic theory has traditionally paid very little attention to the impact of the therapist's gender on the group's development. This is a valid point. However, her own observations, a bit like Elliott's, seem to reflect particular assumptions about women's views of other women, including those in authority, that are not fully congruent with contemporary attitudes towards gender. For example, at a time of greater female empowerment, women may appreciate and admire rather than repudiate other women's authority and their more active, 'masculine' role. However, it is the case that there is still considerable ambivalence about these gender shifts and Conlon alerts us to the continuing complexities of negotiating gender and the way this is represented and mediated by the group therapist.

Rose (2002) picks up on another important but relatively neglected aspect of gender representations in groups: language. She emphasizes that language has a major function in the creation of our gendered sense of self, with linguistic styles and patterns stereotypically associated with male and female. She argues, too, that language is inseparable from experience: it is not just a translation of experience but constitutes experience. Similarly, meaning is not simply expressed in language: it is created by language. Hence, language is an intrinsic part of the social construction of gender. Often, this is unconscious: it happens at a wider cultural level and is continually filtered to the individual who in turn filters it back into the culture: 'within this unconscious linguistic patterning, the role of gender is enacted' (2002: 526).

Rose notes that group psychotherapy is dependent on verbal language: who says what to whom and in what manner. She argues that gender identifications are continually revealed and reinforced through language in the group and that this can become stuck in rigid patterns and styles of communication. Quoting Schlapobersky (1994) and Wodak (1986) on language in group therapy, Rose sees the possibilities of change and transformation. Potentially, there is a movement away from stereotypical patterns of speech to a flexible, mixed style. As something that is performed, language is amenable to scrutiny and review. The individual has the possibility of choice, of agency and creativity and this can help to reshape gender attributions in the group.

Burman (2002) extends the theme of women's gender issues in groups, with particular reference to sexuality and power. She emphasizes the 'silence' within group analysis on the erotic, especially homo-erotic transference and counter-transference. Although this, in her view, mirrors the long-standing neglect and pathologization of homosexuality in the psychoanalytic domain, she notes that psychoanalysis has engaged with feminist theory in widespread debates about gender and sexuality. This, however, is missing in group analysis. Her surprise is underlined by the observation that gender and sexuality are key acknowledged areas of subjectivity – central to the psychotherapeutic endeavour – while at the same time there are profound social influences on gender that invite, indeed demand, a group perspective.

The problem with the non-discussion of gender, Burman suggests, is the implication that gender is a 'fixed constant': 'This treatment stands against the drift of much psychoanalytic theory which emphasizes gender as a construction that (like the rest of the edifice of subjectivity) is always fragile and incomplete' (2002: 545–6). The 'silence' also compromises the identities of gay men and lesbians. These are either invisible or tend to be discussed only when problematic. Yet, Burman argues, the issues which are paramount for homosexuals, such as desire, agency and authority, are universal concerns. Hence, the lack of attention to homosexual identity may reflect a broader disregard for issues of human concern.

The paper includes two examples of groups which illustrate contrasting forms of transference towards a female conductor, highlighting the intricate and ambivalent gender and sexual attributions that occur in groups. Burman concludes that group analysis needs to take far greater account of these subjects, with particular reference to 1) socially gendered processes that reflect the operation of power and authority and 2) the transmission of these processes through the transference relations of the group.

It is worth noting that, as far as I can see, Burman's is the first group analytic paper to address openly the subject of homosexuality. That this needed to wait until 2002 is indicative of the conservatism that resides in psychotherapy, even in a field like group analysis that aspires to a 'radical' representation of its subject (Dalal 1998; Stacey 2003). The positive perspective is that Burman's paper is part of a shifting consciousness that makes it more difficult to sustain this conservatism and that provides a framework for an exploration of sexuality and desire in groups that is inclusive of diverse identities.

The Oedipal situation

While a variety of papers refer broadly to manifestations of the Oedipus complex in group therapy, a small number make this their specific focus. This includes the primal scene, which is generally regarded as a component of the Oedipal situation. These papers are important because they explore triangular group processes, albeit that the concepts through which they do so are controversial. As noted previously, Foulkes believed in the concept of the Oedipus complex but proposed a group perspective by linking it to the family as a whole and suggesting that sibling rivalry has an Oedipal aspect to it.

My own paper on the primal scene in group analysis (Nitsun 1994) went out on a limb to suggest that the primal scene may be at the 'centre' of the group. By this, I meant a metaphorical or epistemological centre concerning the fantasy of coupling and the way this is linked to parental sexuality, rather than a literal centre. The primal scene is the fantasy of parental intercourse in an encoded, largely unconscious form. In line with wider definitions (Samuels 1985), I suggested that the primal scene touches on questions of family history and how the parental relationship reflects a coming together of two separate social histories. Sexual intercourse, then, is not just a physical act, with its exciting and aggressive aspects, but a symbol of cultural and historical interpenetration with themes of power, gain and loss.

My hypothesis is that the analytic group reactivates unconscious fantasies of parental union and that the particular configuration of sexualities in a group evokes particular versions of the primal scene. This in turn reflects the way the group deals with sexuality, how sexual identifications and attractions occur in the group and what forms of sexual enactment or acting-out take place. The creative and destructive components of the fantasized primal scene have an influence on the group. The anti-group, I suggested, is linked to both negative associations of the primal scene and an anti-libidinal conception of the family group.

The idea behind this hypothesis originally came from a statement by Bion (1961) about the role of the primal scene in the formation of the basic assumptions. He postulated that 'the basic assumptions are secondary to an extremely early primal scene perceived in part-object terms and associated with psychotic anxiety and mechanisms of splitting and projective identification' (1961: 164). Brown (1985), supporting this interpretation, suggests that the basic assumptions serve as a defence against the deep ambivalence and anxiety experienced in relation to the parental couple. Bringing in the notion of the primal scene is a way of bringing together the male and female principles in our understanding of the group. Foulkes (1948) and numerous other writers have portrayed the group as a feminine body, a womb or a breast, and the concept of the primal scene adds to this the notion of a masculine force in interaction with the feminine.

My use of the concept of the primal scene, as with the anti-group, is not meant to imply a concrete presence in the group. Rather, I invoke the concept in the spirit of an enquiry, an exploration, in a metaphorical rather than a concrete sense. To what extent metaphorical explanations of this sort are necessary I now question in the light of the clinical findings of the present book (see Part 3), since sexual desire, fantasy and anxiety can be sourced within the current sexuality of group members. At the same time, the secrecy and anxiety about sexuality, especially erotic fantasies, suggests that encoded unconscious historical and family influences have an important influence and that family myths concerning partnership and sexuality are inscribed in this process.

The primal scene is usually regarded psychoanalytically as a precursor of the Oedipus complex. The nature of the primal scene in the child's fantasy has a strong influence on the Oedipal configuration, in which the child now enters the stage as a player, taking the role of a rival who seeks intimate closeness with one of the parents to the exclusion of the other. Halton (1998) makes a determined case for the Oedipal situation as the defining parameter of group psychotherapy. He proposes that the main conflicts in the group are around desires and fears of inclusion and exclusion centring on the person of the therapist, standing for the desired primary object. The desire for favoured inclusion by the therapist arouses intense rivalry that contributes markedly to the group dynamic but is often hidden or disguised. Halton suggests that it is vital for the therapist to interpret the transference to themselves as well as the feelings this evokes among group members.

Halton is critical of the contributions to group therapy of both Bion and Foulkes. He regards both their approaches as 'minimalist' in terms of their attention to group members' relationship to the therapist. Neither saw eliciting the transference of individuals as central to their technique. Bion's predominantly group-centred interpretations rendered him unavailable for intimate relations, with little interest in the needs or desires of the individual. Foulkes saw the therapist's responsibility as empowering the group, avoiding transference interpretations which he thought might lead to idealization and dependence on the therapist. But Halton believes that this is an evasion of the essential asymmetry of the parent-child or analyst-patient relationship: a denial of the reality of generational differences, including the analyst's authority.

Halton argues that this is not only a missed opportunity but that it can produce distortions in the group. Unless the therapist recognizes and actively interprets the Oedipal transference,

> false and collusive cultures develop which inhibit emotional progress and inhibit the emergence of real dependence and associated Oedipal struggles. Who feels left out, who projects what into whom, becomes the work for the entire group to engage with, including the therapist who has to privately monitor his or her countertransference.
>
> (Halton 1998: 248)

Halton provides several examples of what he considers to be manifestations of Oedipal transference and rivalry in the group and how he interpreted these in the group context. His interventions would strike most group therapists as highly therapist-centred, but Halton would argue that this is the only way to tackle head on the Oedipal tensions of the group.

The resolution of the Oedipal dilemma, Halton suggests, is in the depressive position, in which the loss of an exclusive claim on the desired object is mourned and the feelings of rivalry and resentment integrated into ongoing sexual development. He also makes clear that taking up group material in this way is not easy. The therapist may feel uncomfortable about being an object of desire as well as interpreting this to the group. However, Halton is so convinced that this is the right way to address the group process that he advocates using it as a parameter for formulating clinical objectives, selecting patients for the group and developing an appropriate group technique.

A feature of Halton's paper is the absence of any reference to sexuality as such in the group. This echoes a familiar theme in this book: the cryptic nature of sexuality in group psychotherapy. In this case, it is striking that even in a paper which elevates the Oedipus complex, a concept so linked to sexuality, the theme is absent from the discussion.

Apart from challenging conventional non-analytic ways of work-ing in groups, the distinction of Halton's paper lies in his tackling the difficult issue of what happens when the therapist, rather than the group, becomes the object of desire. This is a common experience in groups, not necessarily envisaged in the way Halton suggests, but potentially creating a challenge to both the therapist and the group.

The Oedipal theme is also the subject of a paper by Hadar (2004). She argues for the value of the concept, particularly regarding the two areas that Halton emphasizes: the transference to the therapist and the rivalry among group members. She suggests, however, that the therapist needs to be 'known' by the group, showing more of themselves as a person than is usually anticipated. The approach is therefore based not on the interpretation of transference but on the inclusion of the therapist themselves as a real figure struggling with their own Oedipal dilemmas. This, Hadar suggests, will offset rather than exacerbate the intensity of the Oedipal situation. The process, she suggests, is closer to the value system of group analysis which tends to defuse the vertical patient-therapist transference in favour of the spread of transference across the group.

Summary and conclusion

After a long period of reticence about sexuality in group psycho-therapy, a number of papers, starting in the mid-1980s, begin to establish a fruitful discourse about sexuality in the group. Some of these approach the subject from a broader perspective, such as desire in general and gender identification, and the number of papers which tackle sexuality directly is small. However, they are useful in indicat-ing both the constructive potentials and the problems of developing a sexual discourse in the group. The potentials lie in the opportunity to integrate sexuality into the overall functioning of the group and thereby challenge the secrecy and shame often surrounding sexuality. The problems concern the fears of exposure, the potential for sexual intrusion and re-shaming in the group and the risk of sexual enactment outside the group.

The papers highlight the fact that sexuality cannot be looked at in isolation, either in terms of the individual personality or of wider group processes. So, for example, gender issues relating to feminine and masculine identifications are not only crucial in the group gen-erally but intimately influence the expression of desire and sexuality.

Several papers highlight paradoxical messages concerning sexual-ity that are transmitted to participants in group psychotherapy.

On the one hand, there is the rule of abstinence: no socializing and no 'sexualizing' outside the group. This in itself is likely to whet the sexual appetite and stimulate fantasies of sexual transgression. On the other hand, there is encouragement to explore and even experiment with repressed or inhibited aspects of the self, which include the sexual, and to do so in the here-and-now of the group. The group puts participants in a form of sexual bind which is seldom acknowledged or addressed. The positive perspective is that the containment of sexual tension in the group, through the naming of desire rather than its enactment, is likely to strengthen the understanding and integration of sexual impulses and fantasies in members' lives.

The papers emphasize the role of the group therapist in representing and handling the sexual subject. Far from being a neutral observer of the sexual currents in the group, the therapist is an individual with their own sexual desires, attractions, anxieties and prejudices, all of which must be transmitted in some form, conscious or unconscious, in the group. This is likely not only to influence the atmosphere around sexuality in the group but to be part of the stimulus for erotic feelings, including sexual transference and counter-transference. Whereas the traditional culture of group psychotherapy may have regarded this as signalling the need for great caution, some of the present writers suggest that there are valuable opportunities here for dealing directly with problems of desire, intimacy and rivalry in the group.

While these papers provide a useful start to a more open discourse about sexuality in the group, there are several areas that, to my mind, are insufficiently addressed, allowing for the early stage of the debate. These include:

- the concept of desire is somewhat reified and abstracted in a way that obscures its detailed, embodied expression;
- sexuality itself as a subject tends to remain rather elusive – the papers address broad aspects of sexuality but more intimate narratives are lacking;
- the bodily aspect of the group, and the way this is linked to sexuality, is assumed rather than explored;
- the aggressive aspects of sexuality are rarely mentioned, although we know that aggression is an important aspect of sexuality;
- sexual diversity is barely acknowledged; several authors refer in their clinical illustrations to homosexual participants in groups, but with few exceptions there is no discussion of the subject;

- the social and political aspects of sexuality and their reflection in the group are not generally considered;
- the affective constellation of shame, jealousy and guilt pertaining to sexuality is touched on but not dealt with in detail;
- the approach to sexuality in these papers is generally not situated within any established group psychotherapy model, which makes it difficult to align sexuality to group psychotherapy principles as well as to link the papers within a coherent frame.

The extent to which the typical once- or twice-weekly psychotherapy group, with its limitations of time, can consider all the above, ranging from the intimately bodily to the widely social, has to be considered; equally, whether group therapy can encompass in its usual format the deeper, more diverse and darker aspects of sexuality. However, the answer may lie not so much in the actual limits of time and space in the group as in the attitude towards sexuality itself: whether sexuality is regarded as a legitimate subject for the group; what priority sexuality is given in the understanding of individual and group development; whether the group is ready to respond to the challenge of openly exploring sexuality in its diverse aspects; and whether there is some confidence about dealing with the inevitable desires, tensions and frustrations, as well as the risk of enactment, that arise in the embodiment of the sexual subject. Part of the problem is the lack of an adequate theoretical discourse concerning sexuality in group therapy. In the next chapter I explore how the field of group analysis has dealt with this issue and, in the subsequent chapter, I attempt to formulate a more specific group psychotherapy perspective on sexuality.

6

DESIRE IN GROUP ANALYSIS

In this chapter I explore the representation of desire and sexuality in my own field of training and practice, group analysis. Having concluded in Part 1 that the psychoanalytic approach to sexuality reached an impasse because of its failure to address the impact of social processes and change on sexuality, the next step is to consider how this differs in a *group* analytic approach which espouses an articulate model of social process. Further, given the lack of a coherent group psychotherapy perspective of sexuality in existing publications, it is instructive to explore whether this exists or is possible to achieve within the group analytic frame.

Having said that psychoanalysis reached an impasse in its exploration of sexuality, of which its prejudicial thinking and pathologizing tendency are reflections, it is important nevertheless to recognize its generativity in creating a significant sexual discourse. This, as will be seen, stands in marked contrast to the almost total lack of a sexual discourse in group analysis. The exceptions are papers by Burman (2002) and Moeller (2002) – reviewed in Chapter 5 – which strongly challenge the status quo. In this chapter I suggest that the absence of a sexual discourse in group analysis can be linked to a fundamental cleavage between a more psychoanalytic approach and a more sociological approach that is to some extent inherent in the field and that the problematic representation of the individual within this gap accounts for the absence of a discourse of desire. The individual voice, and with it sexuality and desire, are suspended in an ideological void. I suggest that the group analytic perception of the individual as an abstraction, a being constructed artificially from within a social matrix, makes sense from a theoretical perspective but that, in addition to constraining the sexual subject, marginalizes two crucial considerations in group analytic psychotherapy: 1) existential experience, which rests on the experience of human beings of themselves as individuals; and 2) clinical application, in which the individual is an indispensable focus and point of accountability. Both of these considerations are integral parts of the clinical imagination and so the absence of a discourse on desire relates in important ways to the problematic theory-practice link in group analysis.

Foulkesian group analysis is probably the major approach to group psychotherapy in the UK and parts of wider Europe. Unlike the USA, where there is a diverse range of group psychotherapeutic models (Dies 1992), in the UK the group analytic approach largely holds sway, in terms of training and professional practice (Nitsun 2002). This is a further reason to focus on group analysis in my search to evaluate the place of sexuality in therapy groups. Group analytic therapy in the UK reaches many patients in a wide variety of settings and the responsibility and influence we hold as practitioners makes it important to identify and understand any hidden and repressed discourses that weave through the fabric of the discipline.

S.H. Foulkes, the founder of group analysis, was a Freudian psychoanalyst who continued to practise both as an individual and group analyst until his death in 1976. Although he of necessity – and desire – departed from his psychoanalytic heritage in the shaping of group analysis, he also imported into it much that was psychoanalytic in essence. This might presuppose that as a Freudian he would bring to the new project an emphasis on sexuality, or at least a strong consciousness of it, and that this would be reflected in the emerging theory and practice. However, this is not the case. Not only did Foulkes not address sexuality in any depth but the subject has had an increasingly limited valency in the progression of group analysis. Why this should be is in large measure the subject of this chapter.

In describing group analysis, I am aware that I may have given the impression that this is a unitary, internally coherent and consistent body of discourse, particularly when I compare it to the diversity of approach in the USA. This is hardly true. The approach originated not only in psychoanalysis but drew from Gestalt therapy and sociology. Since Foulkes' death, group analysis has taken several different directions. These have all struggled with the question of the individual in the group. However, in my view, no adequate discourse of desire both in a general and a specific sexual sense has emerged. Further, in so far as sexuality in its diverse forms is strongly influenced by social and cultural processes, this perspective is also lacking in group analysis. Hence, neither an individual nor a social perspective of desire and sexuality has emerged – nor, more importantly, an integrative perspective that potentially links the two.

In order to establish why this is, I propose to follow a more or less developmental line, starting with Foulkes' basic model of the analytic group. I then explore the contributions of writers who I have roughly categorized as 'developers', since they have clarified and/or extended Foulkes' thinking in significant ways. Highlighted here are Pines, Brown and, in a qualified way, Hopper. I then consider later contributions to group analysis, focusing on my own concept of the anti-group as a critical principle and Schlapobersky's perspectives of language in the group. Finally, I go on to evaluate the recent sociological turn reflected by Dalal and Stacey. In each case, my main focus is on individuality, desire and sexuality, and how this configuration is represented – or not – in the particular version of group analysis. Since my focus is specific, I am not attempting anything like a comprehensive review of the group analytic literature. I am also aware that the theme of sexuality may not have been a priority in the writings of the writers I consider – but this in itself does not mean that they would deny its importance. At the same time, our published texts are instrumental in transmitting messages about our work, our beliefs, as well as the discipline of which we are part. Hence, they bear scrutiny as reflections of the absence or presence of a discourse.

My exploration of sexuality in group analysis continues within the framework of the group as an object of desire. Here, I use the notion of desire in a broader sense. It is the desirability of the group – as a therapeutic medium, as a place where the deeper aspects of personhood, including sexuality and desire, can be expressed – which is under scrutiny.

Foulkes

When Foulkes originated group analysis in England in approximately 1940, he made a bold leap from his psychoanalytic tradition to a socially orientated form of group psychotherapy. Instead of the individual being at the centre of the theory, the group now takes precedence. The concept of the individual is regarded as an abstraction, a reification, the figment of a western line of thought that presupposes the separation of individual and group (Foulkes 1948). In Foulkes' view the individual is permeated by the social to the extent that there is no separation: individual is social and social is individual. This means that the psychoanalytic givens of development, innate drives, instincts, the internal systems of id, ego and super ego, are all culturally defined. Instead of inheritance, there is transmission. This is particularly striking in relation to the id, the primitive pool of desires and impulses that is assumed to arise from the deepest unconscious of the individual: this too is a product of culture. In this view, the social unconscious looms large – the repressed aspects of cultural memory and experience that are transmitted from generation to generation.

There is huge promise in this vision for a more radical perspective of sexual development than could ever be achieved by psychoanalysis, since the widening social framework anticipates the liberalizing of sexual identity and morality in the later twentieth century and early twenty-first century. Coming from the Freudian school, Foulkes was also aware of the restricting and inhibiting effect of a conventional social conscience, inscribed in the censoring role of the super ego. His views of these phenomena were influenced by his close colleague, the sociologist Norbert Elias. However, 'radical' is mixed with 'conservative' in confusing, unresolved ways in Foulkes, as Dalal (1998) has pointed out, and the potential to develop an original and challenging vision of sexuality appears not to have been part of his plan.

The tension between Foulkes' orthodox and progressive views is exemplified in his Basic Law of Group Dynamics. In this principle, Foulkes (1948) asserts that the momentum of the therapy group inevitably, and of necessity, leads towards the norms of the society of which it is part. His assumption is that group members – patients in a therapy group – all deviate in some way from the social norm. Through the work of the group, this deviancy is modified and the group as a whole is normalized. I have previously criticized this perspective for its apparent conformist assumptions (Nitsun 1996), a criticism which in the context of the sexual subject becomes all the more trenchant. The 'law' of group dynamics, itself a prescriptive concept, places under duress the whole notion of sexual diversity and compromises the opportunity in the analytic group to freely and openly express sexuality and sexual difference.

Brown (1998), while recognizing the potential in the Basic Law to be seen as coercive, gives it a more benign and liberal interpretation. He argues that Foulkes was not promoting uniformity, merely stating that the membership of each group has more in common than it at first realizes. Foulkes (1948: 30) wrote: 'It is struck by its differences, which provoke curiosity, hostility and fear. As it proceeds it finds more and more of common ground, and less and less contradiction between individuality and community'. This describes the group analytic vision of healing. Through the mirroring processes of the group, members see themselves reflected in each other, the painful edges of their differences are dissolved and they gain a greater sense of belonging to a common humanity.

The jury, in my view, is out on which is the more accurate reading of Foulkes' Basic Law of Group Dynamics: the coercive or the creative. Certainly, it is apparent that when Foulkes gets 'down and dirty', down to the nitty-gritty of sex, he adopts a very careful, cautious and conformist approach. This arises as a hypothetical question he imagines being asked by a reader of his text:

> How can these people possibly talk about their intimate, personal private affairs, thoughts, feelings and phantasies, in the presence of a number of others, total strangers at that? I understand that you can't cure them by talking about the weather. You have repeated yourself, already this Freudian stuff about children's sexuality, repressions, dreadful unconscious phantasies and so on, so I suppose you can expect them to talk about that, too. Do they? Can they?
>
> (Foulkes 1948: 28)

Raising this question so vividly, Foulkes is clearly aware of a problem, the problem of whether sexuality has a place in group analysis, and the fears and curiosities surrounding this. His answer starts off somewhat affirmatively: 'Yes, these people can talk to each other – within certain limits – about their own very personal affairs . . .' (p. 29). But he quickly goes on to qualify the 'certain limits'. He suggests that the standards of the group are automatically the same as in life 'outside', the standards of 'the larger group' (p. 31). He continues:

> the Group's emphasis is more on the present than on the past, it is more progressively oriented than retrogressively. *Accordingly it need not deal in so many words with the infantile, instinctive eroticisms and the concomitant details of intimate sex life, perversions, excretory activities and so on.* It can therefore express its problems sufficiently within the acceptable boundaries. Where this is not sufficient for any one individual, it is a sign that deeper, earlier, regressive levels are too active. This, significantly, coincides clinically

with the need for individual interview, where these manifestations of regression can be worked through, or calls for
individual Analysis.

(Foulkes 1948: 31, emphasis added)

Foulkes' notion of 'acceptable boundaries' tends to reinforce the
conformist interpretation of the Basic Law. He reveals firm views
about what constitutes progressive and regressive, consigning much
of sexuality to the regressive (with 'excretory activities'!) and regarding it as unfit for group analysis, particularly in relation to the
conformist notion of the therapy group aspiring to the standards of
'outside' society. Although it is realistic to say – as he does – that
some problems require individual psychotherapy, it is noteworthy
that he applies this particularly to 'regressive' sexuality. The problem, of course, is that sexuality cannot be so easily divided into
progressive and regressive and that the over-categorization of sexual
experience in this way is likely to make it difficult for anyone in the
group to talk about sex, not just the so-called 'regressed'.

It is important to recognize that Foulkes formulated the above
half a century ago, at a time when the prevailing sexual ethic was
considerably more restrictive than it is now. He was the voice of his
time. However, this was a far cry from the promise of a radical social
vision. His writing reflects a distinctly guarded attitude towards anything other than mainstream heterosexuality. He described homosexuality as 'a severe personality disorder' (Foulkes and Anthony
1965) and suggested that homosexuals should be treated in homogeneous groups – a view faintly reminiscent of Fairbairn's advice
that homosexuals be placed in rehabilitation camps (see Chapter 3).
Some of Foulkes' clinical examples also illustrate a problematic view
of homosexuality. There is the case of the 'young man who had been
discharged from the army because of a nervous breakdown and had
reason to fear trouble in connection with his homosexual impulses'
(1948: 27). Foulkes goes on to describe how this man participated in
the group, did not speak about his homosexuality, listened when
others mentioned the subject – and ended up much improved. His
depression lessened and 'his libido turned definitely towards the
other sex' (p. 28). Although it is difficult to know how to interpret
this example, there is an air of judgement about the man having
reason to fear 'trouble' in relation to his homosexual impulses
and the rather miraculous way, by concealing his sexuality in the
group and hearing others talk instead, he emerges seemingly as heterosexual. An example of the Basic Law of Group Dynamics in

operation? If so, it is difficult to escape the impression that com-munity, in this rendering, is constructed through conformity rather than diversity.

The above, written in 1948, appears to have been the most comprehensive statement about sexuality in all of Foulkes' publica-tions. From then on, until and including the publication of his last paper in 1976, there is very little mention of sex. In the index of his last major work, *Therapeutic Group Analysis* (1964b) there is no ref-erence to it at all and there is precious little in the text itself, as if sexuality has now slipped off the agenda. A late paper on the Oedipus complex (Foulkes 1972) usefully reinterprets the 'complex' in group terms as linked to family dynamics as a whole and also suggests that Oedipal phenomena are played out interactionally in the therapy group. The examples are very broad, however, and lack any sense of sexuality as embodied in the immediacy of the group. Sex has become increasingly marginalized in group analysis. Either the parameters surrounding sexuality in Foulkes' model have tight-ened further or he chooses not to report or theorize sexuality as communicated in the group. Whether and how this is connected with Foulkes' increasing move towards a more socially orientated group analysis – as reflected in his later publications – is difficult to say. My guess is that it is connected in so far as individual subjectivity becomes less interesting and relevant and, unfortunately, with this goes sexuality. So, whether the constraint comes from his conserva-tism about matters sexual or from his developing attraction to the social and the cultural, is unclear. Either way, sexuality practically disappears from view.

There is another version of Foulkes' group – by himself – which I find more encouraging. This is summed in his notion of 'the Group as a Forum' (Foulkes 1948: 167). Here, arguing the therapeutic potential of the group, Foulkes conjures a vision of the group clearly not as a mouthpiece for conventional society but as a form of alter-native community. He talks about the individual being able to see themselves in a new light, in a way in which the boundaries of the ego can be revised:

> The same is true for the super ego, which represents in the last resort the restrictions imposed by the community on the individual as imparted by parental authority and incorpor-ated into the mind. By its rejection, or tolerance, or approval, the group seems able not only to revise but also to modify this formation efficiently. Its effect can therefore be

said to be a genuine reconditioning of the structure of the
ego and super ego.

(Foulkes 1948: 168)

This, to my mind, is a vision of the group far more as an agent of
social change. It contrasts with a picture of the group slavishly
struggling to fulfil the norms and standards of society. It is this
vision of therapeutic change that I see as more genuinely radical,
more intrinsically about social diversity and a template for a perspective of sexuality that may be appropriate and beneficial to group
psychotherapy. Interestingly, Foulkes' notion of the Group as a
Forum is a far less prominent feature of the group analytic culture,
less recognized and less debated, than his Basic Law of Group
Dynamics. There are reasons, I suggest, to correct the discrepancy.

Before leaving Foulkes to explore more contemporary group
analysis, I wish to refer briefly to his biography. In my work on the
anti-group, in which I questioned the idealizing tendency in Foulkes'
account of the group and his neglect of group antagonistic and
destructive processes (Nitsun 1996), I highlighted his experience as a
refugee from Nazi Europe in the 1930s and the apparent contradiction between biography and theory. I wondered if this vein of idealization could be understood as a defence against the ravages of a
world war as well as the inevitable anxieties attendant on immigra-
tion to a new country, with its differing social and professional
demands (Bledin 2003). In other words, too great an emphasis on
the disruptive and destructive potential of the group might have
endangered the optimism of his project. Could the same be said
about his minimization of the sexual agenda? Like aggression, to
which it is closely related, sexuality is potentially explosive, disruptive, even destructive, putting the group at risk. Is its slipping off the
group analytic agenda then a reflection of fears of the underlying
fragility of the group?

The developers

Foulkes drew around him a loyal group of followers who took forward his teachings and went on to make distinctive contributions to
group analysis in their own right. This was largely within Foulkes'
own frame of reference, psychoanalysis and sociology sitting
together, somewhat awkwardly at times, but still the bastions of a
group psychology. If there was a bias in either direction, it was
almost certainly towards psychoanalysis, probably because some of

the developers, as I call them, were psychoanalysts themselves. Among the best known figures associated directly with Foulkes and the origins of group analysis are Dennis Brown, Lionel Kreeger, Malcolm Pines, Robyn Skynner and Meg Sharpe. A further group of figures coming from different backgrounds, such as Liesel Hearst, Harold Behr and Jeff Roberts, to name but a few, brought additional insights and applications to the field through their writing. In this section, I propose to evaluate the contributions of three group analysts who cross the time divide and who may be regarded as developers who made distinctive contributions: Pines, Brown and Hopper. These three writers are linked through a common pathway to group analysis through psychoanalysis but also reflect important differences in the evolution of group analysis.

Pines

Malcolm Pines has been described metaphorically as Foulkes' 'eldest son' (Hopper 1998: 11). Both a psychoanalyst and psychiatrist, Pines did much to substantiate and interpret Foulkes' theory and to put it in context with contemporary psychotherapeutic approaches, particularly self-psychology. Pines (1982) elaborates Foulkes' concept of mirroring, giving it central importance in the group analytic understanding of relatedness, which focuses on the interdependence of self and other through mutual recognition. He (1987) sees the therapeutic development of both individual and group towards increasing coherence and gives this an important place in all psychotherapy.

In line with Foulkes' increasing marginalization of sexuality as an aspect of group analysis, Pines writes very little directly about sexuality but instead approaches it as part of a dominant Freudian perspective of human behaviour that requires reinterpretation in cultural terms. Here, Pines identifies with Foulkes' radical social position and is influenced by Norbert Elias who challenged the Freudian concept of drives as universal. Elias generated a 'historical psychology' which questioned the concept of an id without history and emphasized that the relationship between id, ego and super ego changes in the course of the civilizing process: 'The drives are not timeless, universal, outside of history' (Pines 1998a: 137). Pines is also interested in the suppression of discourse that results from the dominance of a prevailing discourse. Citing the work of the Russian scholar, Bakhtin, he questions the Freudian division between conscious and unconscious as a division between secondary and primary process. Instead, he suggests, the division is between an 'official language' and an 'unofficial language' that is suppressed and repressed. In this case, the denied social 'reality' of man is the unofficial language and the biological monad that constituted 'Freudian' man the official language (Pines 1998a).

Pines' critical position in relation to classical psychoanalysis narrows into a particular perspective of the Oedipus complex. Observing the emphasis on patricide in Freud's version of the story, Pines (1998b), following a commentary by Ross (1982), notes that Freud, while focusing on Oedipus' dilemmas, completely left out the destructive rage of his father, Laius. In the original myth, Laius is a violent man with a traumatic history of his own who acts destructively towards his son. By emphasizing Oedipus' tragic fate, however, Freud creates a view of the violated child as the source of sexual desire, hatred and envy, while ignoring the envy and hatred of the parents. Pines' reinterpretation is in line with the recognition of external social reality as constructive of the sexual subject and harks back to Freud's seduction theory, which attributed responsibility to the parents but was later abandoned in favour of a view of the child's inherent sexuality. Pines' comments reflect an attempt to reinstate the social world of relationships, particularly those of parent to child, as a formative influence on sexual development.

While these views help to establish the sexual subject as part of a revised theoretical discourse, Pines, in none of his writings it seems, attempts to embody these understandings in the analytic group itself. How sexuality enters the group, how 'internal' individual factors interact with 'external' social ones, how this impacts on the group, how the group deals with issues of judgement and morality – none of this is given voice. Sexuality and desire are among the many subjects that combine to form a group analytic value system but they are not presented as an embodied presence in the unfolding of the actual group. In line with Pines' own interest in the work of Bakhtin, sex appears to be the 'unofficial', repressed language of group analysis.

Pines contributed elegantly to the interpretation and development of group analytic theory. He helped to launch the analytic group as an object of desire – in the broad sense of a meaningful and humanizing psychotherapeutic medium. However, the sexual object of desire is in essence missing from this vision.

Brown

Dennis Brown offers a balanced voice in the tension of opposites that begins to mark the evolution of group analysis. Interested in intersubjective psychoanalysis, he brings this directly in to group analysis (Brown 1994) and finds new ways of making sense of communication in the relational sphere of the group. He describes an emergent process of self-and-other discovery in the intersubjective dialogue as the core of the analytic group. Through this, Brown gives substance to Foulkes' concept of 'ego training in action' (Foulkes 1964), helping to clarify how group analysis actually works.

But Brown (1998) is also fully aware of the potential for derailment. Citing my own work on the anti-group (Nitsun 1991, 1996), that of Kreeger (1992) on envy in groups and Zinkin (1983) on destructive forms of mirroring, he recognizes the negative processes constantly shadowing positive processes in group life. He attributes much of this to the hatred of sharing, which he links to sibling rivalry and the exclusion from parental sexuality. Further, he sees this hatred and the associated anxiety as potent factors in the reluctance of many people to join a therapy group. He gives a particularly vivid example of a woman who described a group as terrifying: 'It was them or me', she said, 'I'd not give an inch, or give everything so as not to be found out' (Brown 1998: 396). Although he does not use quite these terms, selfishness and selfhood become crucial themes in his writing. He further relates these dilemmas to wider groups in the culture, noting both the cohesive and destructive representations of identity and difference in social groups.

Brown's (1998) interest in ethics is another distinctive contribution. He formulates the notion of group analysis as an ethical activity, a way of changing people psychologically through processes that hinge on representations of interpersonal justice. He identifies four main components of justice in the therapy group – entitlement, fairness, equality and impartiality. Brown does not relate these processes to sexuality as such but we can see how they have an important bearing on the mediation of desire and sexuality in the group. Entitlement, for example, originates in the sense of claiming one's own rights but it can also represent an excessive demand for special privileges and gratification, in which case it becomes a form of pathological entitlement. This parallels Lacan's notion of demand, in which groups can obscure the fuller recognition and sharing of desire (Giraldo 2001; Tylim 2003). These 'ethical' considerations highlight the important point that desire is by definition 'selfish'. When we desire something or someone we usually want it entirely for ourselves. We do not want to share it with others. How this selfishness is accommodated in the group and how the tension between selfishness and sharing is negotiated depends to a large extent on the group culture, its notion of justice, and how the therapist monitors and mediates the different components of group justice.

Sexuality lacks a significant presence in Brown's writing. He makes reference to parental sexuality, the impact of the primal scene, and the child's sense of exclusion from the parents' intimacy. However, this is mainly in passing and without any substantive sense of a discourse. Yet, Brown's recognition of the individual in the group, the importance of subjectivity and intersubjectivity and the challenges of both entitlement and sharing, provide a useful framework for the representation of sexuality.

Hopper

The inclusion of Earl Hopper in the group of developers highlights the diverse paths group analysis has taken in the decades since Foulkes' death and the vagaries of desire as represented in the different approaches. Hopper brings to group analysis a background in both sociology and psychoanalysis, imparting to his writing a width and depth that is unusual and illuminating. At the same time, he throws up problematic questions about the nature of group analysis, as well as the representation of sexuality in the group.

Hopper's main contributions, I suggest, are his elaboration of the notion of the social unconscious and his development of the theory of a fourth basic assumption. Building on Foulkes' emphasis on the pervasive influence of social processes on human development, Hopper (2003a) looks particularly at unconscious social processes, all the more powerful because they are unseen, unknown, marginalized or denied. The notion of a fourth basic assumption is an elaboration of Bion's theory of the three basic assumptions. As described by Hopper (2003b), the additional basic assumption refers to aggregation/massification as aspects of group fragmentation or incohesion, strongly linked to fears of annihilation engendered by psychological/social trauma.

Whereas the social emphasis potentially draws away from the psychoanalytic roots of group analysis (as it does in the work of Dalal and Stacey, who are discussed later in this chapter), Hopper remains steadfastly committed to classical psychoanalytic concepts, particularly transference and counter-transference. While this is a strength in some respects, these elements are incorporated in his clinical work – illustrated in a series of detailed examples – in a markedly self-referential fashion that creates a difficult tension between the breadth and democratic spirit of a social consciousness and the sometimes categorical, coercive and analyst-centred approach of certain forms of psychoanalysis. By analyst-centred, I refer to the consistent emphasis on the analyst as an 'object' in the mind of the patient, including sexual desire and fantasy concerning the analyst. Hopper's illustrations, in my view, highlight the particular question of who or what the object of desire in group psychotherapy is: the other patient/s; the group as a whole; or the therapist? While all of these may apply at different times, or even simultaneously, there may be a particular tension between the group as an object of desire and the therapist as the object of desire. This is because patients do not unusually fantasize a special closeness to the analyst, to the exclusion of the rest of the group, sometimes making it difficult to share the therapist and hence to tolerate group membership. How we as therapists deal with this, I believe, varies considerably and has major implications for the group process.

In an example titled 'Pandoro', Hopper (2003b) describes a group in which there is predominating anxiety about a wasps' nest directly outside the consulting room. The nest is beginning to intrude into the wall between two windows, staining the wall, while the buzz of the wasps grows continually closer. The group is traumatized by the intrusion of the nest and the analyst's apparent failure to do anything about it. Hopper links the potential trauma of a wasp invasion to an impending summer break. His interpretation suggests that the real trauma is the analyst's absence for several weeks and the fears of abandonment this provokes in the group. Pandoro is a patient described as a young, drug-addicted, homosexually-inclined man who leads a defensive aggregation process in the group through contempt, distancing and ironic humour. Hopper reports his own interpretation to the group as follows:

> Without much hesitation, I interpreted these 'teasing' remarks about WASPS in terms of what I believed was an envious attack in response to the helplessness that they felt about my taking a holiday in a few weeks' time, and specifically in terms of the cutting and stinging of separation anxiety. I said that their attack was expressed in their understandable preoccupations with the brown stains and yellow liquid, *which involved unconscious projections of their desires to make anal and urethral attacks on my eyes, which were displacements upwards from my analytic breasts, as symbolized by the windows.*
>
> (Hopper 2003b: 117, emphasis added)

120

This is possibly the most penetrating and symbolically complex interpretation I have yet seen reported in the group analytic literature. Foulkes himself discouraged what he called 'plunging interpretations' on the grounds that they might empower the analyst at the expense of the group. Group analysts also tend to veer away from transference interpretations, reflecting a concern that emphasis on the relationship to the analyst will foreclose the open discourse of the group. Hopper's interpretation is both plunging and transferential, making the analyst unequivocally central to the group. It is one of several transference interpretations made in the course of this group, each time reinforcing the analyst's centrality. Further, the interpretation of envy implies desire, since there can be no envy without desire. Through both the mode of transference interpretation and the particular content of the interpretation, the conclusion might be that the analyst, and not the group, is the object of desire.

I further have reservations about the standard psychoanalytic interpretation of holiday breaks as invariably generating anxiety about failed dependency on the analyst. Such an interpretation ignores the possibility that patients may be *relieved* at having a break, that they might be happy to temporarily see the back of the analyst and that if they are going to miss anyone it would be each other or the group as a whole, rather than the analyst. These interpretations credit the group with a sense of belonging in its own right, a libidinal connection between the members themselves and an ability to see the analyst as one of the group rather than the supreme being upon whom all in the group must inevitably depend.

Transference undoubtedly occurs in groups and interpretation may well be necessary for recognition and working through in the group. However, transference is a way of organizing and mediating desire in the group and so its active use as an analytic tool requires careful consideration. Also, how we as therapists use ourselves as transference objects, including objects of desire and envy, I suggest, is highly individual and influenced as much by our own self-representations as those of our patients.

It is, however, necessary to qualify the above comments. Hopper points out that over time his technique has become more 'transparent' and 'supportive' (2003b: 113). Even in the present example, he later describes a greater openness on his part when he acknowledges his failure to protect the group from the wasps and their right to feel disappointed and angry. However, his initial interpretative stance stands out in sharp relief.

Sexuality is far more evident in Hopper's clinical material than in most group analytic illustrations. This can be dramatic in its expression. In one example (Hopper 2003a: 181), he describes himself attempting to grapple with the difficult dynamics in a group and offering his own spontaneous free associations. The central image in his associations is that of 'men fucking their brains out' all over a village which has been ravaged by trauma and deprivation. As in this example, sexuality is largely linked in his illustrations to the themes of trauma, anxiety and defence, so that we get a picture more of sexuality under duress, in states of psychic conflict and regression, than of sexuality as a natural part of group relations in which libidinal feelings contribute to the group bonding process.

Hopper often refers to perversion. There is a strong leaning towards orthodox psychoanalytic categorizations and explanations of sexuality. Homosexuality appears in a number of examples, accompanied by interpretations of the assumed pathology of homosexual group members, particularly as a defence against violent impulses (Hopper 2003b: Ch. 5), a defence against psychotic anxiety, and an expression of sado-masochistic desires (Hopper 2003a: Ch. 6). In these interpretations, Hopper follows a pathologizing tradition in psychoanalysis, influenced by the work of Limentani (1989), who has been cited in gay affirmative psychotherapeutic writing as an example of prejudicial theorizing (e.g. Magee and Miller 1995). In a further publication, Hopper (1995: 1126) categorizes homosexuality as 'based on the eroticization of hatreds and violent impulses' and/or 'based on imitative identification with the "female" object, transsexualism and narcissistic object choices'. There are other instances in Hopper's examples in which homosexuality appears to be discussed in groups in a more sympathetic, even empathic light. However, the possibility that there is a natural form of homosexuality, originating in sexual development in a non-defensive, non-narcissistic and non-feminine fashion (in men) that involves loving and affectionate feelings, and that this is experienced in groups, as well as the more problematic versions of homosexuality, is missing. This is set within an emphatic heterosexual value system that inevitably influences the normative culture of the group. There seems to be very little recognition, moreover, of the power of the analyst in influencing the group culture.

Given Hopper's recognition of social processes as constructive of individual development, it is surprising that there is so little seeming regard (in this context, at least) for the relativity of sexual identity and orientation and the way in which social attributions, including psychoanalytic categorizations, both create and maintain the marginalization and pathologization of sexual diversity. Adopting a critical perspective, we may question whether the anxiety, rage and shame that are so often cited as components of homosexuality – as in some of Hopper's examples – are intrinsically present, defensively marshalled or an appropriate response to cultural repudiation.

Drawing together my impressions of the three 'developers' I have chosen to consider, we find significant discrepancies. Pines and Brown are similar in presenting a wide-ranging, liberal vision of the group in which intersubjective responsiveness is emphasized and sexuality underemphasized. Hopper also presents a wide-ranging vision, impressive in its attempt to understand the impact of trauma on the group, and additionally giving sexuality a vivid place in the discourse. However, this is sometimes in a categorical, pathologizing way that appears to derive from psychoanalytic prejudice and instead of opening up a sexual discourse, in my view, potentially closes and constrains it. Whereas Pines and Brown move away from psychoanalysis towards a decentring of the role of the analyst in the group, Hopper moves back to psychoanalysis in reinforcing the analyst's centrality, with implications for the locus of desire in the group and, with this, the nature of group analysis itself. These discrepancies reveal the considerable impact of analyst differences on the conception of the group, coupled with the great difficulty of establishing a discourse of desire and sexuality that is open, challenging of orthodox constraints and that draws creatively on contemporary perspectives of sexuality.

Later contributors

The post-Foulkesian period ushered in a wide range of contributions, further extending the theory and applications of group analysis. I could not possibly do justice here to this host of contributions and so confine myself to my own writing, specifically the concept of the anti-group, and Schlapobersky's treatise on the language of the group. If these approaches seem at first to deflect from the sexual subject, they come back to both desire and sexuality.

The anti-group

I originally formulated the concept of the anti-group towards the end of my training as a group analysis in the late 1980s. I was responding to what I experienced as an idealizing trend in group analysis. Both Foulkes as the originator of group analysis and his product, the group analytic method, were in my view the objects of idealization. The group as an object of desire, in a metaphorical sense, was writ large. This was understandable as the response of a relatively new psychotherapeutic form seeking to assert itself, particularly, as in this case, against the often rigid orthodoxies of psychoanalysis. Group analysis also needed to distinguish itself from the influential theories of Bion (1961), who presented a very different, darker and more pessimistic account of the group. This, however, led to the creation of two extremes occupying a position which could be described in terms of 'the structure of opposition' (Dews 1987). In this, the positive and negative potentials of a given phenomenon are subjected to a cultural and institutional split, which makes it difficult to achieve, or even consider, integration.

Apart from these ideological issues, I was concerned about the absence of discussion about the problematic aspects of group analytic psychotherapy, including the real and troubling difficulties practitioners encountered in the conduct of groups. As an NHS head of department, clinician and supervisor, I became aware of the many difficulties of setting up and maintaining groups. These ranged from patients' fear and reluctance to join groups, often stating a preference for individual therapy, to unpredictable impasse and fallout in the actual group. This was paralleled by suspicion of groups in the organizational matrix and devaluing opinions such as 'the group is second-best to individual therapy' and 'groups are destructive', reflecting the group as an object of non-desire. Several of the themes pertaining to patients' resistance to group therapy in the NHS have now been confirmed in a research study by Bowden (2002). But if group practitioners and students were faced with an overly optimistic group culture in their own institutes, how could they deal with the discrepancy between expectation and experience? My aim in formulating the anti-group was in large measure to legitimize the difficulties that group therapists encountered and to promote a culture of realism and support that strengthened the constructive potentials of this powerful therapeutic medium (Nitsun 2005: 115).

In a series of publications (Nitsun 1991, 1996, 1999, 2000a, b, 2005), I presented the anti-group in essence as a critical principle, a broad construct within which it would be possible to debate the problematic aspects of groups. In trying to make sense of the phenomenon, I sought to understand the conflict between members' individual needs – their hopes, desires and longings – and the requirements of group membership, in which individual needs may have to be suspended. The frustration of individual desires in groups is frequently superseded by a realization of commonality and the developmental potential of mirroring and exchange with others. However, in some cases the frustration festers and grows and the group is felt to be inimical to personal needs. Common group tensions that can usually be dealt with constructively acquire a negative and destructive charge and, if inadequately handled or resolved, escalate and undermine the group and its therapeutic task.

Returning to sexuality, I suggested (Nitsun 1994, 1996) that the anti-group could be seen as an anti-libidinal group. Based on Fairbairn's (1952) concept of the anti-libidinal ego, this viewed the anti-group as reflecting fear of the expression of libidinal need in the group, constraining the potential for intimacy, sexuality and play. This could be represented as a direct inhibition of libidinal expression or a more covert attack on desire and sexuality. I further looked at sexuality in terms of the fantasy of the primal scene in the group, seen in symbolic rather than literal terms as expressing underlying conceptions of sexual relationships and the way these influence the nature of intimacy in the group. This theory, described in greater detail in Chapter 5, reflected my attempt to consider sexuality in the group, although in a metaphorical and theoretical way that is different from the more direct approach I follow in the present book. However, the overriding issue in both contexts is similar – what it is that creates the group as an object of desire as opposed to an anti-group, how we can generate a group culture that inspires and attracts rather than alienates and antagonizes and to what extent the representation of desire and sexuality are part of this process.

The two missing discourses I set out to explore – aggression and sexuality – are closely interrelated. Aggression is an intrinsic aspect of sexuality, in the same way that sexuality is often at the root of aggression. Both are aspects of group interaction that are frequently perceived as threatening and destabilizing and, in my view, both have been marginalized in group analysis.

Schlapobersky

John Schlapobersky (1994, 1996) has made a novel contribution to group analysis through his use of language as a frame of reference for group development, within the scope of Foukes' concept of 'free-floating discussion'. He highlights three linguistic analogies – monologue, dialogue and discourse – as defining the group process in its movement from the dominance of an individual voice (monologue), to the intimacy of two individuals in communication (dialogue), to the comprehensive representation of all voices in the group in creative interchange (discourse). This does not describe a linear sequence as much as a communicative sequence that varies in its expression in groups. Schlapobersky's contribution lies in the originality of his linguistic frame, paradoxically unusual yet crucial in a field as verbal as group analysis, as well as the inclusion of individual, pair and group domains as experiential entities in themselves, notwithstanding the social thread that links all these domains into one.

Schlapobersky also illustrates how sexuality can find its voice in the communicative sphere of the group. While this is not his primary theme, several of his clinical examples illustrate the entry into the group of significant material about sexuality and intimacy. He attempts to link this to his notion of the language of the group, so that in at least one example (Schlapobersky 1994), communications about desire, sexuality and disappointment in intimate relationships are seen in the light of discourse, the overall group's immersion in a theme that unites the members in a shared communicative space. This demonstrates not only that there is time and space in the group to explore sexuality but that the theme, in all its complexity, can be binding rather than threatening or fragmenting. This is close to the thesis that I seek to develop in this book.

The sociological turn

In the late 1990s the sociological influence embedded in group analysis through Elias' influence on Foulkes came to the fore in new writing that challenged the psychoanalytic tradition and proffered a purportedly far more radical vision. This writing, identified particularly with Dalal and Stacey, presented a theoretical reconstruction that aimed at the same time to re-envision the psychotherapy group. It is perhaps too early to evaluate the influence of this development but not too early to draw out some major themes and assess the implications for a discourse of desire and sexuality. The philosophy, tone and value system changes markedly here from that of most of the previous writers considered, as we follow the complex evolution of group analytic thinking.

Dalal

Farhad Dalal (1998), in his book *Taking the Group Seriously*, was the first group analyst to confront in detail the inconsistencies arising from the forging of group analysis from Freudian psychoanalysis.

Dalal also highlights the influence on Foulkes of a different 'theoretical master', the sociologist Norbert Elias, and how Foulkes was unable to resolve the contradictions between Freud's individual, instinct-driven approach (which views individuals as precipitating the social through repression and sublimation) and Elias' more authentically social emphasis (in which the social precipitates the individual and vice versa in a mutually generating process). Dalal describes Foulkes as 'continually torn' between the two and the resultant group analytic theory as an uncomfortable hybrid. Dalal's epithets, 'radical Foulkes' and 'orthodox Foulkes', sum up very well this contradiction.

Dalal also sets himself the difficult task of taking forward the radical agenda in group analysis, aiming to generate a 'philosophical and metaphysical' framework for group analysis that would constitute 'a new way of experiencing oneself and the group' (Dalal 1998: 12). Implicit in this is the model of group analytic psychotherapy. In other words, the project concerns not just groups in general but *therapy* groups, and this is reflected in Dalal's ongoing reference to psychoanalytic and other psychotherapeutic constructs. His work then draws together several strands of thinking about group, social and cultural processes and ends up with a dense tapestry of ideas and thoughts that define a more thoroughly social perspective of the group experience. An important aspect of this is the concept of the social unconscious, in which cultural history, often forgotten, repressed or unknown, profoundly influences current identity and relationships. This concept has also been taken up by other group analysts, notably Brown (2001) and Hopper (2003b, see above), and represents an important alternative to individualized notions of the unconscious.

There is much of value in Dalal's thinking about group identity and the role of both conscious and unconscious social forces that shape individual experience. But, in my view, the emphasis on the social, while meant to reconceptualize rather than replace individuality, ends up marginalizing individual subjectivity. This includes individual desire and sexuality.

It is beyond the scope of this book to elaborate further on his contribution but I will stop briefly to consider Dalal's emphasis on belonging. He notes that Foulkes regarded the need to belong as one of the most fundamental motivating principles of human behaviour, further that this distinguished his approach from the Freudian ethos of instinct. What brings people together is their wish to be part of a group, to have a sense of attachment that transcends individual attachment and gives them a place in the social order. Hugely important, I agree, but where does sex fit in? To challenge the supremacy of instinct is understandable, because of its biological and universal connotations and the constraints these place on the human subject. But by de-emphasizing instinct there is a tendency to de-emphasize anything to do with desire and sexuality. This sometimes seems convenient: sexuality and desire are just too 'personal', too 'private', too messy to fit into a socially orientated discourse. Burkitt (1998) notes that sociological approaches generally fail to represent sexuality, in the same way that they also fail to recognize a sense of individual conflict, expressly that between individual desire and group morality.

Not surprisingly, sex hardly gets a mention in Dalal's treatment of the group. There are several references to 'life and death instincts', however, these are treated very broadly in terms of cultural transmission, with reference to libidinal phases and bodily functions but, as far as I can discern, not one reference to sexuality. Even a sizeable section on the id does not mention sex.

This seems to me a significant omission in a project that seeks to articulate a comprehensive analytic theory of the group, particularly one that aspires to changing our experience of the group and that has relevance to the group as a therapeutic medium. But rather than this being a criticism of Dalal himself, who in other respects does an impressive job of reinvigorating Foulkesian theory, it is a statement of the failure of group analysis, starting with Foulkes and continuing with a new generation of writers, to find a place for sexuality. The problem is that this must influence the way group analysts work with sexuality – or not – in their therapy groups. Our published discourses recurringly reflect and inform our clinical practice. As has been pointed out by various writers, prompted by Foucault's work on the creation and dissemination of knowledge, our institutes and publications play a vital and often unreflective part in the reification of theory. This is also the point Pines made when invoking Bakhtin's notion of the official and unofficial languages that are constituted by discourse. I am anxious about a group analysis that so lacks a sexual presence. I am also anxious about an escalating drift to the social in such a way that the individual, the subjective, the bodily and the sexual are so lost to view.

This brings me to the omission of any clinical illustrations in Dalal's work. The major thrust of his theoretical challenge seems to be towards the explication of the psychotherapy group, but in the last chapter of *Taking the Group Seriously* it becomes disappointingly clear that this is not going to happen. Dalal recognizes this himself and claims that 'the translation of these themes into the consulting room is enormously difficult' (1998: 218). But why should it be so difficult? If a theory has clinical applicability – and we might question the point of theory in psychotherapy if it has no clinical applicability – this should, at least to some degree, be evident. The only explanation I can find is that in an emphatically social theory which eschews the individual perspective, the clinical subject is decentred and therapeutic practice compromised. The reason for this is that the individual is the key focus of clinical practice and that whatever else the theory says, the individual is the speaking voice. Without this, there is no practice. Sociology and psychotherapy are very different discourses. If we want to utilize sociological insights, we need a bridge, a more substantial link.

Stacey

Ralph Stacey's (2003) book, *Complexity and Group Processes*, follows a similar line to Dalal, arguing for a radical 'new' social approach to group analysis. Unlike Dalal, however, he makes it clear from the beginning that his main aim is to understand and strengthen the psychotherapy group.

Stacey rejects all psychoanalytic formulations of groups – and practically all psychoanalytic formulations in general – on the grounds that they fail to provide a satisfactory explanation of human behaviour, given their reification of the individual and their neglect of the social. Instead, he draws strongly on the thinking of the social theorists, Elias and George Mead, constructing a theory of human behaviour that is 'social through and through'. He also introduces a new element to the debate, that of complex responsive processes, which is derived from complexity theory and provides a more detailed account of concurrent group process. This is an 'action' theory in which experience is understood as direct inter-action with others and the therapeutic function of the group lies in the transformative potential of communication. Group communica-tion generates a series of narratives which provide continuity in the group and facilitate the modification and transformation of these narratives, particularly regarding individuals' 'second natures' or unconscious experience which inscribes their sense of identity and group belonging.

Whereas Dalal's version of this approach allowed for consider-ation of a wide range of theories, including psychoanalysis, Stacey dichotomizes the field and rejects virtually, if not all, psychoanalytic, systemic *and* group analytic writers. Since the therapeutic process is seen as residing in the group itself, there is no recourse to explanatory concepts 'above' or 'below' the group, particularly 'universalized' psychoanalytic concepts such as intra-psychic fantasy, infantile sexuality and the Oedipus complex. However, there is some recognition of the attachment-separation process and its link to the dynamics of inclusion-exclusion in the group, as well as the power relations implicit in this process.

There is considerable power in Stacey's unitary and uncompromising vision of the social as penetrating human behaviour through and through. It is also an uncomfortable vision that, taken to a logical conclusion, invalidates much of the conventional psychotherapeutic discourse. It is a particular ideological version of the group as an object of desire in the sense of conviction and commitment to the group. However, the question, as with Dalal, is what it contributes to the clinical application of group analysis and, in the present context, how it addresses subjectivity and sexuality.

Stacey does provide clinical illustrations, albeit just two examples in a strongly theoretical text. I want to look in some detail at the longer of the two examples in order to discover whether in this vision desire and sexuality have a place in the therapy group. I also offer my own reading of the group material, which I recognize is limited, if not biased, by my not having been present in the group.

The clinical illustration

Stacey's description of the group focuses on a recurring problem of dissatisfaction with the group on the part of several members, particularly two men called Ben and Terry. They complain bitterly about the perceived lack of emotion in the group, one stating that feelings are 'banned'. They perceive the group as going around 'the same circle of behaviour over and over again' in superficial and fruitless discussions. They explode angrily against the group and the therapist. Although Stacey initially describes the group as cohesive and committed, there are reports of frequent disruptions, departures, erratic attendance and secession from the group. Some of the men seem to take it in turn to justify or demand extended breaks from the group, giving the impression that they are fairly desperate to get out. One says the group feels 'completely unsafe'.

Looking further at the main interactions in the group, Stacey describes a series of splits, centring on an 'in' group which comprises himself as conductor and the female members who idealize him, and an 'out' group which consists entirely of male members. It is this split which fuels the jealousy, rage and hatred in the group. There is no evidence of the healing of this split. The impression is that when the group ends after two and a half years, the problem still exists: the men are still angry.

It is difficult to see this as an entirely positive example of Stacey's theory of complex responsive processes, in the sense of therapeutic progress. Although there are periods of movement in the group, there is a high level of ongoing frustration and the pattern of communication is often circular and unproductive, leading to stasis in the group's development. I do not get a sense of the constructive change and transformation that Stacey suggests is the outcome of the process. If anything, the illustration gives the impression of an anti-group. Many of the anti-group characteristics I describe (Nitsun 1996, 2005) are present: a high level of frustration and doubt in the group process; irreconcilable conflict; attacks on the group and the therapist; splitting processes; group secession.

Another characteristic of the anti-group that I describe in the above publications is feelings of hopelessness in the conductor. This too exists in the example, since Stacey shares very openly with the reader painful feelings of confusion and incompetence in his running of the group. He says, 'This left me feeling particularly helpless and despondent. I was disappointed at my inadequate understanding of what this repetitive pattern of dissatisfaction with the group, and angry explosions at it, was all about . . .' (2003: 146). Stacey adds that he understood this process better when reflecting on it subsequently from a complex responsive process perspective. This reflection is then shared in detail with the reader. There is much in it that is meaningful and makes sense of the group tensions. I will return to this in a while but for the moment need to go back to the themes of sexuality and desire.

Desire and sexuality are absent as themes in Stacey's description of the group. At first glance they may seem irrelevant to what was happening, but on closer inspection, it becomes apparent that this is a group in which it is very difficult for some members to express desire. Ben and Terry seem to feel that the group allows them to be neither the subjects of desire nor the objects of desire. Desire is very close to the subjective, the personal and the individual and it is on this point that Ben and Terry seem to feel most frustrated. They complain bitterly that they cannot express their feelings – that they do not feel heard, that they are not recognized as individuals.

In Stacey's own analysis of the group, he places some emphasis on processes of inclusion and exclusion – and the shame resulting for those in the excluded category. This is seen as the source of the men's hostility and attack, since it is easier to attack than to reveal the shame and the longings for dependence (the desire) behind this. I agree very much with this formulation – and I feel that here Stacey gets close to the heart of his patients. But I wish to highlight another source of shame – the shame of feeling treated as an object to be made sense of rather than as a person to be understood empathically from within one's own subjective feelings. Hence, when Ben and Terry complain about the group, they seem be saying that there is something wrong with the therapeutic approach. It does not work for them. It is constraining rather than freeing. As Casement (1985) points out, our patients' responses often tell us not only about themselves but about *ourselves*, including how we work as therapists and where we may be going wrong. I have moved here from desire as sexual to the desire for recognition, for empathic understanding – a different kind of desire but crucially important and not unrelated to sexual recognition.

Returning to the sexual, there is no mention of sexuality in any part of the group material. Nor is there mention of a related phenomenon – gender. This applies to both the clinical material and Stacey's theoretical analysis. Yet, gender differences are implicit in the fact that it is mainly the men who attack the therapist and the group while the women idealize the therapist and seem content with the group. There appears therefore to be a split in the group along gender lines. This is an important group process that may be contributing to some of the other splits or, conversely, reflecting them. Gender, we know, is strongly related to power, a theme that has been raised by several group analysts (Elliott 1986; Burman 2002; Rose 2002). It could be aspects of this 'hidden' discourse, the gender/power configuration, that explain more fully the considerable tensions that arose in this group. In this sense, I disagree with Stacey's assertion that there is nothing above or below the interaction in the group itself that is worth pursuing in understanding the process. There is usually some or other hidden discourse that may not come to light, yet is deeply formative of the group process.

It is in the light of this notion of constructs outside the sphere of interaction that I plump for a psychoanalytic interpretation that Stacey rejects unequivocally because of its apparent assumptions about innate and universal processes – the Oedipus complex. My argument is as follows. In Ben and Terry's disenchantment with the group, there is a configuration of relationships which is strikingly evocative of the Oedipal drama. The male therapist is seen as powerful and charismatic. The female group members idealize him. There appears to be an 'in' group of him and the women, although the membership of the 'in' group sometimes varies. The 'out' group of all male members feels rejected and excluded, giving rise to jealousy and anger. In their rage, they repeatedly attack and denigrate the therapist. He ends up, by his own admission, feeling impotent and helpless. It does not require much imagination to see this as 'Oedipal'. The dynamics Stacey emphasizes in his own theoretical interpretation fit in here since the same themes of power, inclusion and exclusion are at the heart of the Oedipus situation, with one difference – desire. What I am suggesting therefore is that the hidden discourse in this group is sexuality and that the story is one not only of relationships of power but of gender, desire and sexuality.

I am treating the above more as a stimulus for debate than a statement about what the 'right' interpretation is. But if the interpretation happens to be even partially right, it indicates that there is a use for explanatory constructs outside the sphere of immediate communication and that in this case there appears to be a hidden sexual discourse in the group.

The clinical subject

Throughout this chapter, I have expressed concern not only about the marginalization of desire and sexuality in group analysis but about the marginalization of the individual perspective and how this compromises the clinical aims of group analytic psychotherapy. The question of what sociology has to offer group analysis must be judged not so much on the basis of theory and what constitutes a radically social vision of the group, but on what is clinically meaningful and what works for our patients. The clinical imagination, as opposed to the sociological imagination, is one that recognizes the centrality of the individual, including individual subjectivity and individual preference. In our clinical work, the individual is our point of accountability. We are answerable *to* the individual and *for* the individual. Accepting this as integral to the clinical task is, in my view, not a choice but a responsibility.

It is worrying that the ideological turn in group analysis may obscure its clinical task. In its preoccupation with theory and the differentiation of its discipline, group analysis has tended to distance itself from mainstream clinical development and research. Carter

(2002) raises serious questions about the conceptual looseness of the approach, its weak theory-practice link and lack of clinical evaluation. He goes as far as to question its long-term viability as a form of psychotherapy, particularly in the NHS in Britain. The group as an object of desire appears to be under threat.

Possibly, there is a distinction to be made between group analysis and group analytic psychotherapy. It could be argued that group analysis is a broad discourse about the meaning and process of the group (theory) while group analytic psychotherapy is a clinical medium (application). However, creating such a split would lose the creativity, coherence and utility of our approach: what is more desirable is the close interrelationship of theory and practice.

Discussion

This chapter, broadly covering the development of group analysis from Foulkes to the recent sociologically-orientated writers, confirms the absence of a sexual discourse of any substance in this field, with desire and sexuality under-represented and under-theorized, as well as at times, in my view, misrepresented. With some exceptions, these themes remain to a large extent hidden, indisputably there but hovering in the margin between expression and repression. This mirrors the denial and concealment of sexuality in conventional social groups. The parallel may not be surprising, given the powerful influence of social convention, but it is disappointing nonetheless. The aim of the therapy group, in my view, is not to imitate society but to challenge some of the orthodoxies that constrain individual lives.

Depending on how one looks at it, this could be an opportunity missed or an opportunity waiting to be found. For all its 'private' connotations, sexuality, as many writers have noted (O'Connor and Ryan 1993; Domenici and Lesser 1995; Denman 2004), is in many respects socially constructed. Like all human behaviour, it is influenced by relationships of power and knowledge, by institutional orthodoxies and by the inscriptions of language. Given the interest of contemporary group analysts in all these matters, there is considerable scope for group analysis to bring sex and desire back into view. But this cannot be achieved without a bridge between the social and the individual. It is insufficient to say, as Dalal and Stacey do, that the social is always individual and the individual always social, without detailed attention to what this means, how it is reflected in the speaking voice of the individual and how this translates into the dialogues of the consulting room.

This undertaking, I believe, would be facilitated by a more generous attitude towards individual subjectivity. Burkitt (1998) has drawn a distinction between individualism and individuality. Whereas individualism implies a cult of the individual, individuality reflects the sense of an authentic self that is yet moulded and defined by the world we live in. This, surely, is what psychotherapy is all about. If we could see subjectivity as itself socially constructed, then we could utilize it as the necessary bridge between the individual and the social. Subjectivity could provide a mirror to the social. There are precedents here, writers in other fields who are grappling with the same conundrums but who suggest ways through the impasse. Burkitt (1998) talks about the 'dialectics of social individuality' and O'Connor (1995) about the 'social character of subjectivity', reflecting a sense of the interconnectedness of the individual and the social. In any case, as I argue earlier in this chapter, the disregard of subjectivity – and the individuality that underlies it – constitutes an empathic failure. The experience of one's subjectivity being ignored or opposed is a source of anxiety, shame and anger. Since desire and sexuality are so often associated with shame, it makes it all the more necessary to emphasize an understanding of subjectivity within group analysis, if we are serious about claiming the sexual subject for group analysis.

Another weakness of socially constituted theories is that they tend to neglect the embodiment of human behaviour (Nightingale and Cromby 1999). But sex, by definition, is of the body. Much of the anxiety and shame about sexuality concerns the body and it is this area of sensitivity that also makes desire and sexuality so difficult to talk about in psychotherapy (Mollon 2003), let alone group psychotherapy. Group analysis places enormous emphasis on verbal communication in the group. I agree with this but am concerned about the absence of a critical perspective: a lack of recognition of the limitations and distortions of verbal communication, as well as the importance of non-verbal and bodily communication. Foulkes (1948, 1964) originally encouraged attention to non-verbal communication in the group process but this aspect has been neglected in the subsequent development of group analysis. In order for the sexual discourse to unfold, recognition of the body, embodied relationships and non-verbal communication is essential.

A further unresolved area is the relationship between group analysis and psychoanalysis. It seems clear that there is much in the psychoanalytic sexual discourse that remains of value to practising group analysts: the emphasis on desire, the exploration of the erotic imagination, the focus on embodiment, the recognition of erotic transference and counter-transference and the understanding of the subjective and interpersonal experiences of shame, guilt and jealousy, partly as envisioned through the Oedipus complex. That these come from an 'individual' perspective should not debar their use. In much of the supervision of groups that I am involved in, as well as the peer supervision I attend, these concepts are freely invoked in the understanding of the group process – at the same time as group analytic perspectives are valued and utilized. To say that psychoanalysis has no relevance to group analysis, to exclude it, is to make of it an 'unofficial language' in Bakhtin's terms.

Equally, group analysis needs to maintain a critical stance towards some of the worst excesses of psychoanalysis – its categorical and prejudicial thinking and its confusion of psychopathology with personal and moral choices. Without this, it may be assumed that group analysis identifies with some of psychoanalysis' restrictive normative values and prescriptions – as in some cases it appears to do. In an age of sexual diversity, a position must be identified and stated.

In sum, the potential in group analysis to develop a discourse of desire and sexuality emerges specifically in its dual origins in psychoanalysis and sociology. This conclusion is different from that of the more socially-orientated group analysts who seek to tease apart and separate the psychoanalytic and sociological perspectives of group analysis. I argue that there is value in keeping them together, seeing them as complementary rather than contradictory discourses. There is value in the contributions of those I have called the developers who emphasize the individual, the subjective and the intersubjective, while recognizing the influence of the social. Equally, there is value in the contributions of the more socially-orientated writers who extend our understanding of the cultural creation of self and group. However, with slight exceptions, neither approach has considered sexuality and desire to any appreciable degree. In the next chapter, I attempt to use the convergence of these two approaches as a basis for developing a group psychotherapy perspective of sexuality.

7

A GROUP PSYCHOTHERAPY
PERSPECTIVE OF SEXUALITY

The crucial question informing the writing of this book concerns whether sexuality, including the subjective states of desire, is a valid subject for group psychotherapy. Underlying this question are two linked considerations: 1) the extent to which it is possible to talk openly about sexuality in a group, given the continuing restraints surrounding the public expression of desire and sexuality; and 2) the question of how constructive an open sexual discourse is likely to be, for both individual and group, relative to the potential risks of enactment, transgression or undue and damaging exposure. These questions are linked to an overarching consideration of whether a more active, explicit representation of desire and sexuality in group psychotherapy would contribute to the group as an object of desire, in the sense of an open, challenging and enlivening experience that is acceptable and meaningful to a wide range of people seeking psychotherapeutic help. This is etched against recognition of the anti-group, a broad term describing fairly widespread negative attitudes of fear and doubt towards the concept of group psychotherapy (Nitsun 1991, 1996) that challenge the therapeutic task and potentially render the group a *non*-object of desire.

The articulation of these questions highlights, to my mind, the near phobic dread of sexuality erupting in the therapy group. It seems clear to me that behind the dissociation and marginalization of sexuality in group psychotherapy is an anxiety that could amount to panic if sexuality threatened to get out of hand. To some degree this is understandable given therapists' accountability for their clinical work, a consideration which has sharpened in recent decades, particularly regarding questions of sexual misconduct. However, I believe that the continuing anxiety about sexuality in group therapy is reinforced by the absence of a theoretical discourse of any substance concerning the development of sexuality in its diverse forms, including the major tensions of adult sexuality; the social influences on sexuality and the way these processes are transferred to the therapy group; the intricate subjectivities of sexuality; and the potentials and risks in group psychotherapy for the embodiment of the sexual discourse.

The position I take is that there is far greater potential to embrace sexuality constructively in group therapy than is commonly recognized, that this is not without risk but that, if undertaken in a consensually agreed, theoretically informed and clinically responsible way, it would undoubtedly strengthen group psychotherapy practice. I also take the position that not talking about sex is *not* necessarily a safer alternative, nor that 'leaving well alone' is the answer to the challenge presented to us by the uncharted territory of sexuality in the group. The assumption in this way of thinking – leave well alone – is that minimizing attention to sexuality is likely to avoid untoward stimulation and sexualization and hence prevent any form of enactment or transgression outside the group. Precisely because the group is such rich ground for the evocation of desire and sexual feeling, I suggest – to the contrary – that non-recognition and non-expression may create a culture of collusion or complicity in which transgression is more, rather than less, likely to occur.

I set out in this chapter to provide a theoretical foundation for the sexual discourse in group psychotherapy that might help to assuage some of the doubt, anxiety and stigma associated with the subject and that could make sexuality a safer province for the group. I draw on the findings of the existing literature on sexuality in the group, reviewed in Chapter 5, as well as the essentials of the group analytic paradigm, explored in Chapter 6. In the latter, it is the link between the social and the individual, the cultural and the subjective, that I seek to embrace within an overall framework of sexuality in the group. Unlike most psychotherapeutic discourse that moves from inner to outer, I start with the outer and move to the inner, establishing a broad social framework that narrows down to the individual, internal representation of sexuality. However, the focus continually loops back into the social, since ultimately the relationship between individual and social is mutually constitutive.

A social perspective of sexuality

Sexuality is usually conceived theoretically from an individual perspective, at best in the dyadic relational context, but seldom from a social or group perspective. No doubt this reflects the biological basis of sex, its physical expression and, in particular, the intensely individual experience of sexuality with its particular subjectivities. All these facets are vital in the understanding of sexuality but tend to detach the sexual subject from the broader context of group, society and culture. Sociologists such as Burkitt (1998), as well as group analysts such as Dalal and Stacey, while not particularly addressing sexuality in any detail or depth, nevertheless challenge the conventional western division between individual and social and, with this, an ontological perspective of human beings as inherently asocial. In Burkitt's words: 'The isolated individual therefore becomes not a historical and social product but a biologically given entity whose individuality is contained inside itself from birth' (p. 17). Burkitt goes on to point out the persuasiveness of this way of thinking because it corresponds so closely to a common-sensical western perspective. However, he argues that the basis of human difference and individuality resides fundamentally in society and the social relations between individuals.

Commentators on sexuality from a contemporary social perspective, particularly those criticizing the individualistic and normative stance of psychoanalysis, have picked up on this perspective to situate sexuality in the social domain. O'Connor and Ryan (1993: 22) comment: 'Sexual identity permeates, mediates and is mediated by all our social and cultural interactions. Sexual identity is not simply a question of isolated individuals repressing or discovering their "true" desires, or of a logical definition, but is variously inscribed in cultural, religious, legal and political systems and practices'. These systems have been analysed by sociologists as transmitting profound and long-standing constraints reflecting relationships of power and submission, inclusion and exclusion, and the shame that binds human beings into conventional groups with their conformist pressures. One illustration of this, particularly relevant in this context, is the difficulty people have in talking openly about sexuality, when it pertains to themselves personally. If this seems to us at one level appropriately 'modest', a natural response to social requirements, this modesty is itself not only socially inscribed but precludes the possibility of questioning the constraints that bind us into established and approved identities and roles.

The idea of an intra-psychic world in an 'encased' individual then needs to be suspended in favour of a view of the inner psychological landscape as constructed through social relations and symbolic interaction. Sexuality, too, becomes not purely a product of biology but an experience, a set of desires and impulses that derive their meaning and purpose, fulfilment and frustration, from a social context that has both contemporary and historical roots. According to Mead (1934), the intentions and motives of individuals are always to be found in the group with its own developmental processes. Burkitt (1998) suggests that the key to unlocking some of the secrets of the self is the study of the social group of which the individual is an active member. This throws a very different light on the premise of a unique sexuality that is self-generated. Although I believe that people do find unique adaptations to social processes, and that this applies in complex, highly individual ways to sexuality, these are nonetheless within a particular set of constraints and influences that are culturally rooted.

This point about social constraints is fundamental to group psychotherapy since the therapy group, a social unit in itself, has its own constraints and potential freedoms and it is useful therefore to explore a bit further what the sociologists say about the subject. Elias (1978), who took account of psychoanalysis and was interested in group analysis through his association with Foulkes, linked analytic notions of individual repression to social processes of control. Freud's categories of id, ego and super-ego are placed within a historical framework, super-ego, in particular, representing internalized social restraints with concomitant fears of judgement and censure. Elias argues:

> The pronounced division in the 'ego' or consciousness characteristic of man in our phase of civilization, which finds expression in such terms as 'super-ego' and 'unconscious', corresponds to the specific split in the behaviour which civilized society demands of its members. It matches the degree of regulation and restraint imposed on the expression of drives and impulses.
>
> (Elias 1978: 190–1)

Burkitt compares this idea of Elias' to Lichtman's (1982) concept of the structural unconscious in which the entire psychic structure, including the desires and drives within it, is created by a social process of which the individual is generally unaware, since its lacunae stretch way beyond the individual self. This also contains the theory of the repressed unconscious since it explains how feelings which can be expressed in public and those which must be hidden in private – usually secreted within the self – are created in the same social process. This explains the marked cleavages in sexuality between a publicly represented sexual persona and a privately experienced sexuality which contains secret fantasies and relationships that may be quite different from the public presentation of self.

The consequence for the individual of adhering to dominant social values is that the internal contradictions are likely to generate anxiety and the potential for shame. The breaching of social values usually arouses painful feelings of inferiority and deviance, self-loathing and shame. It is this process, for example, which underlies the internalized homophobia – that is, the repudiation of homosexuality – of gay and lesbian individuals themselves. There is a further question of how social and cultural processes enter the body itself, in terms of bodily self-perception and perception by others, an area of experience that influences sexually intimate relationships as well as sexual alienation through disgust, shame and prejudice. Hodges (2004: 86) suggests, in line with Turner's vision (1996: 34), that we currently live in a 'somatic regime' in which 'the body has become perhaps the key conduit for fundamental moral and political problems'. The view of Giddens (1991) and Shilling (1993) is that the centrality of self in contemporary discourses on identity has been eclipsed by the centrality of the body.

These perspectives are relevant to group therapy in so far as they highlight the potential of the group to replicate the same oppressive conditions that individuals have encountered outside the consulting room, to exercise the same constraints, both consciously and unconsciously, and to fail to recognize the particular tensions surrounding the sexed body. If this were to happen, it would be the equivalent of Foulkes' Basic Law of Group Dynamics in its constraining version (see Chapter 6), in which the therapy group is seen as moving, of necessity, towards the norms of the society of which it is part. However, there is an alternative vision of the therapy group as able both to recognize and challenge these constraints and to go some way towards the freeing of the sexual discourse. This is reflected in group analysis in Foulkes' notion of the Group as a Forum, a group that aims to interrogate orthodox norms and helps to redraw individual boundaries in the social context.

Elias' distinction between necessary and unnecessary social restraints has an important bearing here. Necessary restraints are those that may be required for a well-regulated social existence, guarding against chaos and loss of control. Unnecessary restraints are surplus to these requirements and serve to keep ruling groups and vested interests in control. Elias expresses his hope that by recognizing the impact of the civilizing process there may be the potential to distinguish unnecessary or surplus restraints, although he does not go as far as to suggest that these can be eliminated. Burkitt, however, refers to the work of Wouters (1977, 1986) who perceives a process of gradual change towards the liberalizing of social values. While the constraints imposed by civilized society are not removed, there is a progressive shift on the limits of behaviour, a widening of the boundaries that limit self-expression and a move towards the communication of feelings and desires that were previously concealed. This must be the aim of group therapy in addressing the sexual subject.

Burkitt raises the question of social reconstruction. To what extent is a more democratic cultural transparency possible in the kind of society in which we live, a transparency which challenges the constraints, which allows for more genuine communication between people? This macro question concerning society as a whole translates into a micro question concerning the therapy group: how far can the group go in challenging the orthodoxies contained within members' problems, in particular the sexual orthodoxies that permeate their lives, and how will this open up communication?

It is important at this point to highlight that a social perspective of sexuality, in my view, in no way denies the importance of either biology or individuality. Reflecting on George Herbert Mead's (1934) seminal contribution, Burkitt points out that the function of the mind, seen as socially constituted, is not to replace the requirements of the body but to recontextualize them so as to increase the possibilities of satisfaction. O'Connor (1995) similarly argues that the social perspective is not meant to deny a biological or individual self: recontextualizing them ideally enhances and frees them. The force of desire, the passionate subjectivity of self and other, are essential elements of a sexual discourse. The challenge to group psychotherapy in articulating the sexual subject is to sustain the creative tension between individual and group, biology and society, the subjective and the cultural, since these are ultimately not distinct but implicit in each other.

From group to individual

Before moving on to the therapy group *per se*, I want to look broadly at the process of social influence on sexuality and how this takes place. The most obvious site of influence is the family. There are innumerable versions in psychoanalytic and psychotherapeutic literature of parental influence on sexuality, whether in the dyadic formation of one parent with the child or the triadic relationship of both parents and the child. As reviewed in Chapters 2 and 3, I suggest that much of this theory and observation is useful, including the Oedipus complex, and that it adds significantly to the understanding we bring to our groups. However, there is much less written (except to some extent in the family therapy literature) about the family as a social unit, situated in its own cultural and familial history, and the sexual injunctions that are brought forth from this background. Equally, there is little attention in this literature to the family, the parents in particular, as the conduit for wider (and deeper) cultural representations of sexuality, with both overt and hidden constraints. Further, the family is not just parents but (usually) siblings and there is strikingly little written about the impact of the sibling configuration on sexuality, or for that matter, the denser configuration of parents *and* siblings on sexuality. However, it is clear, without being able to trace this here in further depth, that the individual is enormously affected by the family – and later the peer group – in the way sexuality is presented, stimulated, facilitated, constrained, repressed, denigrated: all condensing in acts of judgement the confluence of family history and cultural standards.

The family is the individual's first group. It is also an intensely intimate group, in which ancestral and social history, as well as genetic and biological influences, filter through each and every relationship to constitute the nature of desire and sexuality. Anxiety and defence concerning sexual desire originate here too, influenced by individual differences concerning gender, birth order and sexual orientation. The idiosyncratic roots of desire, the origins of the lovemap – Money's (1986) description of the character of an individual's sexuality – exist in this dense family matrix. Every patient joining a therapy group comes with a sexual template of this sort. The therapy group thus represents a series of overlapping templates in which there is both divergence and convergence in the themes of desire and sexuality. Some of the detail of this process can be found in Chapter 2 on sexual development and is illustrated in the clinical examples that form the substance of Part 3.

The sexual self

I find it useful to consider the notion of a 'sexual self'. Without wanting to reify this or suggest that a sexual self exists independently of the rest of the person's self, I nevertheless think that some notion of the particular character of an individual's sexuality is worth considering. In part, this encourages attention to the particularity of that individual's sexuality and in part provides a frame within which can be considered the social influences which have helped to mould that sexuality.

I further suggest that it is useful to consider different facets of the sexual self, in so far as the individual is a specific sexual person with a specific body and a specific set of sexual relationships. At the risk of atomizing the overall sexual experience, we could consider the following aspects: 1) an individual sexual self which contains the private subjective realm of sexual experience and includes the erotic imagination and auto-erotic sexuality; 2) a relational sexual self in which there is intimacy with another through relationships ranging from flirtation to foreplay to sexual intercourse; and 3) a social sexual self in which the individual takes their place, through sexual identity, orientation and role, in a wider community, including both conventional family-based communities and alternative sexual communities.

These facets are of course interrelated, although configured differently in different individuals, so that, for example, some individuals have an active sexual self in each of these dimensions, others not. All three dimensions, even the most subjective and personal, are socially constituted, in so far as they reflect the same individual in the same overall configuration of social relationships, past and present.

Does this model predicate any specific patterns of group relating for the different forms of the sexual self? Could there, for example, be a parallel with Schlapobersky's formulation of group communication reflecting the three linguistic forms: monologue, dialogue and discourse? The analogy does not translate in any concrete way to the three forms of the sexual self. However, we can see how the varied representations of the sexual self could find expression – or not – in the therapy group in different ways, be they the privacy of the individual sexual self, the intimacy-seeking nature of the relational sexual self or the communally-orientated aspects of the social sexual self.

The formulation of these three aspects of the sexual self has implications for notions of adjustment and maturity. Conventional norms of sexual maturity, reflected in orthodox psychoanalytic viewpoints, concern the achievement of a particular kind of sexuality based on preconceptions of what is socially appropriate and acceptable. In the alternative formulation I suggest, maturity might be judged on the basis of the integration and balance of different representations of the sexual self. Ideally, the sexual self would consist of all three parts in a flexible and recursive relationship – the individual, relational and social sexual selves interrelated in a way that is satisfactory to the individual and meaningfully positioned within a social context.

I wish to emphasize the close links between the subjective and the social in the emergence of the sexual subject. In order to explore how deeply represented the social influences might be, I consider key aspects of the three sexual selves I have delineated. Firstly, I consider masturbation as the auto-erotic aspect of the individual self. This is commonly considered the most private and solipsistic of all sexual activities. Mollon (2003) suggests that masturbation is inherently asocial. But this is questionable if we see the act as a form of social withdrawal or temporary isolation – which in itself is a social gesture. It would also appear to reflect a form of sexual freedom, to be free of social constraints since, in fantasy, the person can have whatever they desire. But this is a paradoxical freedom in so far as masturbatory fantasies, if examined in any detail, often reflect the profound social and interpersonal forces that entrain the body. Themes of dominance and submission, power and helplessness, reward and punishment not uncommonly permeate sexual fantasy. Fantasies also strive to attain the unattainable, to appropriate the forbidden, all of which is also socially constructed, since there are deep-rooted representations of the forbidden in society. The moment of apparent separateness in masturbation is therefore a heavily inscribed social moment.

Moving on to the relational sexual self, we may consider sexual intercourse as the defining act, the quintessence of the sexual relationship. Here, we see an intimate bodily encounter in which sexual penetration ideally culminates in the intense pleasure of orgasm. Many aspects of the relationship, if not the whole of it, however, can be understood as embodying or transmitting a social process. For example, who, sexually, takes the initiative, how it is taken, who is more active in the relationship and who is less active, how satisfaction levels are achieved, and so on, are all reflections of gender representations that are socially inscribed and individually translated. Further, each partner comes to the relationship with a complex social history in which sexual identity and object choice reflect a long line of cultural and family expectations – or opposition to these expectations. In this sense, a couple's genital penetration is at the same time the interpenetration of two social histories. When two bodies meet in intercourse, there is a meeting of two social worlds (Nitsun 1994). Although Kernberg (1995) describes sexual coupling as socially transgressive – reflecting an attempt to debar society from the intimacy of the couple – the rest of the world is not only all around but *inside* every gesture and action of the sexual couple.

The third area of the sexual self I posit is the social sexual self, by which I mean the role or identity the individual assumes through their sexuality in the wider community, for example, wife, husband, father, mother, boyfriend, girlfriend, and so on. On the face of it, this is the aspect of the sexual self that is most congruent with the social world. This is where the social process is externally presented. However, on closer inspection, these apparently straightforward social roles, and the decision-making processes that are entrained in an individual's choice of a role, are often fraught with conflict or tension, reflecting a struggle with social values: for example, the husband who feels under pressure to be married but longs to be promiscuous, the wife who resents the confining nature of her husband's sexuality but feels she can do nothing about it, the adolescent girl who seeks sex not so much because she wants it but because she feels under peer pressure to prove her sexuality. Often, these public roles are the most difficult to sustain because of the sense of imposition and the fear of a more authentic private self erupting into view. Social roles are often compromises, in which an important aspect of self is felt to be at variance with the role, and sexuality frequently inhabits this conflicted inner space.

According to the above argument, the sexual self in all its profound subjectivity is saturated with the social. While I have chosen to tease apart three aspects of the sexual self, these are inextricably interwoven in the fabric that binds the individual to the social domain.

The developmental pathway

How do we integrate into a group perspective the individual pathways of sexual development? This is the territory of developmental psychology and the psychoanalysis of sexual development (covered in greater detail in Chapters 2 and 3). Although these conceptions of sexuality sometimes appear to underemphasize the social, not only can they be recontextualized within a social perspective but they are useful reference points for understanding sexuality in group psychotherapy. In any case, however much group psychotherapy is equated with a social perspective, it cannot lose sight of individual development. The three developmental points I wish to revisit briefly here are the mother-infant relationship, the triangular schema of the

Oedipus complex and the impact of peer relationships – not to impose an individual model on the group but to highlight aspects of individual development that have significant social implications.

The mother-infant relationship

The mother-infant relationship is widely considered to be influential in the relationship of the sexual self to one other person – that is, the relational sexual self. Support for this view ranges from psychosexual therapists such as Hiller (2005), who see the experience of physical and emotional stimulation in a secure mother-infant relationship as an important precursor of later sexual relationships, to psychoanalysts such as Kernberg (1995), who see sensual bodily contact between mother and baby as the origin of erotic desire. The significance of this for group psychotherapy lies partly in the fact that the group precludes an intimate relationship with one other person (group member or therapist) and this, I suggest, contributes to people's resistance to group therapy and the frustration experienced at not being able to get individual needs satisfied within the group. This happens particularly when there has been significant emotional and sensual neglect in early development, often leaving residues of intense longing for the enveloping intimacy of a sexual partner. To some degree, this is part of the configuration of lack and desire that Lacan (1988a) postulates and, with it, the inevitability of a degree of frustration and disappointment in all sexuality. But it is necessary for the group to take seriously the need for the intimate other, to facilitate the potential for realizing such a relationship and to recognize this longing not necessarily as a defence against the group but as the expression of a legitimate developmental need. The same applies to pairing relationships within the group. Although they may reflect defiance against group norms or a defence against sharing more widely in the group, they may also express a developmental imperative that is still seeking expression.

The triangular relationship

It seems impossible to me to consider sexuality in the group without some recognition of the particular dynamics commonly described as 'Oedipal'. I do not subscribe to the theory of the Oedipus complex as a universal phenomenon that inevitably occurs in the same programmatic way in all of childhood. Nevertheless, I believe that the predominant tensions it describes – a relationship of jealousy and rivalry in the context of threatened exclusion from an object of desire – occur in many if not most sexual relationships. As Kernberg (1995) suggests, there are probably few intimate relationships in which, at some point, the fear of being displaced by a rival does not arise. Sometimes, of course, the fear is realized and the loss sets in train painful feelings of abandonment and anger. The anxieties attendant on this constellation may account for the retreat from the relational sexual self, as well as the social sexual self, into the individual sexual self with its self-protective auto-erotic proclivities.

In therapy groups, the presence of a number of people inevitably creates alliances and rivalries, including the rivalry among members for the special attention of the therapist. This touches on deep sensitivities about inclusion and exclusion, often historically inscribed, and the particular intensities of feeling evoked may be another reason why people are afraid of joining therapy groups and why sexuality is avoided as a subject in the group.

In my paper on the primal scene in group psychotherapy (Nitsun 1994), I suggested that fantasies about parental sexuality, largely unconscious, as well as the child's exclusion from this relationship, may have a bearing on the way sexuality is dealt with in the group. But even without positing an unconscious fantasy of this kind, the triangular dynamics of self, desired other and rival are an important part of group life. Halton (1998), in one of the very few papers dealing with this subject, argues that the main work of the group is to deal with the problems of inclusion and exclusion inherent in the Oedipal situation, particularly regarding the therapist as the desired object. He suggests that the therapist should be active in interpreting these dynamics and that the group is incomplete without this. While this may be taking the point to an unnecessary extreme, the argument gives food for thought about the basis of rivalry in the group, to what extent this is sexually driven and what implications there are for the therapist's role.

While the configuration of envy and rivalry can be potentially destructive in a group, this is often counterbalanced by the altruistic and constructive aspects of members' relationships. In this sense, it is important for the group to be able to mobilize its cooperative potential when faced with the potential ravages of rivalry. This may depend on the therapist's capacity to recognize the roots of envy and rivalry, to deal with this openly and at the same time to facilitate the expression of reparative tendencies. In Brown's (1998) terms, this may be part of the ethical function of the group, in which entitlement and demand can be matched by sensitivity and fairness.

Peer relationships

In Chapter 2, I highlighted the importance of the peer group as a source of sexual identification in childhood and adolescence. From childhood play to the experimentation of adolescence, the peer group constitutes the main social context, outside the family, that influences sexual development. There are important issues of inclusion and exclusion here, with peers representing attitudes towards sexuality that require conformity to the group. The process draws together prevailing attitudes concerning gender identity, same- and opposite-sex identifications, sexual orientation, the nature and pace of sexual experimentation and the requirements for public acknowledgement or concealment of sexual behaviour. This is the individual's first concentrated encounter outside the family with sexuality in its social manifestations, and contributes to what I refer to as the individual's social sexual self.

The therapy group in some respects parallels the peer group and group members may transfer issues from the earlier peer group to the new group. Some of the anxiety about sexual expression in the therapy group may reflect experiences in the original peer group. Particularly in areas of sexual diversity, such as homosexuality, there may be heightened anxieties about acceptance and rejection that mirror earlier experiences in peer relations. At the same time, the therapy group has the potential to constitute a different form of peer group that deals more openly, fairly and compassionately with the challenges of the sexual self.

Transferring the social perspective to group psychotherapy

Which aspects of their sexual selves do people bring to the group? Is this as marginal an issue for group members as it is for the existing theoretical and clinical discourse concerning group therapy? If this is the case, there is no pressing need to consider sexuality to any appreciable extent. However, I suggest a radically different perspective: I suggest a pervasive sexual undercurrent in the therapy group.

Contrary to the acknowledged aims of the group, some people come to therapy groups looking for an object of desire, a fantasied sexual encounter, a fling, perhaps even a long-term partner. Their curiosity on joining a group is often sexual curiosity. Who is in the group, who will they find attractive and who will find them attractive? In turn, when a new member is due to join a group, the curiosity stirred up among the old members is similarly sexual. In the actual process of the group, the close physical and emotional proximity of members further triggers sexual desire, fantasies and impulses. In a mixed group, there is probably a range of opposite- and same-sex desires. The feelings are probably also not just positive and appreciative. There may be feelings of sexual distaste and rejection as well as attraction.

Inevitably, much if not all of this remains concealed in the group. To some extent, this serves the group task in so far as there would not remotely be enough time to absorb all of this desire and distaste in the group. Much of it might anyway not be productive and some of it, particularly negative sexual reactions, could be destructive. In this sense, the concealment might be akin to Elias' 'necessary restraints': social restraints that support a constructive social process. However, in so far as the hidden themes reflect deeper and more pervasive patterns of sexual relating in people's lives – unsatisfied longings, failures of sexual intimacy, transgressive desires, feelings of inadequacy, unvoiced jealousies, envy, guilt and sexual shame – their remaining hidden is a lost opportunity, a psychotherapeutic omission. Further, the unspoken attractions and rejections in the group are likely to influence current group relationships, alliances and attachments, rivalries and hostilities, in ways that elude understanding in the absence of a sense of where they are coming from.

The upshot of this is that the therapy group not only mobilizes the same forms of sexual attraction and tension that exist in other groups – it exacerbates them through the intimacy of the group. But the therapy group also parallels other social groups in the active operation of restraints. Group boundaries, prohibitions of contact outside the group, the requirement to report back even chance meetings and discussions external to the group, all confirm that this is a group with its own powerful constraints. Again, this is necessary to protect the integrity and functioning of the group but, at the same time, it duplicates the constraints of conventional social groups. And, necessary as it is, what does it say about the freedom of discourse in the group? What other constraints are concealed within the obvious constraints that are part of the therapeutic frame? Who decides what is spoken about and what is not? Where does the power of influence lie? We can begin to see how the therapy group may simply mirror the conventional social group unless there is a conscious recognition of what all this implies for the sexual subject and a readiness to confront the parallel.

What emerges then is a series of options for the group. It could simply ape conformist social groups, aiming to realize Foulkes' Basic Law of Group Dynamics, which proffers that the group moves towards the norms of society, cancelling out excessive diversity and certainly deviancy. But it could also capitalize on being a different kind of group, a temporary social unit which has the potential to question and to generate a new, more discursive morality. As we have seen throughout this book, the main enemy of desire and sexuality is the super-ego, the individual conscience with its proneness to harsh judgement and prohibition, acting in tandem with unnecessary social restraints which may be similarly oppressive. The therapy group has the possibilities of providing a fairer, kinder morality.

Linked to this possibility is the observational function of the therapy group, whether vested in the therapist, the group members, or the group as whole. This is similar to Britton's (1989) concept of triangular space, in which a person can both observe the relationships of others and be observed in relationship with others, a valuable source of learning and development. Britton sees this function as a positive consequence of the Oedipus complex, but even without utilizing this concept, we can see how the group, probably more than any other psychotherapeutic form, provides possibilities of self- and other- observation. This has the potential for freeing the sexual subject from its conventional restraints. In Chapter 11, I introduce the notion of the group as witness. This extends the present argument to suggest that intimacy in a group occurs not in a vacuum but in a context of social observation in which qualities of support, empathy and tolerance from other group members can make the difference between guilt and shame and a sense of valid entitlement and support. In theory then it is possible to renegotiate the sexual self in a more supportive, less restraining social context. Of course, there is no guarantee that it will work this way. The group may reflect exactly the same prejudices as society, even worse, and this is why a discourse in the field is so badly needed. But the fact that this is group therapy, not individual or any other therapy, augurs an unusual if not unique opportunity for social influence.

Brown's (1998) view of group psychotherapy as an ethical activity is relevant here. While dreams of sexual freedom are a common preoccupation, there remain constraints which every individual has to negotiate. How the group deals with the conflicting pulls towards sexual liberation and towards identification with social norms is an important process, in which notions of entitlement and equality, as well as conformity and non-conformity, require consideration.

Of course, group psychotherapy is in essence a verbal and not a bodily medium. The task is to talk about sex and not do it – part of the paradox of the group. This itself may be problematic. Some people find it very difficult to convey bodily states in words. The requirement to do so may create its own frustrations and tensions. Others find it easy, perhaps too easy, to talk about sex. Davies (1998b: 807) refers to the 'performative nature of sex talk' – the way in which two or more people talking about sexual feelings contributes to the experience of desire and even constructs it. This may lead to a form of sexualization, which may in turn prompt enactment. Davies agrees with Hoffman (1994) who, talking generally about psychotherapeutic discourse, postulates an oscillating, unpredictable synergy between word and experience. She goes on to say: 'We cannot always know when talking about sexuality will intensify sexual feelings; we cannot know what words will arouse and what words will contain, what words will help soothe and what words will contribute to dangerous overstimulation' (Davies 1998b: 807). However, Davies is strongly of the opinion – one I share – that not talking about sexuality is *not* a safer alternative. At the same time, the possibilities of inappropriate and unhelpful sexualization, including the eroticization of non-sexual problems, need to be recognized.

The other important omission in much group psychotherapy that I mention at different points in this book concerns the body. I have already highlighted the paradox: the group has such a strong physical presence, the body (even while clothed) continually exposed to view, and yet there is seldom reference to the body in groups. Even the few writers on sexuality in groups hardly refer to it, particularly the body in the immediacy of the group itself. We may speculate that this again is part of the modesty of the group, its concession to civilized values, in line with Elias' observations. But we can also see how the dissociation of the body may contribute to the encapsulation of the sexual discourse. And by ignoring the body we lose a valuable, if not essential, medium of expression and information. In the words of the Gestalt therapist, Fritz Perls (1972), 'Words lie, the body does not'. Bodily posture, movements, gestures, facial expressions, eye contact and avoidance, and vocal utterances, all consciously and unconsciously communicate the sexuality of the group.

The upshot of this is that however much we embrace a social perspective in our understanding of sexuality and its expression in group therapy, there are two aspects that we cannot afford to lose sight of: individuality and embodiment. Individuality refers to the particularity of sexual experience, the intimately personal, subjective representation of sexuality. Embodiment refers to the recognition of the intrinsic bodily components of sexuality. A social perspective of the subject must allow sufficient openness and flexibility to accommodate both these aspects. It is this recognition of the individual embodied nature of sexual experience, within a broadly social perspective that, in my view, makes it entirely possible to embrace psychoanalytic and other individually-focused approaches to sexuality within the group psychotherapeutic frame. The notions of a sexual self I suggest earlier invite psychoanalytic understanding, once we have established the social frame that generates and contains the individual self. The problem, as in all psychotherapy, and particularly group psychotherapy because of its greater complexity, is one of focus. There is so much going on in a group at any one time that there are real problems of where to focus attention: individual, pair, sub-group or group as a whole. But, in line with Foulkes' figure-ground principle, the answer lies in the oscillating attention between individual and group, which requires an ongoing awareness of the figure-ground link and the process of reversal from moment to moment. It also involves listening in different ways to patients' material: listening to the social within the individual and to the individual within the social.

The transformational potential of the group

Stories of desire are often tinged not only with shame and guilt but with sadness – about lost love, love unfulfilled, love never experienced. Sexuality itself is also often experienced as a difficult, awkward, incomplete part of the self, reflected in ruptures in the different areas of the sexual self – individual, relational and social. These are among the reasons why people seek psychotherapy in the first place, their stories of desire often hidden by their presenting problems and symptoms. Part of the work of psychotherapy is the uncovering of these stories. In the safe, supportive space of a well-functioning group these narratives usually emerge, revealing the person behind the patient. Further, in the dense interpersonal sphere of the group, there are opportunities to review, redraw and reconstruct the stories of desire. Often, this happens through group relationships themselves, through new forms of intimacy, through mirroring and understanding of sensitive affective states. Many of the examples in Part 3 of this book illustrate such processes. This reflects the transformational potential of the group (Nitsun 1996: 197–215), the potential to help members to repair their sense of self and their capacity for relationships. We should be careful here not to idealize the therapy group, since relationships in the group are often also ambivalent, hostile and frustrating. There may be insensitivity and indifference to individual desire. But within this ambivalent matrix, there are opportunities to deal with love and hate, engagement and withdrawal, in ways that provide a rehearsal for relationships outside the group and that may help to free the flow of desire.

From theory to practice

In the remainder of this chapter I briefly suggest ways in which some of my theoretical proposals might be translated into the practical imagination of the group therapist. I am all too aware of the difficulty of applying theory, particularly group analytic theory, to the conduct of groups, and I want to grapple with this rather than avoid the problem. This also anticipates the clinical emphasis of Part 3, hopefully providing a bridge between theoretical perspectives of sexuality in group therapy and what actually happens in practice. I am not so much offering technical guidance here as suggesting approaches and areas to be thought about.

The four levels of the group

Foulkes (1964) delineated four levels of group functioning which group analysts find useful in making sense of the complexity and elusiveness of the group process. These are the current level, the transference level, the projective level and the primordial level. Relating these to the sexual subject, these levels have the following significance: 1) *the current level*, also referred to as the social level, is a useful way of comprehending the spread of group membership – the mix of gender, sexual identity and sexual orientation within the context of members' present and past relationships; 2) *the transference level* refers to the recapitulation in the group of sexual relationships that have had an important bearing on members' development, including the potential for erotic transference and counter-transference; 3) *the projective level* consists of 'part-object' attributions through which members mirror each others' perceived and imagined qualities, expressed for example in the erotic imagination and the introjects of the sexual self; 4) *the primordial level* refers to archetypal images of the collective unconscious. Within the terms of this book, I suggest this could be reconceptualized more broadly as the social unconscious, in which archetypal images contribute to

154

the unconscious constellation. The transmission of sexual behaviour and morality through the social unconscious has a major influence on sexual selves.

Boundaries

Group therapists generally agree on the importance of boundaries as an essential part of the therapeutic frame (Behr and Hearst 2005; Cohn 2005). Boundaries contain and protect the safety of the group. If this is important generally, it acquires an even stronger significance in the context of desire and sexuality. Since sexuality concerns the penetration of boundaries, its presence in the group is likely, in isomorphic fashion, to challenge and potentially rupture boundaries. This is most evident in the sexual enactment of a pairing relationship outside the group. The therapist has an essential task in monitoring and maintaining boundaries in the presence of the sexual subject, both as it emerges in the group and is potentially enacted outside the group.

Boundaries might include a judgement of the readiness of the group to deal with sexuality at any given time, as well as the impact of expressed desire and sexuality on boundaries of safety and personal integrity. Although boundaries need to be kept intact, there is also a point to be made about the meaning of boundary crossings if recognized and understood. As Cohn (2005) suggests, they can provide opportunities for individual and group learning. This applies especially to the consideration of conventional sexual restraints, particularly 'unnecessary' restraints and their need to be confronted in the group. Here, the rigidity of boundaries around encased sexuality comes in for scrutiny. Valuable information about the operation of restraints and counter-restraints is to be found in the expression of boundary problems and incidents.

Confidentiality is another crucial aspect of boundaries. Roback *et al.* (1992) report particular sensitivities about confidentiality in relation to sexual confidences in groups. In a study of group confidentiality they found that boundary violations were both expected *and* found to occur with greatest frequency in relation to sexual material in the group. Boundaries of confidentiality concerning sexuality must constitute among the most important structural requirements of the therapy group and it may be necessary to redraw them from time to time in the course of the group, but in a way that facilitates safety of expression rather than promotes rigid group constraints.

Group development

The requirement for trust and safety in the group when dealing with sexuality also has implications for the stage of development of the group. The privacy of sexual experience, the anxiety about exposure, the potential for shame, all within a socially-constructed morality, mean that in order for individuals to take the risk of revealing their sexual selves, the group has to feel safe enough to do so. Trust in the group does not usually come at the outset. It takes time for members to trust in each other as well as in the group as a whole. Hence, the timing of communication about sex is important and it is more likely to occur, at least to occur openly and constructively, at a stage of relative maturity in the group. Experience suggests that sexual confessions and sharing of sexual trauma very early in the group's development may have a negative impact, alienating the group and leaving the 'confessor' feeling isolated and unheard (Nitsun 1990). Of course, trust does not just emerge from nowhere. It requires a degree of risk in the first place, a testing out of the group's responses. In this, a judicious risking of the sexual subject in the group may be a valuable testing ground, an indication of the level of intimacy attained, as well as a point of connection that deepens trust in the group.

The stage of group development may also influence the nature of the response to sexual communications, along the lines suggested in Whitaker's (1985) focal conflict theory. The act of talking about sex in the group, about revealing the vulnerabilities, longings and particular dilemmas of sexual relationships, may elicit, in Whitaker's terms, either restrictive or enabling solutions. The group may close down sexual communication, it may obstruct a member seeking a solution to a sexual problem or it may ignore or punish a member struggling to establish intimacy in the group. These are all restrictive solutions. However, if the anxiety and ambivalence about such communication can be managed, the response may be facilitative and enabling. In such a case, the sexual discourse is supported and shared. The latter response is more likely to occur at a stage of relative maturity in the group. In addition to other requirements of the therapist, attention to the stage of development of the group may help to clarify processes that are otherwise difficult to understand and manage.

The group therapist

Much of the foregoing highlights the crucial role of the therapist in facilitating the sexual discourse in the group. There are considerable challenges to the therapist in managing the complex representations of sexuality in the group and how their own sexuality, attitudes and anxieties are likely to influence the unfolding of the sexual subject. Because of the importance of this role, Chapter 15 is devoted entirely to the therapist.

Summary

A model of sexuality that is relevant to group psychotherapy is proposed, allowing for both the social influences on sexuality and the internal, individual nature of sexuality. Passionate desire and cultural process may seem like opposite ends of a spectrum but are intertwined in subtle and profound ways. However, while recognizing the overall configuration, it is necessary to understand each aspect as a reality in itself. Hence, the subjectivity of sexuality remains the essential parameter of the therapeutic enquiry and patients' experience cannot be eclipsed by so sweeping a social emphasis that the individual is lost to view.

It is suggested that the therapy group, while subject to the necessary sexual restraints that are part of constructive social relating, has the potential to challenge the unnecessary restraints that bind individuals into a sexual armour that impoverishes their lives and their relationships. The recognition and alleviation of shame, a pervasive feature of sexual morality, encourages sexual disclosure and freer exploration. This might happen through the development of a more benign morality in the group, which gives the individual a push, however small, in the direction of emancipation. Further, within the transformational space of the group, relationships are formed which help to illuminate and repair the desiring self. Within this frame, there is place for the elaboration of the erotic imagination, the representation of sexual diversity and the unfolding of sexual selves.

Part 3

THE CLINICAL DISCOURSE

INTRODUCTION TO PART 3

The move from the theoretical to the clinical in Part 3 highlights the complexity of the sexual subject in group psychotherapy – its pervasive presence, its multitudinous forms, the contradictory nature of its presentation, its sometimes subtle and sometimes powerful impact on the group, and its elusiveness when we attempt to capture the essence of sexuality and desire in group therapy. Not surprisingly, in a group of eight people or so, all coming with their unique sexualities, the subject is dense and multi-faceted. However, without attempting to account for these complexities, we cannot address the potentials and tensions surrounding sexuality in groups. We are left with a meagre discourse, the weight of theory coming from psychoanalysis, developmental studies and cultural perspectives of sexuality, unable to tie these influences clearly into the discipline of group therapy itself and to evaluate them from the perspective of the group.

Two factors render the presentation of the clinical material a daunting task. One is the embeddedness of the material in the detailed textures of the group, the other is the particular sensitivity surrounding the representation of sexual material in group psychotherapy, given the complex nature of boundary management in group therapy and the heightened concern about confidentiality – itself an important theme in the emergence of sexuality in groups. The illustrative material comes from a variety of sources – my own group psychotherapy practice, the work of colleagues that has been shared with me and the experiences of supervisees who bring their groups for discussion, in either individual or group supervision. This body of work crosses the private practice-NHS divide, yielding groups of diverse populations and levels of disturbance. I concentrate on mixed-sex groups comprising males and females of varying sexual persuasions. Although single-sex groups are not uncommon in our services, the mixed therapy group is closer to the social spread of sexualities and provides greater opportunities for exploring the complex interaction of gender, sexual identity and sexual orientation that is germane to this book.

Readers will find that the clinical illustrations are presented in varying degrees of detail. This is only partly intentional. Since many of these groups were not run by myself, I had varying access to the clinical material. This includes the role of the group therapist, where in some cases I had very clear knowledge of conductor responses, in others less so.

In order to maximize confidentiality, I have followed the guidelines for published clinical material of the Institute of Group Analysis (London). I have either sought permission for publication or disguised the material by 1) combining several examples into one and 2) disguising significant features of group participants and therapists. However, I have attempted to preserve the flavour of the examples so as to illustrate as closely as possible the relevant thematic concerns.

I aim to illustrate the potential in group psychotherapy not just for the expression of sexuality but for the enriching of the erotic imagination and the development of greater awareness of self, other and *others* in the understanding of the sexual subject. At the same time, the illustrations highlight the ambiguities and risks encountered along the way, the dissociative and repressive processes generated by desire and sexuality, the potential for failure as well as success and the considerable technical and personal challenges facing therapists in dealing with sexuality in groups. From this, I hope will emerge a contribution to the discourse that is grounded in clinical experience and that provides a basis for further development in theory and practice.

8

THE EROTIC CONNECTION

Group cohesiveness, described by Yalom (1985) as the most important therapeutic factor in group psychotherapy, is frequently cited in
the literature as a criterion of the group's development and progress.
Cohesion in the group is usually associated with factors such as
interpersonal bonding, group commitment and motivation to attend.
There is typically no reference to erotic connection as a possible component of cohesion. I am not so much suggesting the inclusion of an
overt sexual connection as I am referring to the energy that comes
from libidinal attraction and connection in a broader sense. The sexual may be part of this. Maturana's (1988) concept, 'the passion for
proximity', which he uses to describe the attraction that motivates
people to stay in intimate relationship, comes closest to defining this
phenomenon. However, the sexual aspect of group psychotherapy is
usually problematized, some writers regarding it as regressive – for
example, Tylim (2003), who, in line with Freud's (1921) original
hypothesis, views the erotic in groups as a manifestation of the
excitement generated by the leader and spread contagiously through
the group. Other writers, without necessarily saying as much, regard
sexuality in the group as dangerous and disruptive.

What if we were to reverse this and see sexuality in the group as
something natural and bonding rather than unnatural and disruptive? This is in line with the principle of Eros, which Freud originally,
and various subsequent writers (Samuels 1985; Thompson 1999),
have described as the principle of connection. Eros is not only about
the explicitly sexual but about the connecting and unifying process,
as well as the paradoxical differentiation that occurs as part of the
unifying trend. Laplanche (1970) portrays it thus: 'the life drive
contains within it a mixture of the optimism borne by the ideology of
progress or evolution: Eros is the gatherer and tends to form per-
petually richer and more complex entities, initially on the biological

level, then on the psychological and social one'. In some respects, what better definition could we have of the group? Of course, Eros is a metaphor rather than a concrete force, a name for a spectrum of desires that stimulate intimacy and excitement, but one, perhaps, that needs to be revived in order to recognize the erotic connection in our work.

In this chapter, I illustrate the notion of the erotic as an underlying principle in the development of the therapy group, showing how a group is created, enlivened and strengthened by this connection. Through the mobilization of desire and the interlocking of desire between individuals, the group itself becomes an object of desire.

I present two examples. The first is of a children's psychotherapy group. This differs from the usual format of this book, which is in essence about adult psychotherapy, but I have deliberately chosen the example as it reveals some important themes, highlighting both the potentials and limitations of adult group psychotherapy in dealing with the affectionate and playful aspects of sexuality. The second example is of an adult group in which the attraction is mainly between two people but shared and supported in the group. The two groups illustrate in different ways the generative power of the erotic connection.

The children's group

This was a weekly psychotherapy group for the children of traumatized refugee families who had been referred to a specialist treatment centre. The group therapist described the group as frozen. While language differences between some of the children affected their ease of communication, the real problem seemed to go deeper. The children appeared to have absorbed the family trauma, the sense of fear, displacement and alienation that pervaded their experience. They could communicate neither verbally nor non-verbally and they made scant use of the toys available in the room. Occasionally, a child retreated into solitary play, well away from the others. They could not play together. Paradoxically, a painful sense of isolation seemed to bind them together.

The therapist considered that the children might need a different approach, a change, a new challenge. She decided to take them on an outing to the sea. Several of the children had never seen the sea, so this was a rare occasion. A few days later the group of seven youngsters, accompanied by the therapist, took the train to a beach some 30 miles from London.

It was a fresh, early summer's day. The children, at first overwhelmed by the vast expanse of sea and sky, initially responded with shy, reserved interest. But gradually they began to play. Shoes and socks came off, one or two children dipped toes into the edge of the icy water, others took to the sand, scooping it up and building little sand edifices. They began to relate freely to each other, unselfconsciously. They relished ice cream and cold drinks.

On the train journey home, the spontaneous play continued. Jokes were shared, imitations and role-plays enacted. There were smiles, eruptions of laughter. One boy took it upon himself to show the other children how to kiss. The group gathered eagerly around him as he demonstrated an artful use of the lips. The kissing became contagious as the children tried it on each other. There was a frisson of excitement in this but essentially the kisses were about contact, about connecting, about affection, perhaps about imagined romances.

As the train drew closer to home, the tired children grouped together in a close huddle, holding each other, arms on shoulders, hands clasping, legs intertwining. One or two fell asleep in another's arms. As the train pulled in to the station, they brightened up, peering out of the windows, showing a new interest in their environment, as if they were seeing London for the first time.

The sense of friendship and intimacy that had grown between them reappeared in the next psychotherapy group. There was a fragile trust and interest in each other where previously there had been suspicion and avoidance. Communication improved. They played together. And later they began to speak about some of the traumatic experiences they and their families had suffered – not long soliloquies or detailed stories, but fragments that began to connect them in their shared pain. This alternated with periods of light-hearted play and boisterous confrontation. The group had changed. Although complications occurred later on as the group progressed, a small miracle had occurred.

This vignette illustrates some important themes in the discourse on sexuality in group psychotherapy. I am not suggesting that what happened between the children, the kissing specifically, was sexual in a frankly erotic sense, but a libidinized and playful attachment that arose unexpectedly and served to unite the group. In this sense, it illustrates the thesis developed in this book that Eros as a connecting principle is a fundamental paradigm for the therapy group. But there are other themes that are linked to this, including the deadening and disconnecting effect of trauma – the group as it was at the beginning – and the question of whether vitality and intimacy can be reclaimed in the face of trauma. That the children could achieve this, I suggest, was to some extent a function of their youth: they were young enough, open enough, playful enough, to respond to a new opportunity for engagement and pleasure. They had development on their side.

That the opportunity arose in the first place was made possible by this being a child psychotherapy group – and one with an imaginative therapist. It would not have happened in an adult group: the group could not have left the confines of the consulting room and physical contact of the sort the children engaged in would have been prohibited. Even in a child therapy group, the initiative took some daring. Yet, the therapist must have been in touch with some potential in the children, some capacity for wonder, for desire, for play – and the need for a new stimulus to awaken their potential.

Our adult psychotherapy groups similarly consist of individuals whose freedom of expression has been damaged by experiences of trauma. Sexuality is likely to have been compromised – undermined, repressed, dissociated. The group allows them the opportunity to confront the trauma in the hope of an amelioration, of gaining distance and perspective, while at the same time exploring their anxieties about emotional and sexual connectedness. That the adult group has to do this symbolically, in words rather than actions, is part of the limitation and frustration of the group but also part of its protectiveness. To be able to play, in thought and imagination, with kissing and touching, with desire and intimacy, is part of the journey back to the sexual self.

The adult group

The group is a twice-weekly analytic psychotherapy group in private practice consisting of three men and four women, with a male therapist. This is a relatively mature 'slow-open' group which has met for three and a half years. The example focuses on the relationship that develops between two people, Melvin and Imelda, in the context of the overall group.

Melvin (38), an anxious, depressed solicitor, described the traumatic impact of his wife suddenly leaving him eight months after they were married. Although this happened almost ten years ago he was still preoccupied with the event. He had lost confidence, had been unable to form a relationship with another woman and, to make matters worse, had developed erectile difficulties. He was wary of sexual relationships because of a fear of impotence. A feature of his presentation to the group was the sense of guilt he felt about the failure of his marriage. He believed that he had been over-involved in a demanding job in the early part of the marriage and had not given the relationship the attention it needed. It was not surprising, he felt, that his wife had strayed. Coupled with this, he revealed an idealized view of his wife: how attractive, intelligent and vivacious she was. In his mind, he had lost the love of his life.

The group challenged his perception of his failure in the marriage and his idealized view of his wife. She had let him down, after all, betrayed him, left him. What was so good about that? If anything, she was to blame and he should feel angry with her, not the other way round. Where was his anger? The therapist and other group members had on numerous occasions attempted to persuade Melvin of this view but he remained unconvinced. When members expressed exasperation with his rigid interpretation of his marriage and his resistance to any alternative view, he responded that he could see their argument at an intellectual level but this did not change his feelings.

Imelda (42) a striking, dark-haired woman, also a successful estate agent, had joined the group because of problems of managing conflict in her relationships, including her marriage. She felt that she was unable to assert herself without becoming angry and explosive and this led to considerable friction and instability in her relationships. In the group, members noted her prickliness and how quick she was to take offence, even though she could show compassion and insight when it came to other people's problems. She rowed with some of the group members and tended to react negatively to the therapist's interventions. She became known in the group as 'the bossy woman' and this was said to her with a mixture of humour and annoyance.

Melvin and Imelda had overlapped in the group for approximately a year, their relationship undistinguished other than as two members of the group who were gradually getting to know each other. This changed in a series of groups shortly before a holiday break. There was an edgy atmosphere in the group, with an outbreak of irritable spats between members. The therapist interpreted this as anger with him about the impending break but most of the group denied the connection and one or two members chided the therapist for his predictable interpretations about breaks.

Melvin, however, stated that he *was* anxious about the break. He had been feeling isolated recently and was worried about being on his own for several weeks. When he was on his own he would go back in his mind to his lost wife, reliving the good times in their relationship and regretting what had happened. Group members became critical about his continued obsession. One female member, June (46), tried to defend him, saying it was understandable that if he was isolated he would think back to his wife. Imelda became critical of June, saying it was typical of her to play the 'nice guy'. June objected to being called a guy and to Imelda's insinuations. Melvin came to June's defence, saying she was the most sensitive person in the group and the only one who really understood him. Imelda then flared up at Melvin, saying she was sick and tired of his whingeing and his complete refusal to deal with his problems. She had seen not the slightest hint of change in him since the time they had been together in the group. No wonder he liked June since she was just as soppy as him. He then, to the group's surprise, rebutted sharply, saying that Imelda was out of order, that she behaved badly in the group and showed no inclination to get to grips with her own problems. She was 'a nasty piece of work'.

In the remaining sessions before the break, the row between

Melvin and Imelda simmered, flaring up again in the last session. Group members expressed surprise at the change in Melvin. There was an overall feeling that this was a positive development. They had never seen him as assertive as this. There was less support for Imelda, who argued her case up to a point but also said she felt unappreciated in the group. She complained that she would say things that everyone felt but was then attacked for saying them.

In the second session after the break, Melvin revealed that he had had a dream one night and woke up with an erection. He could not remember the content of the dream. When members probed, asking him if anything came to mind, he volunteered tentatively that that he thought the dream might be connected with Imelda. There was initially a titter of laughter in the group, with a roar of surprise from Imelda. In this and the next few sessions Melvin's feelings about Imelda came under scrutiny. The group was quick to interpret his erection as a result of his assertiveness, his literally 'standing up for himself'. There was some humour and enjoyment in the sharing of the analogy. The group was less quick to make the obvious connection: that Melvin fancied Imelda. When the therapist pointed this out, there was some agreement overall but an absence of response from Melvin and the group moved on to another topic. The therapist, noticing himself submerged by the flow of the group, pointed out that the group, Melvin included, had managed to avoid talking about sexual feelings. They were more comfortable talking about Melvin's assertiveness than his sexual attraction to Imelda and the fact that one member of the group had an erection dreaming of another.

In subsequent sessions, the sexual discourse in the group opened up significantly. There was some change in Imelda as she revealed for the first time the deterioration in her sexual relationship with her husband. This had been lively and satisfying in the first few years of their marriage but had increasingly lost its excitement. Imelda felt that her husband was uninterested and depressed and her own sexual responsiveness had waned considerably. Sex between them was now infrequent and difficult and they were unable to talk about it. Melvin, with some prompting from the therapist and the group, spoke about his feelings for Imelda. He had found her very attractive from the moment he first saw her in the group. He thought her looks and her personality were great. Even 'the bossy woman' aspect appealed to him. He further made a connection between Imelda and an aunt, his mother's younger sister, whom he had adored as a boy. Unlike his inhibited mother, the aunt was lively, warm, sexy. He admitted with some difficulty that he had had sexual fantasies about this aunt: in fact she was the subject of his masturbatory fantasies. The therapist, sensing that this was an area of some significance and that the group could easily slide away from it, encouraged him to talk about it. What emerged was his guilt about these fantasies. He had been unable to take his eyes off the aunt in public, particularly her breasts, and had been ashamed of his intense fantasies and the frequent masturbation that accompanied them. The therapist interpreted his guilt: it was as if he was actually having sex with his aunt. The parallel with his relationship to Imelda in the group was implicit in this discussion.

The admission of incestuous desire opened up a period of discussion about the naturalness of sexual curiosity and fantasy in the family context. This was at first tentatively broached. The therapist was active in supporting this discussion, noticing when members tried to avert attention from the sexual material and drawing attention to this. There was a considerable sense of connection in the group during these discussions, a sense of real intimacy. The relationship between Melvin and Imelda receded into the background, then emerged again as the focus. During these times, they were able to talk quite honestly about their perceptions of each other, not just sexually but as people in general. The group commented that in these discussions Imelda seemed quite different, a softer, gentler woman than the bossy one who dominated the group. When members commented how much more likeable she was in these moments and how these were sides of her she hadn't previously shown in the group, she cried. She admitted that Melvin's attraction to her had meant a great deal to her. Once she got over the embarrassment and anxiety about it, she said it made her feel appreciated as a woman in a way she had not felt for years.

This fertile period in the group ushered in changes in several members. Imelda became less tense and prickly and said that she and her husband had spoken about their sexual problems and decided to seek help. Melvin had joined a gym, was feeling fitter and less depressed and had started dating women after a long period of withdrawal. He felt more confident sexually. The group as a whole continued in a period of intimacy.

This group differs from the children's group in so far as the libidinal connection was mainly between two members, Melvin and Imelda, rather than generalized across the group. However, the group's support and involvement and the impact of the pair connection on the other members reflected an overall libidinization and deepening of the group. The group also differs from the children's group in the absence of physical contact. Whereas the children were able to freely play together, to touch, kiss and hold each other, the adults had to explore feelings and desires at a symbolic or verbal level. That they were able to do this without enactment and in a way that was facilitating is a measure of the holding capacity of the group, the safety created by group boundaries and the therapist's close attention to the communication process.

Pairing

Some observations on the process of pairing in this group merit comment. The erotic connection between Melvin and Imelda, although more obviously reflected in him, generated a distinct pair. The positive significance of this bears comment, given the suspicion displayed towards pairing in the group literature. This is epitomized in the Bion tradition in which pairing is regarded as one of the three basic assumptions and interpreted as a collusive defence against group anxiety. The specific interpretation is that pairing enacts an unconscious fantasy of messianic redemption through the fruits of a sexual coupling (Bion 1961). While pairing can be dysfunctional and collusive in the group – and these aspects are explored more fully in Chapter 12 – I would argue that it can also be genuinely creative and growthful, minus regressive and destructive underpinnings. The group's contribution, rather than being collusive, is in the nature of support for a healthy and natural development that may have value to the couple and the group as a whole. The erotic connection in a group is in any case more likely to occur between two people than between everyone in the group and the issue is more whether the group can tolerate this development without undue envy or rivalry.

It is clear that the group as a whole played a significant role in this development. Certainly, they benefited from the libidinizing process that invigorated the group, but their presence, support and encouragement made it possible in the first place for the two main players to 'play'. In this sense, the connection that grew in the group could be seen as circular and interactive rather than emanating from two individuals in isolation. This is probably where the erotic connection is influenced by the group process, holding and supporting a more specific dyadic connection, as represented here by Melvin and Imelda. Throughout this book, I argue for the importance of the social group in facilitating and containing the intimacy of the couple – a point that has relevance to both group psychotherapy and the community outside the consulting room.

Incest

A further theme that emerged concerned incestuous desire. The connection between Melvin and Imelda sparked this off, through Melvin's linking Imelda with his aunt. Group members then picked up on the theme, exploring feelings about sexuality in the family setting. Further, Melvin's expressed sexual attraction to Imelda represented a form of incestuous desire within the group. That this could be spoken about openly helped to embody sexuality in the group, to substantiate the erotic connection and to reduce the anxiety and shame attendant on it.

The theme of incest is very relevant to group psychotherapy, given the analogy of the group as a family, and is the subject of fuller treatment in Chapter 9.

The therapist's role

This example illustrates the value of the therapist's active facilitation of the sexual subject. Without being dominant or particularly directive, the therapist keeps the group on track in its exploration of desire and sexuality. In particular, he observes and comments on the tendency in the group to avoid the theme. For example, where the group initially chooses to focus on the assertive aspect of Melvin's erection, he points out their evasion of the erotic. When they begin to change the subject in the discussion about incestuous fantasy, he similarly brings them back. It is possible that very little of the sexual exploration might have happened in the group had the therapist not been attuned to the subject and commented actively on the communication process.

Summary and reflection

A children's psychotherapy group and an adult group are presented in parallel, highlighting a libidinal connection in each that enlivened and deepened the group process. It brought each of the groups together in a spirit of intimacy. In the children's group this was expressed in physical contact and play, the excitement of an outing to the sea serving both as a real event and the symbolic mediator of a new liveliness. In the adult group, where physical contact was inappropriate, the connection was mediated verbally. In this group, pairing occurred in a way that was constructive and supported by the group.

There is a further parallel in the therapists' role in the two groups. On the face of it, this was very different, the therapist in the children's group going out on a limb and arranging an outing to the sea, and in the adult group actively taking up the sexual theme and tracking communications about it. In the first group, the therapist changed the external boundary by taking the children outside the consulting room. In the second, the therapist held the group boundary intact but pushed the internal boundary of what was acceptable discourse in the group. What they have in common is an intuitive grasp of the libidinal subject in their groups as well as the courage to follow through on their intuitions. This is a useful point on which to conclude this first chapter on the clinical discourse: a point about both the imagination and initiative needed to encourage and support the realization of the sexual subject in group psychotherapy.

9

THE THEME OF INCEST

The phenomenon of incest – sexual relations between family members – has hovered in the shadows of psychotherapy since the beginnings of psychoanalysis. Partly as historical data concerning patients' childhood sexual experiences in the family, partly as a force in transference and counter-transference and partly as a necessary warning to psychotherapists to avoid the temptation of sexual relationships with their patients, the spectre of incest looms large in psychotherapeutic consciousness. Whereas the warning it constitutes has served to limit the incidence of actual sexual transgression in and outside the consulting room – a good thing by any public and professional standards – the anxiety about sexual enactment has also contributed to the desexualization of much contemporary analysis. Samuels (1999) refers to the emergence of 'safe analysis', the institutionalized repression of sexuality in the consulting room. This has created a twilight zone of sexuality in psychotherapy, a form of paralysis about what is obviously present but has to be treated with the utmost caution.

These themes have a particular relevance to group psychotherapy, a constellation not unlike the family with its parental and sibling identifications and hence open to the arousal of 'incestuous' feelings. Further, the group has a strong physical presence: it is an assembly of bodies in close proximity to each other. Usually, group members can see and practically touch and feel and smell each other. While being expected to comply with the boundaries of time and space, members are not constrained by the kinds of formality that exist in individual psychotherapy with its greater hierarchical emphasis. Spontaneity is encouraged. There is of course a prohibition against sexual enactment in and outside the group, but no prohibition can stop the arousal of desire that arises in the group. This includes the desire of and for the therapist who in various ways is more visible and available in group than individual therapy. That the therapy group is such a potential hotbed of desire, with its many temptations, may be one reason why sexuality in group psychotherapy is so marginalized. It evokes the anxiety of incest, the guilt about forbidden wishes. By ignoring or concealing sexuality, there may be an illusion that it does not exist, that there is no wish for – or danger of – enactment. But, of course, concealment usually intensifies rather than erases what is desired.

What is lost in the denial is the opportunity for development. Throughout this book I suggest that it is possible in the therapy group to hold in creative balance the emergence of sexual desire and the recognition that this must be contained without enactment: this is part of the therapeutic work of the group. Having touched on this issue in the previous chapter, I want to look more closely at the theme of incest in group psychotherapy from two perspectives: 1) the representation in the group of incestuous feelings and experiences in childhood; 2) the exploration of incestuous impulses in the here and now of the group. I intend here to look at both these issues through the single example of a group in which the theme of incest was the focal point.

This example derives from a previous publication (Nitsun 1990) on the group treatment of survivors of child sexual abuse. In that paper I highlighted the value of a mixed psychotherapy group for this problem, in contrast to the commonly-held view that homogeneous groups are more appropriate (Ryan *et al.* 2005). Here, I pursue the view that heterogeneous groups are valuable for this population and, additionally, that the incest theme is very relevant to group psychotherapy more generally and reflects the potentials, as well as pitfalls, of openly addressing sexuality in the group setting.

Example

This was a 'mature' group in the group-analytic sense that it approximates Foulkes' (1948) ideal of 'therapy by the group of the group'. The group had acquired a facility for 'free group discussion', Foulkes' description of the conversational process that elaborates and enriches group material. This encourages a horizontal rather than vertical perspective on problems, in such a way that communication is helpful not just to one or two individual members but to the group as a whole.

The incest theme was initiated by Bridget (35), who had been sexually abused as a child by an uncle over a period of years. She had been in individual therapy with the group therapist for two years before joining the group. In this she had developed a strong positive transference towards him but was very anxious about any possible sexual feelings in the relationship. She saw these as severely tainting and damaging. She also maintained that she had no sexual feelings outside her relationship with her husband – which was in any case inhibited – as if her sexuality belonged to him rather than her. I pick up on Bridget's concerns some years later in the therapy group, concentrating on the events of a single group session in which all the members were involved.

Bridget began by saying that she had been disturbed by what she saw as the therapist's insinuation in the previous session that she had sexual feelings towards him. Yet she had recently had dreams about him which she felt might confirm that she did have such desires. If this turned out to be the case, she warned, she would have no option but to leave the group.

The rest of the group reacted against this, saying that her leaving would be an unnecessarily drastic step. Participants encouraged her to consider her sexual feelings as part of an affectionate relationship with the therapist and to see this as natural rather than perverse or contaminating. The topic encouraged further revelations concerning incestuous feelings. Richard (47), who had previously hinted that there were sexual issues in his relationship with his daughter, Miranda, announced, 'I had intercourse with Miranda three nights ago – in a dream'. He went on to talk about a period in his relationship with Miranda, then 15, when she became extremely awkward about any physical contact with her. They had previously hugged and kissed warmly, but now she recoiled from him. On one occasion, she had accused him of being 'a dirty old man'. He then, through anxiety about transgression, had stopped all physical contact with her. He remembered feeling lonely and troubled about the problem. He had not been able to talk to anyone about it at the time, including his wife. He looked tearful in the group as he recalled these events.

Martin (42), an unmarried man who still lived with his parents, joined the discussion. He revealed that as a child he used to get angry with his mother, then apologize and draw close to her for comfort. At these times he would get an erection. He had always worried about this and considered himself abnormal. He had had great difficulty in adulthood forming sexual relationships with women and believed that his feelings towards his mother had something to do with this. He currently had a companion and noticed that when they had an argument he wanted to hurt her and at the same time found himself having an erection. There was some discussion in the group about the place of aggression in sexuality, with a tendency to normalize this. The discussion initially deflected from the theme of incest but members came back to it.

Richard asked the therapist whether mothers had the same problem (incestuous impulses) with their sons that fathers had with their daughters. The therapist replied that Martin's example confirmed that this could well be the case: it was likely that when Martin responded sexually to his mother, she was party to these feelings. The group explored further the issue of aggression and sexuality, saying that these were often linked and that Martin had felt unnecessarily guilty about this.

Another male participant, Paul (24), then recalled that he had had sexual fantasies about his mother and his two sisters, particularly a younger, very attractive one. He had believed that he would never reveal this to anyone and was surprised by the unexpected way this emerged in conversation in the group. June (43) then entered the discussion. She had suddenly remembered a dream the previous night in which she experienced herself as a man having sexual intercourse with a woman. It had been a vivid, exciting dream. Richard commented that June blushed as she spoke. June laughed in an embarrassed way and said she was shocked at having such a dream. Members spoke about how confusing sexual feelings could be and whether it was normal to be attracted to the same sex, even if you were heterosexual. June went on to say that she had wondered if she was a nymphomaniac, not in fact a lesbian but a woman who craved sex with men. She shared the fact that she had been attracted to each of the men in the group at some point. There was a wave of laughter and then Paul said, 'Funny, I've been attracted to most of the women in the group. There are some very nice women here!'

As the session drew to a close, the therapist commented on the openness that had developed in the group. He noted that much of the discussion concerned the ownership of sexual feelings. In some people, like Bridget, past experience had led them to view their sexuality as something put into them from outside: people often felt overwhelmed by the intensity of their sexual feelings, almost as if they emanated from some alien source, but the discussion here gave the impression of participants attempting to locate the sexual impulse within themselves, however exciting or disturbing. In the last few minutes of the group the focus returned to Bridget and her disowned sexuality. Part of this appeared to be guilt about responsibility: she secretly feared that she had been responsible for her uncle's intimacy with her. This made her frightened and confused about her sexuality, needing to deny it even in situations where it was entirely natural. This brought the group back to Bridget's possible sexual feelings towards the therapist, which she was able now to acknowledge with less anxiety and shame. The discussion helped Bridget, who in later sessions delved more deeply into the question of her guilty sense of responsibility, eventually gaining a clearer understanding of which sexual desires were hers and which belonged to another individual.

Discussion

What is the function of incestuous fantasy? Samuels (1999: 155), attempting to go beyond the conventional assumptions about incest – the universal taboo that reflects the urgency of desire, the longing for enactment and the dread of its consequences – raises this question: 'What is the *telos*, the goal, the aim, the magnet, the aspiration, the prospect, the dream of human incestuous sexual fantasy?' Recognizing the dangers of enactment, he nonetheless argues for the positive psychological function of incestuous fantasy. He suggests that its function is growth. He is referring here to psychological growth and the way this occurs through relationship, through the enrichment of personality that comes with intimate closeness to another and the internalization of that closeness. This is especially true in childhood, when the child looks to its parents for an intimate bond – and the parent, whose own growth and seeking continues, albeit in a different time-frame, finds something in the child that mirrors their own desire and quest for generativity (Nitsun 1994). Summing up his views on the theme, Samuels concludes, 'The psychological function of fantasies of incestuous sexuality is to inspire and facilitate that multi-layered closeness we call love. This means that incestuous sexuality and the social bond are also interrelated just as pleasure and power are interrelated' (p. 156).

These points have considerable relevance to the group material I present above. The mainspring of the material – and the organizing theme – is incestuous desire. There is initially anxiety in the theme – the dread of incestuous desire and the shame and fear associated with its recognition – reflected in Bridget's declaration that if she discovers that she does have sexual feelings for the conductor, she will have to leave the group. However, through the contributions of the other members, the theme of incest is expanded in the deepening communication of the group as a whole. Bridget is now freed of the burden of being the only one with this problem. It becomes universalized as each group member shares a particular version of incestuous desire. The feelings of shame, guilt and anxiety associated with it are also shared and in the process the group comes together in a spirit of intimacy and trust. In turn, this enables members to talk about their desires for each other, embodying the incestuous impulse in the here-and-now of the group. The therapist comments that this helps with the location and ownership of desire. At the end of the session, the focus returns to Bridget, who gains something to take her further in the resolution of feelings about her childhood experience of abuse.

It is not entirely a coincidence that this session, which is dominated by the theme of incestuous fantasy, is also a vivid example of the group analytic process at work. The theme has generated a richly associative process in which every member is able to contribute: there is a vivid recall of past experience; the evocation of dreams; a flow of resonance from member to member; an open discussion about transference issues; a capacity to enter fully into the present of the group; and at least a hint of the medium that oils the wheels of the group – play. In this coming together of thematic content and group process, we have a striking illustration of how an analytic therapy group works. It is significant that this is in the context of exploring incestuous desire. Rather than impeding the therapeutic process, which might have been predicted, the theme liberates communication and generates a closely cohesive group. This confirms the point about the interrelationship of incestuous fantasy and the social bond and is a further illustration of the integrating power of the erotic connection.

The success of the group in addressing this highly charged subject must be qualified by reference to this being a mature group in group-analytic terms. The group had been meeting for some years and had built up a level of trust that made it possible to venture where younger, less mature groups would hesitate to go. This, however, is the point of long-term analytic group work – that it strengthens the group's capacity to confront the most difficult areas of emotional development. At the same time, the material shows how the theme of incest lends a greater depth to the process, increasing both intimacy and trust in the group. That the patient with the identified problem of child sexual abuse had been in individual therapy with the conductor prior to joining the group must also have contributed to the process. In some circumstances, an additional link with the therapist can create tensions in the group through the rivalry of other members – and there were aspects of this in earlier stages of the group – but here the contextualization of the individual transference in the group, making the transference transparent and open to discussion, appeared to support the unfolding of the theme of incestuous desire, both for the patient concerned and the group as a whole.

While the present chapter focuses on incestuous sexuality *per se*, it is suggested that the interlocking of theme and process described is relevant to the representation of all sexuality in the group setting. Secrecy, shame and the distrust of sexual relationships – key features in the clinical literature on child sexual abuse (Ryan *et al.* 2005) – form the substratum of anxiety that resides in much sexuality and that creates the defensive narratives required to protect the sexual self. It is this constellation that makes it so difficult for people to discuss sexuality in psychotherapy generally and group therapy specifically. However, it is important to differentiate incestuous from non-incestuous desire, as well as desire from enactment. In a therapy group, members are not biologically related and it is possible to use this difference as a point of departure rather than an occasion for impasse.

Whereas incestuous desire can be seen as linked to social bonding, it is equally true that the enactment of incestuous sexuality is damaging to social bonds. Incestuous fantasy tends to arouse anxiety about social as well as sexual transgression and the ensuing guilt creates a division between the sense of a private sexual self and the representation of the social self. The social group therefore holds the power of judgement and censure – and this is another reason why the psychotherapy group can be so feared, why the opportunity to reveal sexuality in the group is so intimidating. Guilt about sexuality is often in the shadow of incestuous desire. But herein lies an important opportunity for the group – to offer a new kind of morality, an authority that is forgiving and enabling, in the way illustrated in this chapter.

Summary

The theme of incest is illustrated in a mature psychotherapy group which enabled the constructive exploration of incestuous desire, both in members' childhoods and, by analogy, in the group itself. While incestuous impulses are associated with sexual transgression, and this has led to considerable caution about their acknowledgement or expression, the example indicates the potentially bonding function of such desires and the value of sharing incestuous feelings and fears in the therapy group.

10

DISSOCIATED DESIRE

The previous two chapters celebrated the triumph of desire over despair and illustrated the power of the erotic connection in animating and integrating a therapy group. They presented the optimistic side of Eros, the creative, enlivening aspect of connection. But this is by no means always the case in group psychotherapy, where desire and sexuality are frequently challenged by failures of emotional development, traumatic sexual experience and confusion about sexual identity and orientation. This chapter addresses the negative representation of desire in the group, but with the possibility, in some cases, that the group can help to restore hope and reclaim desire.

Throughout the theoretical part of this book, reference was made to the dissociation of desire, the tendency to expel from awareness the full intensity of desire, both sexual and otherwise. Usually, this is a defence against the anxiety aroused by desire, the fear of a loss of control or the fear of injury, physical or psychological. Sometimes, there is a fear of retraumatization, of an earlier injury being repeated. 'Sexuality', says Bollas (2000), 'is inherently traumatic'. The dissociation, then, may serve a protective function – a large degree of repression is a necessary part of socialization and some repression is also needed for survival. But, mostly, the dissociation is at a cost to the individual: a cost in terms of diminished vitality and capacity for intimacy with others. Most people coming for psychotherapy are seeking to reconnect with their desires, to find a way of owning them, fulfilling them or coming to terms with frustration and disappointment – to deal with the sense of lack that Lacan (1988a, b) posits as part of the human condition.

Group psychotherapy offers an unusual opportunity to reconnect with desire. The presence of several others, including the therapist, provides an interpersonal setting in which desire is potentially evoked, mirrored and recognized in myriad ways – a 'theatre of desire', as

Tylim (2003) suggests. But if there is the potential here for the unfolding of desire and sexuality, there is also the potential for renewed anxiety, shame, the compounding of defences and the flight from desire. Groups can be both freeing and constraining, liberating and intimidating. The psychotherapy group may represent a challenge to conventional repressive morality but it can also create a critical authority of its own. How desire and the dissociation of desire are embodied in the group process has a major influence not only on the sexual subject but, I suggest, on therapeutic outcome as a whole.

In this chapter, I consider developments in two contrasting therapy groups. In the first, the predominance of despair makes it impossible for members to access and share their desires. The group is paralysed by an anti-libidinal process that becomes a form of anti-group. A destructive split in the group proves impossible to penetrate. In the second example, the group initially deals with conflicts about sexuality through splitting into a desiring sub-group and a repressed non-desiring sub-group. Libidinal and anti-libidinal tend to be divided between two fairly distinct groups. However, the overall group is open to therapeutic intervention and in time begins to integrate the splits. The contrast between the two groups highlights how differently desire and dissociation are manifested and managed in groups, what it is that accounts for these differences and how they may be linked to overall therapeutic development.

Anti-desire

The experience of running a group that lacks vitality and therapeutic momentum, seemingly devoid of desire, is not that uncommon. It can also be baffling, debilitating and deeply disheartening for the therapist and group members. This is an example of such a group, a weekly group of male and female patients in an NHS setting, run by a male therapist. The patients had serious and long-standing mental health problems, some with psychiatric histories involving hospital admission and attempted suicide. All had severe difficulties in their interpersonal relationships.

The group had a relatively stable core of four men who attended regularly and a shifting, unstable sub-group of women which changed several times in the three years in which the group had been running. The mood of the group was largely dictated by the men: a mood of despair and cynicism in which the hope of a better life was consistently negated. The men's regularity and cohesion, while lending the group a distinct continuity, therefore had a deadening impact on the therapeutic process. The women who came and left the group had difficulty connecting with the men. There appeared to be an unbridgeable gap between them. The women similarly related superficially to each other, failing to establish any kinship or bonding as women, and leaving the men in a position of quietly and destructively dominating the group.

The men's communications were marked by the absence of any positive expressions of desire. This applied to their personal lives, subjective longings and prospects for therapeutic change. Their inability to enjoy life was exemplified in the story of Max's (41) winning a £20,000 prize in a lottery draw. He had won the money soon after joining the group. He had high hopes about what he would do with the money, but he had left it in a bank account where through random spending it had gradually whittled away. Now, two years later he was broke and fighting with social security for a disability allowance.

Sexuality in these men seemed remote, repressed. Yet, there were occasional glimpses of passive longing, unspoken yearnings for an idealized other. Jeff (43) waxed enthusiastic about a woman he saw periodically at the supermarket and admired from afar: a glamorous blonde who drove up in a fancy car and strode through the shopping aisles with great verve. This figure captured the imagination of the men and acquired the nickname 'Marilyn', after Marilyn Monroe. The men's interest in this figure contrasted with their lack of engagement of any substance with the females in the group. Although these were all very different women, in terms of looks and personality, they were treated like a homogeneous blob. The women themselves sometimes revealed worries about their attractiveness and fears of rejection in relationships with men outside the group. When the therapist suggested that this might be an indirect reference to their feelings of rejection in the group, there was a blanket denial all round. Men and women alike expressed irritation with the therapist's constantly bringing things back to the group: this was practically the only time that there was some unity between the sexes.

The lack of engagement with the women was also evident in the men's reactions when, one by one, the women left. Hints of surprise and disappointment were subsumed in an overall reaction of resignation and indifference. Just below the surface, however, there appeared to be a rising sense of panic and despair that they could ever hold onto a woman. Alan (39), on hearing that one of the women, Carrie (29), had dropped out, had an emotional outburst. He admitted to liking Carrie: there was a sense of some connection between them in the group and a glimpse of real regret and disappointment in Alan when she left. However, this quickly turned into an angry generalization about all women: 'They're all the same. They don't give a toss. There's no point in losing sleep over any of them'. The other men concurred and the waters closed over Carrie's departure.

Some themes in the men's past histories helped to make sense of the anti-desire that bound them together. They all suffered from the absence of parental coupling of any depth or continuity. They described family atmospheres of deprivation and neglect. Much of this was interlaced with violent abuse. Dave (47) described his mother 'beating the life out of him'. He revealed in the group that he harboured violent sexual fantasies towards women and that he had had sado-masochistic sexual relationships as an adult. He also admitted that this had started in response to his mother beating him and that he had become sexually excited by the beatings as a child. Alan described a different trauma. At 15, he had enjoyed a spell of popularity with girls and had his first sexual intercourse. Then, in a rock-climbing accident, he had fallen and severely injured his back. The accident left him incapacitated and the recovery was slow and painful. Although he largely regained his physical strength, he lost his social confidence and withdrew from girls. In adulthood, he resorted to drink and drugs and made several suicide attempts. Even now, he experienced a compulsion to walk into oncoming cars. He described being drawn irresistibly to the looming lights of the approaching traffic.

The men's attitude towards the male therapist was curiously distant, and they were scornfully amused by his interpretations. Any attempt he made to confront their defeatist attitudes was met with a retort of 'It's all right for you. You doctors and professionals have it all right. You have no idea of what it's like for us'. The therapist frequently felt impotent and approached the group with a mixture of exasperation and despair. When inviting the group to say how they viewed him as a person, the response was something like, 'You have it all sorted, don't you, with your wife and 2.5 kids and your smart car and golf on the weekends'. This seemed to be the male equivalent of Marilyn, the woman in the supermarket who fuelled their fantasies: an idealized, stereotyped figure with whom they could have no real connection. In the case of the therapist, the idealization was mixed with envious contempt.

The therapist could make no inroad into the group impasse. In the fourth year of the group, in consultation with a colleague, he decided that the exercise was futile. He could see no point in bringing any new women into the group – or, for that matter, men. He decided to close the group. He would start again afresh. Some weeks later he terminated the group.

Piecing together the various themes outlined above in an attempt to understand the profound resistance presented by these men, it would seem that desire was relinquished in the face of early parental neglect, the absence of parental coupling and the threat of violence lurking in the family. Alan's traumatic fall at 15 symbolized the danger of sexual assertion. The fall was like a punishment, a castration. In the absence of desire expressed and realized with a degree of safety and satisfaction, the only solution might be a masochistic one: to enjoy the suffering. This was reflected in Dave's sexual excitement in being beaten by his mother. It may also have been the underlying force that united the men in the group in a form of masochistic submission to their fates. Although seemingly a case of passive resignation, this also reflected an attempt at control. By denying desire, they attempted to deny vulnerability and the pain of loss, change and disappointment. The self-destructive aspect of this was reflected in the mesmeric attraction of the car headlights for Alan: the lure of death.

What remained largely concealed, unacknowledged, was the rage about frustration and deprivation. Only in flashes was this rage revealed in the group. Equally, hostile and competitive feelings between the men were eclipsed by the collusive dynamics that bound them together. They functioned in a way that is reminiscent of 'the gang', Rosenfeld's (1971) description of a powerful internal organization that guards against human vulnerability and narcissistic defeat. Their seeming indifference to the women in the group probably concealed a mixture of frustrated desire and hatred of women. The violent sexual fantasies Dave hinted at were probably hidden or kept at bay in the group, while being secretly nurtured. This was more than the defensive repudiation of women found in male-bonded groups (Benjamin 1990): it was akin to Kernberg's (1995) description of the pathological hatred and envy of women in men who appear to have had early experiences of a sexually tantalizing and withholding mother. Kernberg suggests that these men experience sexual desire for a woman as a repetition of the early teasing and that they unconsciously hate the desired woman. He also suggests a variation in which men fear being rejected and ridiculed by women, which he sees as the projection onto the women of their own unconscious hatred.

Gender representation in the group merits comment. The men's unwillingness to reflect, to open up in any significant way, is a fairly extreme version of Elliott's (1986) description of stereotyped male communication in psychotherapy groups. The women, however, did not conform to the expectation of greater communicative sensitivity in females. If this was potentially there, it was probably killed off by the noxious atmosphere of the group and the men's attacks on the contributions of the female participants. This meant that the reflective process, so important in group therapy, was absent.

The rigid processes of encapsulation and dissociation created a strong anti-group. Resonance and amplification of defences in the male sub-group resulted in a highly collusive entity, holding power over the females in the group as well as the therapist in a way that was probably inverse to the powerlessness in their own lives. It is interesting that the only way the therapist could find to deal with these problems was to close the group. He had to take power into his hands. The 'gang' could not be challenged psychotherapeutically: it would yield only by being broken up.

Divided desire

This contrasting example is of a group of six men and women conducted by a male therapist in a primary care setting (a GP surgery). The therapist was gay – which was unknown to the group – and the members were all predominantly heterosexual. The group had been running for four years. There was an overall sense of therapeutic engagement in the group but there were particular tensions about the open discussion of sexuality. However, this was available for exploration and understanding and the group was able to move forward.

The men in this group (in opposite fashion to the previous group) represented an active, probing sexuality and the women an anxious, inhibited, even traumatized sexuality. John (51) and Phil (48), in particular, gave the impression of being confident of their own sexuality and argued for an open exploration of sexual desire and relationships. Wendy (57) and Jenny (28) actively resisted this and expressed doubts about the value of such openness in the group. They had both been sexually abused. Wendy had been abused by an older brother in childhood and Jenny had been raped by her own husband after five months of marriage (which led to the disintegration of the marriage). These facts were well known to the group but neither woman was willing to discuss them in any depth and both maintained considerable reserve about sexuality. They shared a distaste for all matters sexual. A third woman, Sylvia (35) had a sexual relationship with her husband but was very coy about sexuality in the group. The result was a polarized representation of sexuality, with the men mainly occupying a libidinal position and the women mainly a non-libidinal if not anti-libidinal position.

This constellation from time to time triggered conflict and distress in the group. The men, who expressed feelings of affection for the women, tried to bring them out of their shells, as they saw it. But this was invariably counter-productive. The women felt invaded and the men behaved like frustrated husbands trying to penetrate the defensive walls erected by their wives. There was a sense that intercourse could not take place.

The dynamic started shifting when Wendy was able to begin talking about the sexual abuse by her brother. She did this with considerable difficulty. Years of anguish and anger had left a deep mark and her sharing what had happened was painful and slow. She hesitated several times, stammering, seemingly repressing images and memories that were shameful to her. The therapist, who felt moved and troubled on Wendy's behalf, found himself suddenly voicing a thought that had entered his mind: 'Did he put his penis in your mouth?' Distressed, Wendy confirmed this. There was an unspoken realization in the group now that Wendy, age 13, had gagged on her brother's penis in her mouth – and, further, that she was gagging now on the words that revealed to the group the details of the abuse and the ensuing shame and disgust. But she was helped by the gentle persistence of the therapist's questioning and the empathic attention of the group as a whole. John showed a particular interest, in which one or two members thought he might be too pressing.

Soon after the abuse took place in childhood, Wendy had attempted to talk about it to her mother but the latter, she felt, did not want to know. Wendy had never since discussed the abuse with anyone. The secret she had concealed all those years had left her feeling not just sexually dirty but a social misfit. The experience, therefore, of sharing the information in a supportive group was very meaningful. She said later that the experience had helped her to come 'out of the shadows'.

Wendy's opening up was part of an unravelling of the fixed gender dynamic in the group, a lessening of the distance between the 'sexual' men and the 'non-sexual' women. The men, previously the standard bearers of sexuality, began to share their own doubts, anxieties and conflicts, ranging from difficulties in sexual performance to guilt about extra-marital affairs to homosexual impulses and fears. John reported a dream about a building exploding. The initial image was of a building rising, as if in a process of rapid construction. It then suddenly exploded, leaving debris everywhere. There were a number of associations in the group to the dream – including the attack on the twin towers in 9/11 – but the one that resonated most strongly was that of a sexual orgasm – an explosive, damaging orgasm. This enabled the group to talk generally about fears of destructiveness in intimate relationships and specifically about John's sometimes aggressive entry into the group. Had he been damaging here? Had he damaged Wendy by his questions, in spite of the impression that her opening up about the abuse had been therapeutically beneficial? Through discussions of this sort, group members reflected on their here-and-now interactions and raised questions about the limits of how far they could go in revealing their sexual selves. This helped to regulate intimacy in the group and to give members a sense of shared responsibility for the process.

One important development was the more open expression of affectionate and desirous feelings between members. The men took the lead in this. John tended to focus on Wendy, telling her what a lovely woman she was and how much she had concealed her femininity. Phil was very appreciative of Jenny, the woman who had been raped by her husband. She tended to react to his affection with a degree of irony, maintaining that she remained suspicious and distrustful of men. Phil responded that he would not leave the group until he saw evidence of a change in her attitude to men. He several times said if only she could have a really loving intercourse, this would make all the difference.

The deeper anxiety lurking in this exploration of gender and sexuality was reflected in a dream Phil had about Jenny. In the dream, he saw her riding a bicycle into the distance. She seemed to wobble, then fall over. She lay there motionless for some time. He wondered if she was dead or alive. The dream had a disturbing impact on the group. There were various associations and questions. Did this reflect Phil's anxiety that sexual feelings towards Jenny might in some way damage her? Was there a sense that if Jenny let herself go she would end up hurt? Had the rape left her so damaged that she might never recover?

As the themes of sexual anxiety, damage and recovery wove through the material, members engaged intensely with each other. Their communications gained in resonance. This alternated with periods of disengagement, when attendance at the group faltered and communication froze, but it was usually possible to understand these periods as counter-reactions to the process of opening up. Over the course of time, there were a few significant changes in members' lives outside the group. John linked the problems in his marriage to his attempt to preserve an illusion of continual potency and sexual satisfaction. This made it possible to think of more realistic solutions. Wendy was able to expand her social circle and deepen important friendships, even though the sexual abuse remained a problem. Jenny joined a salsa class, which she thought might help her to regain bodily confidence – and meet new men.

Gender roles in this group shifted in constructive ways. The initial premise of active, confident men and passive, repressed women began to alter slowly, with a greater sense of commonality – as well as difference – between the sexes. At the same time, the interest and affection displayed between the sexes, while at times generating suspicion, helped to heal the splits and facilitate the unfolding of desire.

Comparison of the two groups

The striking differences between the two groups reported in this chapter raise questions about how and why these differences came about – one group that remained stuck in an anti-desire position that undermined therapeutic development, another that was able to confront the problems of desire and sexuality and gain strength and value as a therapeutic entity. The differences are all the more striking given that members of both groups had suffered significant early trauma, sexual and otherwise.

There were some obvious differences between the two groups that should be noted. These were not necessarily constitutive or explanatory and may have been a consequence rather than a cause of the distorted representation of desire. If anything, the causal relationship is probably circular rather than linear. However, the first example was of an NHS group with a highly disturbed population, comprising members with serious psychiatric histories; the second group was in a primary care setting consisting of members who, in spite of significant problems, mainly led functional lives. The first was a once-weekly group; the second a twice-weekly group. The first demonstrated a diminished capacity for psychological reflection; the second was a reflective group.

We cannot generalize from these two groups to others – this is a very limited sample indeed – but the likelihood is that problems of desire and sexuality will be more pronounced in a psychiatric population and that there will be greater resistance to reflection and change in this population. Comparing once-weekly and twice-weekly groups, the twice-weekly format, by definition, offers more time and space for working-through. That this is probably true in dealing with most significant disturbance does not alter its relevance in the present context.

Both groups demonstrated marked splitting along gender lines. In the first group this created an unbreachable gap, probably because of the level of hatred and aggression, whereas in the second there was a dimunition of the split through dialogue and understanding. Aggression was also implicit in the power dynamics of the groups. In the first group, the men in their profound anti-desire held sway over the rest of the group, disempowering in turn the therapist and the female participants. In the second, the male hegemony regarding sexuality was replaced by a fruitful encounter between the sexes and the shared perspectives that emanated from this.

Also significant is the marked difference between the therapists in their reaction to the groups. In the first example the therapist appeared to be drawn into the mood of despair that pervaded the group, struggling to manage the powerful projections transmitted – and not succeeding. In the second example the therapist, in spite of periods of frustration, felt in tune with the group, intervening effectively and remaining hopeful for most of the group. His courage in voicing the unthinkable may have facilitated the more open expression of sexuality in this group. Whether his being gay had anything to do with this is difficult to say, but the point is worth noting, since there may be assumptions that a gay therapist would have difficulty dealing with the sexual problems of a straight group. Whatever the case, this reinforces a theme running through this book: the vital contribution of the therapist in the intersubjective sphere of the group, important in any group but with the added significance here of sexuality.

Summary

Two groups are presented in which the dissociation of desire is a marked dynamic in the group. In the first, this dynamic generates a gender split in the group which becomes fixed and impenetrable. The 'anti-desire' is also an anti-group, highlighting my suggestion (Nitsun 1996) that the anti-group can be understood as anti-libidinal, the attack on life and love making it very difficult to form and sustain a group. With desire vitiated in this way, there is no chance of the group becoming an object of desire. The second example demon-strates the possibility of desire being re-found through interactions in the group. Through this process, splits in the group are gradually dissolved. The differing reactions of the two therapists to their groups, as well as differences in the group setting, are considered as contributing to the contrasting outcomes.

11

THE GROUP AS WITNESS

This chapter explores two interlocking themes: 1) the expression of intimacy in the group and 2) the function of the group as a witness to intimate encounters. This builds on the previous chapters but with greater attention to forms of intimacy and the role of the group in observing or responding to this intimacy. The main thesis is that the group has an important social function in recognizing intimacy and that this distinguishes group therapy from other forms of psychotherapy, particularly individual therapy, in which there is the absence of a witness.

The expression of intimate desire and sexuality is a private matter. It mostly takes place between two people in a setting removed from others. It requires an appropriate boundary. This is consistent with the nature and aims of intimacy, providing a protected space for the expression of longing, excitement and close union. However, it is also in this dyadic setting that that much of the anxiety, tension and frustration associated with sexuality takes place, the hurt and disillusionment – and beyond that, transgression and the abuse of power that can occur in sexual relationships. In the latter case, it is the absence of a social witness, of support, of constructive interference, that renders one or both parties vulnerable to hurt and injury. The opposite also applies: a healthy, intimate relationship that is unsupported or undermined by those in the wider interpersonal matrix is likely to suffer and be derailed. These contrasting possibilities raise the question of what happens in a therapy group when intimacy is expressed in a shared space, in the presence of others. What functions does the group play as a witness to moments of intimacy and desire that arise in the ebb and flow of the group?

A view developed in this book is that while the intimate longings of one person, or the intimate encounter of two people, require a boundary, a separation from the wider community, this boundary is

194

not nearly as firm or opaque as is usually assumed. As in all behaviour and relationships, social processes exert great influence. The invisible social context is paradoxically deeply penetrating. This applies as much, if not more, to sexual behaviour as it does to the full range of behaviour, since questions of social judgement and conformity have a powerful influence on the expression of sexuality.

Kernberg (1995) views the couple as socially transgressive in its attempt to flout conventional restraints. In parallel, he sees the group as highly ambivalent about coupling: resentful, envious, wanting to intrude. This underplays the possibility of constructive social support for coupling: the group's positive identification with the couple and the wish to recognize and nurture the couple, partly in order to strengthen the group through the deepening of bonds.

In this chapter I introduce the notion of the group as witness. This describes the group's functions as an observing and reflecting presence, a presence which provides a constructive and potentially reconstructive social process. As illustrations, I examine three situations in which the group acted as witness in some form or other. All three situations, although very different, involved the expression of desire or a sharing of some traumatic aspect of desire. There were two main protagonists in each situation, with the rest of the group providing a social context which served an essential function in the unfolding or repression of the intimate contact. The overall impression is of a significant interplay between the expression of desire and interpersonal/social processes of recognition and validation in the group as a whole.

Transgressive wishes

How does the father of two small children reveal in a group that he has sexual thoughts about them? He believes he is unlikely to act on these thoughts but is nonetheless deeply ashamed and afraid of them.

Jim (34) is a tense, uncomfortable presence in the group. Prior to joining, he revealed in his assessment interview with the group therapist that for years he has had sexual thoughts and impulses in relation to his children. He believes that he is very unlikely to mention this in the group: he feels sure that the group would despise and reject him. This is the reason for his reluctance to join the group in the first place. However, he is persuaded that he needs long-term therapy, as he has a variety of disturbing problems, and he agrees to join.

In the group, Jim is uncommunicative, defensive, evasive. He worries the group as he has a job which involves the safety of others but is frequently so depressed or drowsy because of the medication he is on that he cannot perform. He struggles to stay awake at work and sometimes drops off in the group. The group is frustrated by his unwillingness to engage. Although members are also supportive and concerned about him, he increasingly feels disapproved of and less inclined to talk about his problems. His tension tends to build up to boiling point and then he lets go in the group, crying and shouting, filled with despair and anger.

A female patient, Joan (54) shows a particular interest in Jim. She is an attractive older woman who describes considerable problems with her own children but brings a quietly maternal quality to the group. She is less likely than the others to push Jim or to berate him for not responding. Gradually, Jim warms to Joan, admits that he likes her, and tends to address her when he talks about himself. He increasingly refers to his family of origin, his harsh, critical stepfather and his mother, whom he felt let him down badly when she remarried and had several other children. He felt marginalized and deprived seeing her raise her other children and wondered whether she had ever cared about him. He has no memories of her being affectionate, of touching him in a loving way.

Although he increasingly feels supported by the group, Jim reaches crisis point in his personal life. His job is in jeopardy, his marriage fragile and his relationship with his wider family at breaking point. He begins to use the group more openly and productively. He has hinted in the group from time to time that he has troubling thoughts that he cannot share with them. Then, in a session in which he shows great distress, he reveals the sexual thoughts which have bothered him all these years. He tells the group that he stopped bathing with his children because he frequently got an erection. He continues to think of bathing with them, however, and has fantasies of touching and exploring their genitalia, as well as images of them playing with his erect penis and bringing him to orgasm. He says he no longer plays with the children for fear of sexual arousal. Yet, he longs to touch them and they are puzzled by his withdrawal.

Jim's anguished revelation makes a great impact on the group. Members are moved rather than shocked or critical, although there is a recognition that these are disturbing and potentially dangerous thoughts, however small the chance of Jim enacting them. The group adopts a questioning but sympathetic position. Part of the discussion concerns the psychological origin of Jim's preoccupations and this is where Joan, his close ally in the group, shows particular sensitivity. On hearing Jim talking about his longing to touch his children, she reminds him that just a few sessions ago he spoke about his mother's neglect of him and how he often wished she would touch him. He once saw her caressing his stepfather's neck and wished it was him. An important connection dawns on Jim and the group. His guilty preoccupation with touching his children reflects his frustrated longing to be touched by his mother. Joan attempts to put this into words and the therapist underscores the link.

This is a moment of significant closeness in the group. Jim and Joan are in sensitive emotional contact. The rest of the group is supportive not only of Jim but of the intimate bond that has developed between him and Joan. Later in the group, these two reveal a degree of sexual attraction to each other. Joan jokes that if she was 20 years younger she would ask Jim out for a date. He tells her that he cannot understand her difficulties with her children since he sees in her such a maternal and loving person. It is as if the mother-son transference between them has enabled him finally not only to talk about the thoughts of which he is so ashamed but to understand their meaning in the context of his own deprivation of mothering. The affection Jim feels for Joan, including the sexual attraction between them, helps to refocus desire in an adult relationship, to transform – at least in this situation – Jim's regressive longings. The fact that there is a significant age difference between them paradoxically serves to dilute the sense of sexual transgression that so worries Jim.

The group as witness provided some crucial functions in this example. At the broadest level, group members acted as witness to Jim's revealing his sexual preoccupations. They represented a benign authority that could hear him and support him but not ignore the seriousness of his problem. They also acted as witness to his growing bond with Joan and the intimacy they developed, allowing and supporting this relationship, which made it possible for Jim both to share his thoughts and regain a sense of self-respect. The age difference between the two was also known and accepted by the group: it is possible for an older woman and a younger man to love each other without this being sexually transgressive. From a group-analytic perspective, the therapy happened through an intense process of resonance and mirroring and an interpretation (the linking of Jim's sexual preoccupations to his relationship with his mother) that emerged in the here-and-now communication of the group rather than being imposed by the therapist from the position of an observer.

A failure to witness

The second example comes from a group at an early stage of development – approximately three months into the life of the group. It concerns the failure of the group to anticipate an intimate encounter and to deal with the negative consequences of the failed encounter. The fact that this happened at an early stage highlights the link between group-stage development and the capacity to deal with intimacy in the group.

In a weekly NHS group, Jeff (29) presented a contradictory picture. An attractive young man, dressed in stylish, even flamboyant clothes, he nonetheless revealed to the group an overwhelming fear of intimate contact with either sex. This was against a background of lifelong social and interpersonal withdrawal. Belinda (25) was a pretty black art student who had sought help because of intermittent periods of bulimia, combined with poor self-worth and bouts of depression. She also revealed a history of failed relationships with men, including attraction to white men whom she felt used her sexually and then rejected her. Whereas Jeff maintained a measured distance from the group, Belinda was an expressive group member who, if anything, wore her heart on her sleeve. She was also the only black member of the group. This had not been addressed in the group, possibly out of anxiety about making too much of an issue of it.

The group was taken aback when soon after a session started Jeff blurted out angrily that Belinda had approached him after the previous group. She had presented him with a figure drawing she had done in an art class. The drawing was of a man who reminded her very much of Jeff and she wanted him to see it. Far from being interested or flattered, Jeff felt invaded. He saw the overture not only as a transgression of the boundary pertaining to extra-group contact but as an intrusive gesture that took no account of his problem about intimacy. Belinda reacted with distress to his account. Crying, she was at first reluctant to say anything about what had happened. Then she explained that she had intended this purely as a friendly gesture. She was surprised by how much the drawing had turned out to look like Jeff and she wanted him to see it. She was aware that this might be contrary to the group boundary but she believed it was a minor infringement. She could not understand his hostile reaction.

The story transfixed the group. The air was thick with the sense of Jeff's outrage and Belinda's humiliation. The group was virtually silent, people fumbling for something to say. What words could express the shock that this unfortunate event had happened, that both Jeff's and Belinda's problems had been enacted so precipitately, so unexpectedly? A tense, uncomfortable session achieved little other than confirming a sense of guilt and helplessness about how best to handle the incident. Subsequent sessions did little to remedy the situation. As commonly happens in groups, competing agendas quickly crowded in and the problem was metaphorically swept under the carpet.

A few sessions later Belinda announced that she was leaving the group. She gave as her reason the increasing demands of her art course, which made it difficult to continue attending. The group was surprised and disappointed. She had been a popular member. Attempts were made to get her to reconsider, at least partly on the grounds that she had been in the group for such a short time, but she was adamant. She would serve her month's notice and then go.

By the time Belinda left, there had been no clear acknowledge-ment in the group of the impression that she was leaving *not* primarily because of time pressures to do with her course but because of the shame and anger she felt as a result of the encounter with Jeff. Nor was the link made with her previous difficulties with white men, how she was repeating these, setting herself up for failure by approaching a man who was very likely to reject her. This was hinted at in the discussion but quickly denied by Belinda – and there was no challenge to her denial. Equally, there was very little discussion about Jeff's role in the incident: how threatened he had felt and how intensely he had rejected Belinda. As a result, there was no learning in the group for either of the protagonists or for the group as a whole. Belinda left and the group was very sad, not only about the premature goodbye, but about the sense of a trauma unprocessed by the group, about an opportunity lost.

A complicating factor was that the therapist was a white South African male. This, too, had not been addressed in the group. The therapist himself had not in his own mind made a link between his being a white South African and the incident involv-ing Jeff and Belinda. He had liked Belinda and had no misgiv-ings about a black woman approaching a white man, other than this being outside of the frame of the group. He was deeply sorry that she had been hurt and had dropped out of the group. Only on thinking this through subsequently with colleagues was he able to consider that the incident might have represented some enactment of feelings towards him. Was Belinda's attempt to get close to Jeff a form of testing out, on her own and the group's behalf, something to do with the therapist – and had Belinda been scapegoated in the process?

Hidden, unexplored factors in the group that may have contributed to the unsuccessful handling of this difficult event include:

- the impact of the event at an early stage of the group's develop-ment so that it was not yet able to address and process issues concerning desire and intimacy;
- feelings about the therapist generally and his ethnicity specifically;

- gender tensions concerning a woman approaching a man rather than the other way round;
- racial tensions concerning a black woman approaching a white man;
- boundary tensions and group norms concerning intimate relationships.

These factors highlight the psychological and social influences on the expression of desire and sexuality that are reviewed in Part 1 of this book. They reflect the operation of power and inclusion-exclusion processes that are intrinsic to social functioning (Elias 1978), and they illustrate how these processes are deeply embedded in all relationships, including sexuality. Had the group been able to address this more openly and courageously, it could have served more as a constructive witness and less as a silent bystander. There was a place here for both the therapist and the group to have been more active. This could have encouraged exploration and growth in the protagonists – and the group – rather than shame and withdrawal.

A homosexual crisis

The third example has a homosexual theme and could equally have been included in Chapter 14, which deals specifically with this subject. However, it is a vivid illustration of the group as witness, this time in a positive sense, and so is included here.

This was a mixed psychotherapy group in private practice consisting of men and women, straight and gay. Two men collided in an intense incident in the group. The men in question were Michael (32), a predominantly heterosexual man anxious about nagging homosexual wishes, and Guy (51), who presented himself as openly and aggressively gay. Michael was struggling to deal with a long-term relationship with a woman who was keen to marry him. A major aspect of his uncertainty was the worry that he was homosexual, which in turn linked to the homosexual longings he frequently hinted at in the group but did not reveal. Guy, the gay man, was sexually promiscuous and had come to the group because of periods of depression combined with drug and alcohol abuse.

The group at times became frustrated with Michael's obsessive vacillations and half-articulated desires. He gave the impression of a very correct young man determined to rationalize and reconcile every aspect of his behaviour. There was little room for spontaneity or play. A suggestion in the group that he might explore his homosexual interests in an actual relationship with a man was rejected as completely unacceptable.

This reached a head in a session in which Michael was relating in a particularly frustrating way, intellectualizing his desires and rebuffing attempts to challenge his defences. Guy, who was visibly irritated through all this, suddenly blurted out: 'I would like to take you home with me, strip off your pants and fuck you right up your tight little arse'. There was a stunned silence in the group, apart from the odd titter of embarrassment. Michael looked abashed. Guy goaded him further: 'Are you up for it? Should we leave the group now and you come and bend over for me?' Michael, frozen at first, now reacted with a mixture of anger and humiliation. Guy was about to taunt him further, when members of the group actively intervened. Several told Guy to lay off. James (52) expressed anger on Michael's behalf, saying that it was unnecessary to go this far and that Guy was totally out of line. The women were also protective. Jane (39) said that Michael should not be afraid of Guy's attack, that he should protect his masculinity and not be intimidated by Guy.

The group's protectiveness of Michael, aided by a quiet but supportive male therapist, helped to restore equilibrium. From this, Michael took the strength to begin to talk more openly about his passive homosexual wishes. Guy, it seemed, had touched on the very issue he found most difficult to talk about: his longing to be penetrated anally by a man. In the next few sessions, he revealed that since his teenage years, in addition to heterosexual desires, he had had fantasies of deep penetration by a man. He felt intense shame on revealing this but the group responded sensitively. Several members revealed their own homosexual experiences. James admitted to periods in his life when he had homosexual fantasies and Melville described sex play with another boy in his early teens. One of the women, Marion, said she had had several passionate crushes on girls when she was younger and experimented with kissing a close girlfriend. The effect of this sharing was to normalize homosexual desire and to encourage in Michael a greater tolerance of his wishes.

Outside the group, Michael continued to resist any possibility of a homosexual relationship but became more decisive in his heterosexual relationship. He initially broke off the relationship, then a few months later made up with his girlfriend. Their sexual relationship improved somewhat and although he still had doubts about his sexuality, he felt less tormented and more in control of his desires.

The group as witness had a major function here in helping Michael to come out of his shell of secrecy and share his homosexual desires. In particular, its witnessing the powerful verbal attack on him by Guy, symbolically enacting the very fantasy that Michael most desired and feared – and supporting him in the process – facilitated a breakthrough. What could have been abusive and destructive was instead therapeutic.

The positive aspects of the group as witness here included:

- the group's capacity to act as a socially responsible agent;
- its representation of a benign authority that could tolerate and accept what it felt to an individual as a pathological desire;
- the group's normalizing and universalizing of homosexual desire so that the individual could feel less isolated;
- the positive contribution of both genders in the group, making it possible to configure male and female, homosexual and heterosexual, in the same sexual matrix.

The strength of the group psychotherapeutic process is highlighted if we compare the process to what might have happened in individual therapy. It is unlikely that this degree of immediacy could have been achieved in a dyadic therapy. Even if the patient and therapist were both male and there was an open and unbiased discussion of homosexual fantasy – which is unusual – there is a difference between the discussion of fantasy and its direct communication in an interpersonal encounter. Further, in individual therapy, there is by definition no witness, no auxiliary group which can provide the valuable functions of observation, reflection and the representation of a considered and constructive sexual morality. To be realistic, groups are by no means always as unbiased and constructive as this one turned out to be – and there is inevitably a risk of impasse, even derailment – but the potential of the group process in witnessing the unfolding of desire is clearly evident in this example.

Summary and reflection

Group psychotherapy offers a function which may be unique in the spectrum of psychotherapies – an observing function which has the potential to adopt a more tolerant view of behaviours that are commonly marginalized and pathologized by society. Although ordinary social constraints often provide the necessary, if not essential, deterrents to transgressive behaviour, they can also be prejudicial and internalized by individuals in repressive and self-destructive ways. In psychoanalytic terms, we are in the area of the super-ego with its critical and demanding morality. Britton (2003: 71) argues for the value of judgement based on experience which 'speaks with the authority of the individual's own experience' rather than parental or ancestral authority. The psychotherapy group is able to offer an observing function in a way which facilitates the individual's own authority through the provision of an alternative social authority.

This is especially relevant to sexuality which so readily evokes moral judgements. The group as witness not only has an observing function but can act as an arbiter on questions of moral responsibility. In two of the examples in this chapter, we can see how it helped individual members to modify the judgement of their sexuality, not just on a cognitive level but through relationships in the group that generated new experiences and facilitated the opening up of rejected areas of the sexual self. In the third example, we see a failure to do so and how the capacity to provide this function is by no means automatic, how groups are not always successful in doing this and how the ability in question has to be acquired as part of the development of the group.

12

SEXUAL PAIRING

In Chapters 8 and 11, I argued for the positive value of pairing in group therapy, in contrast to the commonly-held view that pairing is a defensive and collusive manoeuvre, expressing regressive unconscious wishes in the group. I was referring essentially to pairing as a relationship between two people contained within the boundaries of the group. However, this is different from sexual coupling that takes place *outside* the group, usually in secrecy. This is not an uncommon situation in group therapy, in spite of the usually explicit rule prohibiting intimate contact outside the group. It is a situation that can create a crisis in the group when it is revealed and poses a considerable challenge to the therapist attempting to understand and deal with the transgression.

Of all the potentially difficult sexual situations in group psychotherapy, this appears to be cited most consistently in the literature (Courville and Keeper 1984; Tylim 2003), highlighting both its frequent occurrence and the problems it presents in clinical practice. This also reflects its explicit and dramatic nature as a form of sexual expression compared to the many subtly nuanced and ambiguous ways in which sex is communicated in groups. Opinions on its significance and management appear to be sharply divided. In a recent publication on complex dilemmas in group psychotherapy (Motherwell and Shay 2005), in response to a dilemma concerning extra-group sexual pairing, one author (Hopper 2005) insisted that he might ask the couple to leave the group, while another (Cohen 2005) saw this as important and useful information about relationships in the group. This reflects the complex moral, personal and clinical considerations engendered by group-transgressive sexual coupling in both the therapist and the group as a whole.

In this chapter, I explore sexual pairing in two groups in which the therapists found differing ways of handling the crisis, as well as a third example in which sexual enactment outside the boundaries was prevented by the work of the group. The examples suggest that this phenomenon cannot be separated from an understanding of the group process as a whole and that its management touches on fundamental aspects of authority and boundary-setting.

Dependent longings

A weekly NHS outpatient group run by a male therapist had considerable difficulty becoming a group. Early sessions were marked by feelings of estrangement, heightened by the fact that the group was held in a psychiatric hospital: patients were afraid that the group would reveal them to be mad and that this would lead to sectioning and admission to the hospital. Possibly as a comfort, they brought sweets and biscuits to the group. Passing these around had become a ritual at the start of each group. The therapist saw this as an expression of dependent longings that could not otherwise be met by him or the group. However, interpretations to this effect did not stop the behaviour and the therapist fell short of actually forbidding the ritual. There were also strong bids for individual attention from the therapist, mainly in the form of attempts to engage him before or after the group, when some members would linger in the room.

It became apparent that patients were meeting outside the group. Lifts and bus-rides together were mentioned, usually in passing, and there was report of a post-group group that met regularly in the grounds of the hospital. This was presented as very useful: it helped participants to debrief after the group, to steady them if it had been a difficult group and to ease the pain of saying goodbye and going home alone.

Inside the group, the material often expressed problems in dealing with difference in relationships, differing needs and wishes, and the inevitability of the relationship floundering in the face of these differences. From this, the therapist deduced the existence of a shared fantasy of perfect union, an all-satisfying relationship that would mitigate feelings of frustration and separation. When the therapist interpreted this, highlighting the frustration members felt with him and the group and how they would settle for nothing less than a perfect relationship, patients took his comments as a criticism and this reinforced their impression of him as 'professional and cold', 'a machine', and 'wearing a plate of armour'.

In spite of these difficulties, the therapist felt that there was progress in the group. Patients were beginning to talk more about their actual problems, early abuse, fears of violence, great loneliness, depressive and suicidal ideas. But just at the point of apparent progress the therapist had a shock. He went one day to a local supermarket and saw, standing in a queue, absorbed in deep conversation, touching affectionately, Stuart and Linda – two members of the group. Astonished, the therapist stood staring at them for some minutes. Then Linda caught his eye, whispered to Stuart, and they stared back in anxious acknowledgment. At the following group, Stuart arrived on his own, giving Linda's apologies: she had decided not to come. Stuart then told their story. For approximately six months, he and Linda had been meeting outside the group and on occasion had had sex. Then came another surprise: most of the other group members knew about their relationship. It had actually been discussed in the post-groups, with some members supporting the liaison, others unsure.

The therapist had been torn between feelings of shock, betrayal and worry since seeing the couple in the supermarket. Now, as he heard the story unfolding, he felt a rising determination to put a stop to all the extra-group meetings. He put to the group his conviction that these meetings, especially the affair, were flights from the real work of the group and would end up being destructive to the group. He interpreted the affair as a particular expression of the longing for a perfect but unattainable relationship and the group's collusion as an attempt at vicariously sharing in this relationship. Further, he suggested that members were attempting to leave behind in the group their unwanted, rejected bits and that this was making for a rejected, abandoned group. Although there was initially some resistance to the therapist's interventions, there was a gradual recognition by members that their actions were undermining the group and that their behaviour had been inappropriately rebellious.

Ironically, the group came together around the crisis. Members reported being careful to avoid meeting outside the group and Stuart and Linda began to disentangle themselves from their relationship. This was not without resentment on the part of some members, but the process gained momentum as the therapeutic group itself strengthened.

This example highlights a common development in group psychotherapy: the formation of alternative group meetings outside the main boundary. This often reflects a sense of deprivation and failed dependency. Hyde (1991) suggests that it indirectly expresses an idealization of the unavailable therapist and that the extra-group meetings are a way of mitigating the frustration. In this group, there were clear indications of this frustrated longing, leading to the creation of a couple that enacted the longed-for intimacy outside the group. The couple represented the wished-for perfect union, as the therapist suggested – a theme that is discussed further in Chapter 1 on theories of desire. The fantasy of the perfect couple rules out the need for anything or anyone else and is a way of transcending the dependence on social belonging. However, the idealized dyadic relationship, universal in its representation, runs counter to the purpose of the group and requires active therapeutic intervention. The fact that in this situation the rest of the group knew about the relationship but colluded with it suggests the vicarious fulfilment of idealized longings.

The material can also be interpreted as an Oedipal rebellion, an attack on the authority of the father/therapist. This led to a form of 'barometric event' (Bennis and Shephard 1956), in which the group attempted to overthrow the leader and seize authority for itself. This, in a sense, is the reverse of the previous interpretation of the group enacting a wish for dependence on the therapist, but it is likely that these conflicting impulses – dependence and independence – operated simultaneously, in a complex configuration. That the group responded positively to the therapist's firmness in prohibiting further extra-group contact suggests that the affirmation of his authority and the strengthening of boundaries were major requirements for the constructive progress of the group. It was only once the boundaries were firmly redrawn that the group could both stop its rebellious behaviour and engage with the therapist in a more cooperative relationship in which there might also be greater satisfaction of members' dependency needs.

It is striking that the transgressive enactments in this group needed to go as far as they did before they could be fully confronted. However, it is also reassuring that they could be managed effectively at this advanced stage, suggesting that groups have processes of their own that may have to be lived through before they can be assimilated into the therapeutic consciousness of the group.

A diverse group

The second example is of an NHS group in an inner-city area with a large incidence of ethnic minorities, unemployment and substance abuse. The group, run by a woman, was marked by its diversity on several parameters. The members were: Peter (Irish); Marco (gay Italian); Donald (black Afro-Caribbean); Mem (gay Turkish); Conchi (Spanish); Irene (Cypriot); and Annie (English). The members were generally young adults struggling to survive in a tough urban environment. They showed high degrees of depression, social isolation and cultural alienation. Because of linguistic differences, verbal communication in the group was more complicated than usual, with rather frenzied attempts to relate to each other that usually ran aground. At the same time, silence was very difficult to tolerate and there were frequent complaints of 'What's the point of the group?' and 'What help are you supposed to get here?'

There was also tension between the sexes in the group. Two of the women, Irene and Annie, particularly the former, openly proclaimed their dislike and suspicion of men and the male group members seemed to swallow this without defending their gender. The exception was Conchi, who from early on developed a flirtatious relationship with some of the men in the group. She was an attractive woman who dressed provocatively and behaved teasingly in the group. This tended to hide her underlying depression and make her the focus of attention, with one or two men feeling neglected and annoyed and the other women bristling with irritation. The therapist felt upstaged and marginalized and wondered if this was a form of rivalry with herself. Conchi's behaviour drew increasingly negative attention in the group and the therapist found herself making barbed comments in which she recognized her own feelings of irritation and puzzlement about this behaviour. When two members dropped out within a few weeks of each other, there was a shared sense that this had something to do with Conchi's behaviour.

This was not a happy group. As the time came for the first long break, there were strong feelings of discontent. Some weeks before, a new member, Jash, an Asian man, was introduced to the group. He was responsive and likeable and there was briefly a hope that the group would gain in cohesion and meaningfulness.

On returning to work after the break, the therapist received a letter from Jash saying that in the group's absence he and Conchi had met and were having a sexual relationship. They cared for each other and were unsure of how to proceed. Was it in order for both of them to return to the group? Since they wanted their own relationship to continue, one or both of them was prepared to leave the group, if necessary. The therapist, thrown by the news of their relationship, nevertheless encouraged them both to return.

Their return to the group triggered a highly ambivalent reaction. Some of the group were strongly in favour of the relationship, almost celebrating it, while others were critical, particularly berating Conchi, whom they saw as a seductress and responsible for this complication. There followed a few weeks of turmoil in the group. The therapist felt out of her depth, not helped by her sense of isolation in the unit in which she was running the group. She had very little contact with other staff and practically no support. She found herself identifying with the ambivalence in the group about the relationship, more annoyed than anything else, but drawn into the growing confusion and inaction. Conchi ended up having a furious argument with Annie, who called her in no uncertain terms 'a slag'. Enraged and humiliated, Conchi decided to leave the group. Anger with her escalated in the period before her leaving. Jash, feeling aggrieved on her behalf and finding the group hostile and unhelpful, also decided to leave. The group had lost four members over a space of six months and there was a sense of fragmentation and demoralization.

It was only at a later stage that the therapist, seeking consultation from a senior colleague, began to make sense of some of these events. There was first of all Conchi's provocative behaviour. Her exhibitionistic tendency was in marked contrast to the inhibitions of most other members, reflected in her imperviousness to 'shame signals', which eventually led to her explosive row with Annie. Possibly this was a manic defence against deeper underlying shame, given that in some respects Conchi became the group scapegoat.

Further, there was the question of what Conchi's behaviour represented for the overall group. At face value, this appears to have been a flagrant violation of group morality, acting-out not only her own transgressive impulses but those of other members as well. An alternative interpretation, however, concerns the communication problems in the group. Could Conchi's seductive behaviour be seen as an attempt to deal with the pain of difference and the dysfunctional communication resulting from the unusual diversity of the group membership? By making herself the object of attention, Conchi provided a distraction from the communicative and empathic gulf between the members. Although not consciously supported by at least part of the group, there may have been an unconscious collusion to maintain her behaviour. The fact that the affair took place during the break also suggests that this was a way of dealing with separation anxiety. Although the defence used was an erotic one – it was clear that this was a full-blown sexual relationship – it illustrates how sex serves more functions than sex itself and that sexual pairing outside the group may reflect significant problems in the overall group.

The therapist's isolation in the work setting made it all the more difficult for her to grapple with the untoward developments in this group. There is a parallel here – the therapist had difficulty communicating with colleagues and enlisting their support while the therapy group had considerable problems about communicating: an example of organizational mirroring (Nitsun 1998). We may speculate on whether things might have been different had the therapist felt more supported. Would she have been more able to facilitate a meaningful connection between the patients? Would this have precluded Conchi's seductive behaviour in the group and the sexual transgression outside the group? I make these points so as to highlight the importance of support for the therapist in dealing with group problems, perhaps especially in preventing and/or managing sexual acting-out. The absence of support combined with the great difficulty of communication in a particularly diverse group resulted in a sexual pairing that became damaging to the group as a whole.

Overcoming virginity

The third example differs from the other two in illustrating how a group both contained the potential for sexual enactment outside the boundary and helped a member to progress in his psychosexual development. This was in the context of a long-established twice-weekly private group run by a male therapist.

Jeremy was a shy, inhibited young man who at 28 had not yet had sexual intercourse. He had had very little sexual contact of any kind, largely because of long-standing sado-masochistic heterosexual fantasies that he was ashamed of and which interfered with his ability to initiate relationships with the opposite sex. In his fantasies, he was usually in the masochistic role, with images of bondage and domination at the core of the fantasy. He was both desirous and afraid of these fantasies being realized in actual relationships.

There was a high level of trust and intimacy in this group, the consequence in part of the therapist's tendency to encourage expression of material of a personal sexual nature. Jeremy, with difficulty, was able to share some aspects of his fantasy life in the group as well as his fear that he would never be able to have a 'normal' sexual relationship. The group responded to his fantasies without judgement or censure, so much so that the therapist enquired if they were not all a bit too blasé and if this might reflect a denial of some sort.

Cecile (31) was a single woman who described herself as unable to sustain relationships with men. This disappointed and confused her because she was sexually confident and enjoyed sex. But she invariably ended up feeling hurt and rejected. When one of the other members commented that Jeremy and Cecile seemed drawn to each other and were frequently seen leaving the group together, they admitted that they usually walked together to the Underground station and a few times had ended up on the same train. They had spoken about their own 'matters' at such times and the idea had come up between them that Cecile might avail herself to Jeremy as a sexual partner, for the express purpose of helping him to overcome his anxiety about intercourse. The idea was received by the group with a mixture of surprise, interest and indignation. Some members thought that this was an excellent opportunity for Jeremy, others that it was wildly transgressive. Overall, it was agreed that such a relationship was too risky and complicating, for themselves and the group, but the idea remained in the imagination of the group and was explored from an 'as if' perspective: 'how would it be if . . .?'

The group discussion enabled Jeremy increasingly to see the possibility of his having sexual intercourse. This was helped by a frank discussion in the group about the possibility of an individual having several different sexual sides, a variety of sexual fantasies and activities that could exist together. Members gave examples of such diversity within themselves. This encouraged Jeremy to see that his sado-masochistic fantasies did not rule out either more conventional relationships or indeed other fantasies that might develop if he were freer sexually. He decided to try this out first with a prostitute and reported a difficult but partly successful encounter. This was followed by several more successful encounters. He lost his virginity. He also reported indulging in mild sado-masochistic sex with one of these partners. He felt that this was too contrived and stiff to really excite him but he could see himself taking this further with less anxiety and shame than he previously felt. He remained anxious about unpaid sex with 'ordinary' women, but he also started talking more in the group about women he met on an everyday basis and there were hints that his overall inhibitions were beginning to thaw.

Jeremy's sexual unfolding was part of the continuing honesty in the group about sexual issues, many of which were discussed in frank bodily terms and created an open space for the exploration of sex. This included discussion with Jeremy about the actual mechanics of sexual intercourse. Cecile went through a long phase of having sex with men, without worrying about committed relationships, while at the same time recognizing that her active, even aggressive, sexuality could be threatening to men and that this might be the reason for their withdrawing.

This group differs from the other two in that the potential sexual liaison was revealed to the group before it could happen. The fact that it was picked up by another group member and brought into the group is itself very different from the other examples, in which either the members knew but opted to keep it out of the group or no one knew and the information came as a complete surprise. In these cases, the secrecy of the liaison was a key ingredient, probably one of the motivating conditions for a relationship that transgressed the group boundary. The point in this example is that it was possible for this group not only to intercept such an enactment but to make constructive use of the intended liaison. In turn, the protagonists almost certainly derived greater benefit than they might have, had they embarked on an illicit, short-lived and probably guilt-inducing affair. This is an example of the positive role of a group in both facilitating and regulating intimacy – by encouraging its expression in an appropriate context. That Jeremy sought out a prostitute in order to break through sexually may be open to question but could simply have been a pragmatic solution to a difficult problem.

There are other aspects of the group's functioning that merit comment. Its openness about sexuality – largely encouraged by the therapist – was a major factor in the progress Jeremy achieved. The absorption of his sexual fantasies into a spirit of non-judgemental inquiry in the group, backed up by other members' associations about their own sexual complexities, attests to the power of the erotic imagination in the group. The opening up of erotic possibilities transmitted a message of sexual fluidity to Jeremy, making it possible to view his sexuality in an emergent form rather than through the static preconceptions he had about himself and sexuality in general. This reflects the debate about sexual plasticity that I refer to in the theoretical section (Chapter 2), illustrating how the group associative process can loosen up the fixed expectations associated with too rigid a 'lovemap' (Money 1986). Finally, the freedom of exploration in the group was facilitated by – and in turn facilitated – an embodied view of sexuality as opposed to the more abstract and disembodied discussions about sex that tend to occur in groups.

Summary and reflection

Of the three examples presented, two suggest that sexual pairing outside the group is a reflection of group processes that are not understood or managed adequately. These include unsatisfied dependency needs and rebellious attacks on authority. The sexual enactment may also express the longing for perfect union with another, which is frustrated in the group by the emphasis on having to share space, the therapist and the group as a whole. Sexual pairing of this sort is always a boundary transgression, whether committed in complete secrecy or with the collusion of other members, and requires clear redrawing of the boundaries. The therapist benefits from having a supportive professional environment which makes it possible to recognize and deal with such processes. The third example suggests that in a mature group with a high degree of intimacy it is possible not only to pre-empt the sexual enactment but to use the intended act as a stimulus for constructive therapeutic work.

The theme of sexual pairing outside the group relates to Kernberg's (1995) view that the sexual couple is socially transgressive. This is in response to the conventional morality of social groups which, in spite of messages to the contrary, is a restrictive morality. Sexual coupling, then, even in its conformist manifestations, involves a challenge to authority which Kernberg links to the Oedipal situation. There are strong reverberations of the Oedipal situation in this chapter's examples of transgressive sexual pairing. Particularly in the first two, the pair is set up in opposition to the authority of the therapist and, to some extent, the group. There is a quality of Oedipal defiance in the act. The enactment mobilizes a degree of vicarious enjoyment in the group, probably because it expresses the repressed longings of other members. But it also excites disdain and envy. The group becomes the excluded other. This pertains also to the therapist, who is disempowered, in a reversal of Oedipal strivings towards him.

That in the first example the therapist was able, after some time, to put a stop to the acting-out by adopting a firm, clear line suggests that, above all, what is needed in these situations is a firm authority. This was helped by his analytic authority through interpreting the source and impact of the transgression. This can be compared to the second example in which the therapist was at sea with her authority, unable to hold the boundaries of the group. That she was isolated at work meant that she had no access to a shared professional authority and was thrown onto her own resources in dealing with the acting-out.

The contrasting process in the third example illustrates how in a mature group which addresses sexuality openly and fully, the impulse to transgress is not only contained but shared in a way that strengthens the therapy. Here, as in Britton's (2003) formulation, the authority is one of experience, of self and other observation, of dialogue and reflection, rather than the authority of the parents, society or the super-ego. The emerging morality is a product of the group endeavour and becomes an integral part of the therapeutic process. Through this, pairing becomes an opportunity for understanding and intimacy rather than an act which undermines the group.

13

EROTIC TRANSFERENCE AND COUNTER-TRANSFERENCE

Erotic transference and counter-transference present a particular challenge in group psychotherapy. The intensification and eroticization of the two-person relationship is contrary to the nature of group psychotherapy in which the horizontal transfer of attachment across the group more commonly defines the essence of the approach. Both the meaning of erotic transference and counter-transference in the group, and its clinical management, are therefore more complex than in individual psychotherapy, igniting the spark of deep attraction but potentially creating considerable problems for those involved. This chapter deals specifically with erotic transference and counter-transference as manifested in the relationship of patient and therapist. The forms of transference that may occur between group members themselves, given the intense relationships that frequently develop between participants, are referred to elsewhere. Here, I focus on transference in the therapist-patient relationship because this is potentially the most difficult and the most serious in its consequences and yet probably the most ignored in the group psychotherapy literature.

The problem of recognizing and managing erotic transference and counter-transference in groups is compounded by the lack of discourse more generally on transference and counter-transference in group therapy. Although group psychotherapists vary in the importance they attribute to transference and the extent to which they address it, there is an overall tendency to downplay it. For the purposes of this chapter, I will proceed on the assumption that transference and counter-transference do occur in group psychotherapy and that this can take an erotic form, but that erotic feelings are not necessarily transference-based and that we need to distinguish between spontaneous sexual responses and erotic transference as such.

Even in individual psychoanalytic psychotherapy, where erotic transference is a more widely accepted part of the process, there is continuing controversy about its existence and value as a therapeutic focus. As examined in greater theoretical detail in Chapter 3, Mann (2003) describes this as a debate between the progressive and regressive views of erotic transference. The progressive view regards it as healthy, growthful and potentiating development, whereas the regressive view sees it as unhealthy and deriving from primitive, even psychotic parts of the patient that interfere with and can destroy the psychotherapy. Mann concludes that both progressive and regressive potentials are present in erotic transference and that their actual manifestation depends on the individuals involved and the psychotherapeutic context. Mann and other writers take a similar view about erotic counter-transference, generally agreeing that it can be greatly facilitating in the therapy but that it can also be enormously difficult for the analyst/therapist to deal with. The greatest risk, as is now widely recognized, is the pressure towards enactment – and the serious consequences that are likely to follow in its wake.

That little has been written about erotic transference and counter-transference in group psychotherapy is not surprising given the marginalization of both sexuality and transference in group work. However, as Moeller (2002: 493) points out, there is huge potential in the group for the evocation of sexual desire: 'Incestuous and other erotic impulses are far more strongly mobilized in the group than in individual treatment'. This applies as much to therapist-patient relationships as it does to patient-patient relationships. Moeller, in fact, writes very honestly about his own desires in therapy groups, how as a therapist he is often emotionally and sexually attracted to group members: 'I can give the precise ranking of my libidinal cathexis of every group ... It can happen that members of the group correspond to one's own ideal partner, to someone, in other words, whom one would happily marry on the spot' (2002: 491). Moeller recognizes the difficulties arising from this but maintains an optimistic stance:

> If we develop a space which is so human, and hence so intensely erotic, as that of the group, we must accept that we will sometimes be unable to control the forces we have conjured up, and that love in the group will overwhelm us. However, the liberations which love within the group brings about are far greater ...
>
> (Moeller 2002: 496)

A number of writers, such as Moeller and Burman (2002), recognize sexual transferences in groups but there is a dearth of clinical literature exploring the handling of these phenomena in any detail or depth. Material concerning erotic transference can be difficult to access because of its intensely personal nature, but clinical data are needed in order to clarify the assumptions and beliefs about the subject. In this chapter I present two contrasting illustrations, both reflecting the intensity and gravity of erotic transferential developments in groups, one example highlighting the potentially disintegratory impact of these developments, the other the difficult process of a complementary erotic transference and counter-transference.

Dennis/Claire

Dennis (48), a single man with a history of antisocial behaviour and failed heterosexual relationships, was a member of a mixed psychotherapy group in a social services setting. The group was run by Claire (37), a social worker with an interest in psychotherapy but very little experience of running groups. She had been asked to take on the group following a service reorganization and was offered intermittent supervision by a team member with some group training.

Dennis' first few months in the group were marked by an attitude of amused disdain. He could not see how group psychotherapy could help. How could patients with their own overwhelming problems help each other? It was like the blind leading the blind. Yet, he continued to come, staying on the periphery of the group, guarded about his own problems but occasionally delving into discussions about other people's problems.

In one session, he rather surprisingly reported a dream in which Claire had appeared. He and Claire were walking down a street together. She kept brushing up against him. After the group, Dennis left a telephone message for Claire, asking her to contact him. When she did, he opened up two themes that came to predominate his relationship with Claire and the group. One concerned how difficult he found the group. The other was that he felt he was developing a special bond with Claire. If he continued attending the group, he maintained, it would be only to see her. He asked if he could have individual therapy with her instead. She declined, encouraging him to return to the group and talk about these issues there.

Dennis continued to attend the group but also set up a pattern of telephoning Claire after sessions. Anxious that he might leave and that this might weaken the group, which already felt fragile, she responded each time to his calls. She felt that just a few minutes discussion was enough to assuage his anxieties about the group and that there was no great harm in this. She mentioned it only once in supervision, not giving it much emphasis, and the supervisor did not pursue the subject. She also did not refer to this contact at all in the group. She felt that Dennis would feel humiliated by the exposure and that it was reasonable to provide him with a small degree of support outside of the group.

Dennis started telephoning her more frequently. Instead of the once-weekly call following the group, he now called twice or three times a week. She did not always return his calls and started feeling more and more intruded on. The content of the phone calls also veered increasingly towards his admiration and affection for Claire. He found her very helpful. She made his life more bearable. He had also had further dreams about her. He was always delighted to see her in his dreams, some of which had romantic themes. He was beginning to think how wonderful it would be if they could have a relationship outside the group. She was the kind of woman he had always longed for. He wondered if she felt similarly and he cherished a hope that they would one day end up together. She tended to handle these declarations by saying that she did not reciprocate his feelings and that he should not expect any other form of relationship with her, but that his feelings might be a useful part of his therapy, particularly if he could bring the subject into the group.

This did not happen, however. The precarious balance of his involvement in the group also began to be shaken by the challenges of Matthew (33), a new member, who expressed increasing irritation with Dennis. Until now, the group had to a large extent tolerated Dennis' behaviour, his aloof distance, occasional wry comments to other members, veiled hints about his affection for Claire. But Matthew, an intense young man who took the group very seriously, began to lose patience. In a session in which Dennis had been particularly supercilious, Matthew lashed out: 'What are you fucking doing in this group? Why do you come here if you think it's all such a joke? You've not once spoken about yourself in a way that sounds real and you come here and make the group a bad place for everyone else!' This triggered a mixture of fear and anger in Dennis, who started swearing blindly, furiously. He remained red-faced until the end of the group, when he left saying he was sick and tired of 'the lot of you'.

He continued to attend, but descended into increasing conflict with other members of the group. He responded badly to new members joining. One of these was Diane (26), a very anxious young woman, who drew much of the group's attention. Claire seemed to be particularly absorbed with Diane's entry and focused on Diane's newness and vulnerability. This triggered an outburst from Dennis, who expressed exasperation at new people entering the group and taking all the space. If Diane was so vulnerable and needy, he argued, she should have individual therapy and not bother the group with all her problems. Group members were shocked by Dennis' attack and rushed to Diane's defence. If anything, this only inflamed Dennis and marginalized him further. He also took great exception to the in-group pairing of two members, Jean (48) and Andrew (46), who were open about their attraction to each other. He was enraged by their little asides to each other and their knowing glances and insisted they were only interested in each other and 'having it off' in the group. He berated Claire for allowing this. The rest of the group grew increasingly intolerant of Dennis' behaviour and Matthew called him 'a sick, selfish git who should never have come to the group in the first place'.

Dennis's calls to Claire expressed increasing desperation, both about his wish for individual therapy and his insistence that she was his perfect love-object and saviour. By now, she had used her supervision more fully to discuss Dennis and his demands on her and had been advised that she needed urgently to restore boundaries. She was encouraged not to respond to Dennis' calls and to insist that he bring up in the group his wish for a relationship with her. Although she had not intended an immediate and total break in her extra-group contact with him, he interpreted it this way and in a subsequent group he had a major emotional outburst, shouting, swearing and crying, still not talking openly about his relationship with Claire and blaming the group for its stupid and cruel indifference to him. At this point, Matthew demanded: 'Well, leave, get the fuck out of here. None of us wanted you here in the first place'. At this, Dennis got up and stormed out of the room, banging the door, never to return.

This left the group with an intense mixture of relief, guilt and demoralization. Claire felt increasingly anxious and out of her depth. The group sustained several further losses: three members dropped out over the next few months. There was a sense that members had lost confidence in the group and in Claire's role as therapist. The escalation of Dennis' problems and his dramatic exit had generated deep doubts about the group.

This example vividly illustrates the problems arising from erotic transference in a psychotherapy group. Whether in fact this was erotic in the full sense of the word is unclear. Certainly, there was an idealizing and romanticized transference, and although Dennis did not openly reveal sexual feelings about Claire, it is likely that these existed in some form.

The most crucial aspect of the narrative in the present context is the way Dennis fixated on the therapist – and not the group – as his object of desire. In fact, there was a severe split: Claire was everything desirable, the group everything undesirable. This split – apart from the simple fact that attending the group allowed Dennis ongoing contact with Claire – may be why, paradoxically, he continued to attend. By deflecting his contempt and hatred onto the group, he could preserve the therapist as all good.

Erotic transference in a group is likely to create an intensely difficult triangular relationship, whether the rival is considered to be another patient, all the other patients or the group itself as an entity. If erotic transference is understood as an expression of unresolved Oedipal longings, then tensions in triangular relationships – in which jealousy and rivalry are key components – are inevitable. In individual psychotherapy, this to a large extent is contained within the dyadic relationship. This is not to say that fantasies and preoccupations with 'the third', the rival, are absent or unlikely to create problems in individual therapy – we know that erotic transference in dyads can be highly problematic – but here the rival is not visibly present or competing for the love of the therapist. In group psychotherapy, the presence of several other members, whether singly or in combination, is a constant reminder of the rivalrous other. The dynamics of inclusion, exclusion and specialness in the eyes of the therapist – and the resultant configuration of envy and jealousy – are likely then to be mobilized in full force. Dennis' wish for exclusive possession of the therapist is witnessed in his attack on new group members and his intolerance of other couplings in the group.

There are significant questions to be asked about the therapist's handling of the situation and more generally the challenge of managing erotic transference. Claire's difficulties were no doubt exacerbated by her inexperience as a group therapist. The primary technical consideration was one of boundaries. Her responsiveness to Dennis' calls after the group was the initial problem. Her sense early on that he might need some additional support was understandable but her behaviour reinforced his regular calls to the point that they became an unmanageable intrusion into her private space. Further, this was not discussed in the group. Although she encouraged him to talk in the group about their extra-group contact, as well as his developing attachment to her, he did not – and neither did she. The result was a deepening secret between them that became increasingly difficult to address in the group. In turn, this intensified the good therapist/bad group split and made it difficult to explain his attack on other patients, as well as his vulnerability *to* attack. In the end, his position in the group became untenable and he left.

We cannot necessarily generalize from Dennis and Claire to other patients and therapists in the grip of an erotic transference. There are milder forms of erotic transference which, combined with a greater reflectiveness in the patient and a capacity for group relatedness, may be more successfully managed. However, there are also – though rarely – more extreme forms, which may wreak even greater havoc. Regarding the therapist, experience is obviously an important component of the ability to handle such situations, although it is possible for even experienced group therapists to get sucked into an intense and escalating erotic transference.

The clinical problem here parallels the social implications of sexual coupling in the world outside the consulting room. I suggest at various points in this book that the longing for an all-satisfying one-to-one relationship, universal and natural as it is, has an antisocial aspect to it. It is a way of retreating from the pressures and tensions of social relating. It is socially transgressive, as Kernberg (1995) suggests. Most couples do manage the tension relatively well – by achieving a balance between intimate relating and wider social relatedness. Moeller (2002) refers to the couple itself as a generative group. However, some couples become the focus of social disruption through their exclusiveness, their isolation and their aggressiveness. In the wish to merge in the arms of the beloved, there is a wish to escape the pressures of both social convention and connection.

I have previously suggested that the obsession with individualized desire can constitute an anti-group (Nitsun 1996). The longing for a one-to-one relationship, whether in or out of therapy, can reflect a retreat from the group. The present example illustrates not only the individual patient's severe anti-group but the way in which the uncontained nature of the problem as a whole led to anti-group developments, such as the mass secession of group members following Dennis' dramatic exit. Ironically, it was the therapist's wish to keep Dennis a satisfied member of the group in order to preserve the group – an anxious response born out of the fear of the anti-group – that exacerbated the problem and triggered the group's fragmentation.

Tamara/Brian

Whereas the first example illustrated an essentially one-way transference relationship of patient to therapist, the second example describes a mutually transferential relationship in which the patient's positive transference evoked an intense counter-transference in the therapist. There appeared to be a strong erotic component, particularly in the therapist's counter-transference. The fact that this took place in a therapy group created a complex, fraught and painful process, veering between creative and destructive – ultimately helpful to the patient, but not the therapist.

Brian (54) was a Canadian Jewish group therapist living in London and running a twice-weekly mixed group in private practice. Tamara (33) was an Israeli by birth but had grown up in Canada and come to the UK approximately two years earlier with her male partner. The relationship had broken up a few months previous to her joining the group and this had precipitated a crisis in her sense of identity, career choice and country of abode.

In the period before entering the group, Tamara had decided to give up her legal studies and apply for training as an art therapist. As part of this process, she was required to join a psychotherapy group and had been given a list of names of therapists. Brian was on this list and when she found out that he was Canadian she was drawn to his group and asked to see him.

There was an immediate understanding between the two. She had not previously known that he was Jewish but in fact they shared similar backgrounds and family histories (both families had lost members during the Holocaust). Brian had been unsure about whether he should take another member into an already full group but he found her an ideal potential group member, intelligent, sensitive, thoughtful, and he had no hesitation in offering her a place – which she had no hesitation in accepting. The fact that she was a very attractive young woman, of course, did not escape Brian's attention and he was aware of his attraction from the beginning.

Brian's personal situation was that he had been married for 15 years to an English non-Jewess and had two children. The quality of the marriage had deteriorated in recent years, which Brian linked to the cultural differences between him and his wife. He found her emotionally unresponsive and missed the warmth of his extended Jewish family in Toronto. He had himself felt lonely and depressed in recent years and had maintained links with a psychotherapist through this period.

Initially very anxious in the group, Tamara began to reveal overwhelming feelings of loss and displacement. Although she had registered for the art therapy training, she was filled with doubts about whether this was right for her. This was compounded by her uncertainty about staying in London. There was a tenuousness about her existence and her relationship to the group that was palpable. She tended to relate strongly to Brian as therapist and the group was quick to pick up the similarities between them. He found himself identifying deeply with her, with her sense of loss and alienation, and his feelings were exacerbated by the possibility that she might leave the group and go back to Canada. Although she was confused and depressed – and this mirrored his own state of mind – he greatly enjoyed having her in the group and noticed in himself a new energy for his work.

Possibly because of the subtly erotic charge that had entered the atmosphere, this was a very fertile period in the group. Dreams were reported freely and Tamara shared a dream about her father who had died some years earlier. She had had a close, though ambivalent, relationship with him and had experienced his sudden death as a traumatic loss. In the dream she had hurt herself and he was tending to her. She was half pushing him away. He would disappear and then return. The group suggested that the dream might be about her relationship with Brian. She agreed, saying she had made the connection herself. She had found Brian very concerned and helpful. She began to cry, saying she was very glad to have found him and the group at a time when she was on the edge of despair. When the group ended, she was the last to leave, as was quite often the case. She and Brian were briefly alone together in the room. He felt she looked at him with great affection. Then she left.

In the months that followed, Brian was aware of a deepening closeness in their relationship. This was not spoken about in the group, although there was a sense that the group was aware of it, even took it for granted. Brian was generally regarded as a father figure in the group and there were a few comments about how he represented Tamara's father, but without recognizing the full extent of the transference that might be developing. Tamara's depression was lifting. She started feeling stronger and more optimistic. She felt more committed to life in London and certain that this is where she wanted to be for the next few years.

Things got complicated when she decided to leave the art therapy course. A year into the course she felt dissatisfied and realized that she had made the wrong choice. She decided to go back to legal studies. This threw up the possibility that she might leave the group, since it was no longer necessary for her to be there for training purposes. She decided to stay because she was finding the group helpful. It was during this period that Brian became aware of the depth of his feelings for her. He was mortified at the possibility that she might leave and realized how much she had come to mean to him. The sense of her possible loss also intensified his sexual feelings towards her and he became preoccupied, feeling that he had, to all intents and purposes, fallen in love. This paralleled a further deterioration in his marriage, a growing distance from his wife and a feeling of despair that he could ever do anything about it. He began to have fantasies of a relationship with Tamara. His sexual fantasies overwhelmed him at times and he found it difficult to contain his urges. He found himself working out ways in which he could meet Tamara outside the group, have sex, an affair, go away together, get married, have children. Sometimes when she lingered briefly after the end of the group, he felt an overwhelming urge to touch her, embrace, ask her to stay. She became everything to him.

Tamara's improvement continued. She was glad to get back into legal studies. She felt a renewed confidence in her attractiveness as a woman and started meeting and dating men. One of these contacts blossomed into a romance and within a few months had become a serious emotional liaison. She acknowledged her debt to the group and, in particular, to Brian, whose 'belief' in her, as she put it, had transformed her view of herself. The new relationship was not without its difficulties and she felt she needed to be in the group for the time being. But she began to talk about a termination date. It was during this period that Brian was faced with the full reality of her unavailability and the prospect of her finally leaving the group. He had pictured her leaving therapy unattached to anyone else, creating the opportunity, at least hypothetically, for them to have a relationship post-therapy. This fantasy was now unrealizable. He found himself isolated with his torment, unable to talk to even close colleagues about the problem. He decided to go back into regular individual psychotherapy, where he could speak freely about both his unhappy marriage and his anguish regarding Tamara. When she eventually left the group, in the third year after joining, she had maintained her improvement and her new partnership,

while Brian remained in deep conflict about his marriage and his
frustrated longings for her.

Perhaps the most striking aspect of this example is the different
effect the relationship had on the two protagonists. Whereas the
patient, Tamara, benefited greatly from the bond that developed, the
therapist, Brian, was left with very painful unresolved feelings.
Reasons for this are explored below.

First, it is useful to consider in greater detail the beneficial consequences for Tamara. She clearly had a positive transference to
Brian. Seeking him out as a group therapist in the first place because
of their shared background, she found in him a valuing, affirming
male figure who embodied aspects of both her deceased father and
the lover with whom she had broken up shortly before joining the
group. The relationship helped her to deal with these losses, as well
as the loss of country and identity that contributed to her depression. Undoubtedly, Brian's affection – and attraction to her – was
therapeutic, if not transformational. It illustrates a point that is frequently made concerning the impact of the therapist's affection for
the patient: the more powerful the therapist's feelings are towards a
patient, it is suggested, the more potential there is for therapeutic
success (Weinstein 1998, quoted in Mann 2003). Brian took the role
of a loving, desiring, passionate father, animating the dead space left
by her own father's death and the loss of her boyfriend. Kristeva
(1983) endorses the value of the therapist as a 'loving Other to the
patient', through which he becomes a living, loving father, not a dead
father. The therapist represents the 'father of personal pre-history'
(quoted in Mann 2003).

Samuels (1985) emphasizes the value of the father's erotic interest
in his daughter: not a sexual enactment but a managed admiration
and intimacy that awakens and confirms the girl's sexuality. In parallel, there is a need for 'erotic playback' by the therapist to the patient,
the appreciation of the patient's sexuality but without any form of
enactment.

It is striking that although the group picked up in a general way
the positive relationship between Brian and Tamara, its intense and
erotic aspect could not be discussed. It is possible that Brian contained not only his own but also Tamara's erotic transference, not
stated or explored in the group, and that since, as a patient, she had
the group's support and attention, she was able to resolve her transference in a way that was impossible for Brian. I suggest that in

instances like this, the therapist becomes something of a sacrificial object, having to hold and contain an enormous intensity of feeling which may be more than one individual can bear. Since it is difficult for therapists also to talk to colleagues about feelings of this depth, and more so since the group therapy culture tends to under-emphasize transference and counter-transference, the therapist may be left carrying a considerable burden.

I am aware that in this example I have said very little about the group as a whole, which is a reflection of the meagre information regarding exactly what was happening in the overall group. Possibly a more rounded impression of the group would have helped to deconstruct the problem, offering a group perspective that could take some of the sting out of the two-person relationship. Part of the problem of erotic transference and counter-transference in the group setting is its tendency to become encapsulated. That this might happen with some frequency in group therapy is a matter for reflective consideration.

Summary and reflection

These examples drive home the point that erotic transference and counter-transference can occur with the same intensity in group as in individual therapy, potentially creating more problems in a group because of the plurality of membership and the greater complexity of the process. Both examples highlight the great challenge to boundaries in the group. The erotic impulse seeks to penetrate boundaries, to invade the barriers to intimacy. Since the management of boundaries in group therapy is a crucial and continuing task, this presents a particular problem. In the first example, the therapist's failure to manage the patient's attack on the group boundary is one reason for the disturbing outcome, for both patient and group. In the second example, the therapist succeeds in holding the boundary, avoiding any enactment between himself and the patient – maintaining his professional role and facilitating the patient's progress – but leaving him with painfully unresolved feelings.

Both cases are alike in demonstrating the constraints surrounding group discussion of the erotic in the relationship of patient and therapist. Hypothetically, if such a discussion had been possible, it might have lightened the burden for both the therapists, locating the desire and sexuality more in the group and less in the secret communication of the two protagonists. But is it possible? It is one thing to interpret supposed sexual feelings between patient and therapist but another to reveal the depths of erotic transference and counter-transference. Symbolically, this would be tantamount to exposing the parents' sexuality, revealing the primal scene or the incestuous liaison between parent and child (Nitsun 1994). These questions highlight the problem of how far to go in making sexuality explicit in the group, even if we assume that greater openness is, in a general way, necessary and facilitating.

The examples touch on significant themes of loss, suggesting a link between erotic transference and the experience of loss. This is most apparent in the second example in which the series of losses Tamara has suffered – father, country, lover – appear to contribute to her transference towards Brian, a man who comes to fill the empty spaces in her life, reviving the sense of a deeply valued connection to a male figure as well as to her cultural origins. The therapist's counter-transference is similarly imbued with a sense of loss. In his case, however, the ending of the patient's therapy constitutes not a reso-lution but a *further* loss.

These examples also demonstrate the thin line between the loving aspect of erotic transference and the destructive. Within Mann's (2003) formulation of the progressive-regressive duality of erotic transference, the outcomes in these examples (except in Tamara's case) veer towards the regressive. These findings, although specific to the two examples, confirm the need not just for a sexual discourse in group psychotherapy but one that gives due weight to the occurrence of eroticized feelings between the therapist and the patient. The overall freeing up of the sexual subject in group therapy is likely to contextualize erotic transference in a more meaningful way. In the erotic imagination of the group, there must be a sense of the fan-tasized relationship between therapist and patient. To be open about this is a way of facilitating rather than encapsulating the erotic narrative.

14

HOMOSEXUALITY IN THE GROUP

The changing landscape of sexuality in the last few decades is noted throughout Part 1 of this book, in chapters on desire, sexual development and psychoanalysis. A more diverse sexual universe has emerged. The greater openness about homosexuality, in particular, has been paralleled by an increased representation of homosexuals in psychotherapeutic training and a reduced emphasis on homosexuality as a pathological deviation. The change is also evident in the greater number of homosexual patients presenting in mainstream psychotherapeutic services, more because of their increased visibility than because of any inherently greater disturbance, while at the same time specific services for homosexuals and other sexual minorities have become more focused and extensive, as in the pink therapy movement (Davies and Neal 1996).

The consequence for group psychotherapy is that in the predominant sphere of mixed-sex groups there is generally a greater likelihood of gay and lesbian individuals joining as participants. This creates a more complex representation of sexual identities and orientations than has previously existed, with the diversity consisting of straight men, straight women, gay men, lesbians and all the variations on these identities that make up adult sexuality. That this inevitably and of necessity creates a more complex group process, not only in the sexual sphere itself but in all the linked interpersonal and social processes of identification and inclusion, is clear. This makes it all the more surprising that there is so little published literature on homosexuality in group psychotherapy, particularly in the field of group analysis, which emphasizes the impact of social processes on the individual. An article by Burman (2002) highlights this point and offers some interesting perspectives on the issue, but hers is practically a lone voice in a sea of silence.

What is also clear is that while a landscape of greater diversity has opened up, many of the old problems of fear, prejudice and discrimination remain. This is not surprising: long-standing prejudice does not disappear overnight. Social attitudes change slowly and ambivalently, individuals struggling with their own deep-rooted ambivalence about difference and diversity. With its valuing of difference, it could be argued that group psychotherapy, of all the therapies, is the most relevant to the theme of sexual diversity. That most groups now include homosexuals, in particular, suggests that there are important clinical reasons, in addition to the theoretical and political, to enlarge our perspective and understanding of homosexuality in group psychotherapy.

In this chapter, I present three examples that reflect the homosexual subject in the group, highlighting the complex interpersonal and social processes that both underlie the subject and are generated by it. This complexity resides not only in homosexuals themselves but in each and every member of the group, including the therapist, all of whom may be struggling to some degree with issues about sexual identity and the nature of desire.

To be lesbian

This example focuses on Marian, a 34-year-old homosexual woman, who came to group psychotherapy subsequent to a difficult experience in individual psychoanalytic psychotherapy. The group provided a more tolerant forum in which to explore the various facets of her identity and orientation, including the emotional struggle involved in becoming a lesbian.

Marian was a highly intelligent and accomplished professional woman who came from a conservative Jewish North London family. Although she had dated boys and had some heterosexual experience, she knew from early on that she was homosexual. She had been unable for many years to tell her family and, when she did, she felt that in spite of their attempts to understand, they were shocked, confused and hurt. She was the only daughter and the prospect of her neither getting married nor having children was a source of deep disappointment and shame.

She had entered individual psychotherapy in her mid-twenties with a psychoanalytically-trained female therapist. The therapist, she felt, saw her sexual orientation as deviant and interpreted her sexual wishes as a defence. Some of this was couched in transference terms as a problem about rivalry with the therapist. According to this interpretation, Marian's reluctance to acknowledge her rivalry with the therapist reflected her difficulty in competing with other women for a man of her own and hence her retreat into a homosexual solution. Marian found this form of interpretation dispiriting and confusing. She had struggled to come to terms with her lack of sexual desire for men and experienced the therapist's interventions as invalidating and undermining. What made this all the more difficult was that she found her therapist sexually attractive and was unable to reveal this, for fear of being shamed and rejected. She both resented the therapist for pathologizing her and longed for physical intimacy with her. Eventually, feeling that therapy was intolerable, she terminated after three years.

Marian sought further help approximately eight years later. During this time, she had come out more widely as lesbian and had largely enjoyed her lifestyle, while at the same time finding the unresolved issues about her family and social identity very painful. What precipitated her return to psychotherapy was a relationship she had established with another woman that had run into difficulties concerning her female partner's wish to have a child that would be reared by them as a couple. The prospect of becoming a parent to a child she had not conceived precipitated a crisis in Marian about her sexual identity, reawakening her underlying ambivalence about being a lesbian.

Returning for psychotherapeutic help, and suspicious of orthodox individual psychotherapy, she opted for group therapy in a setting that was known for its open approach to sexual difference. She joined an established twice-weekly group that in addition to several straight members included a gay man, a woman with a homosexual son and a married man struggling with homosexual wishes. The group was run by a female therapist who had been through an actively bisexual phase some years earlier. Although she had the usual anxieties about joining an ongoing group, Marian quite soon felt that she had made the right choice of psychotherapy. Her problems evoked

a strong resonance in several other members and their problems in turn touched her. The straight members were also
mostly attuned to homosexual issues and there were discussions which centred on the common fears of intimacy and
ambivalence in all relationships. At the same time, there were
vigorous and sometimes angry debates about what constituted
homophobia, about the rights and wrongs of children born to
non-normative couples and about the tensions between sexual
conformity and non-conformity. There was a high level of feedback in the group, with moments of pronounced intimacy, the
therapist encouraging a here-and-now approach that enabled
members to talk about feelings of attraction and desire that
arose in the group and that crossed the conventional lines of
gender and sexual orientation.

Belonging to this group of people struggling with issues of
diversity within themselves and within the social sphere
became a very meaningful experience for Marian. She was
increasingly able to address her most painful feelings about her
lesbianism, her alienation from her family and her sense of guilt
about this, as well as her grief about the likelihood of probably
never conceiving a child of her own. Through the latter awareness, she was able to understand her intense distress at the
thought of her partner having a child, a reaction born of envy
(even though she was sure she did not want to have a child this
way) and her overriding sense of what she had lost – as well as
gained – by being a lesbian. Marian's partner eventually succeeded in having a baby. Overwhelmed at first by the arrival of a
noisy and demanding infant, Marian gradually settled into her
role as a parent and in a complex, ambivalent way, grew to love
the child.

It is worth commenting on the difference between Marian's individual psychotherapy and her group therapy. The eight years' difference between her ending the former and starting the latter may
have reflected a cultural change in psychotherapeutic attitudes, in
which a greater openness about sexual difference became manifest.
Marian's experience of a rigidly unyielding approach in individual
therapy was by no means unusual at the time – and for some
decades – as documented in O'Connor and Ryan's (1993) disturbing

account of lesbians' experience in analytic psychotherapy. However, this change was – and is – by no means universal. There remain pockets of prejudice and pathologization in psychotherapy, as well as the continuing problem of heterosexual therapists, with little understanding of homosexual experience, treating gays and lesbians. The problem here concerns not only theory or ideology: it concerns the deeply personal responses that are evoked by sexual difference, which include anxiety and disgust, and how this interacts with power dynamics in psychotherapy, since the therapist is in a position of authority and the patient in a dependent position on that authority.

The constraints inherent in Marian's individual psychotherapy can be contrasted with the group presented here. The group represents some of the key elements of contemporary group psychotherapy: the presence of several individuals as well as the therapist creates a democratic process in which communication spreads across the group rather than being confined within the therapist-patient relationship; the therapist's greater transparency and the checks and balances in the group make it less likely that therapist-based distortion will influence the process; the presence of people with varying identifications enables a greater recognition of the range of human potentials, while, at the same time, the similarity of patients' identifications allows resonance across the group. Finally, the group provides a place of belonging in an often lonely and hostile world. These features are common to all well-functioning psychotherapeutic groups but may be of particular value in the therapy of problems associated with sexual identity and orientation. In this particular group, these processes were combined with an accepting, non-judgemental approach to sexual difference that facilitated an exploration of both heterosexual and homosexual orientations as valid lifestyles. That the therapist had herself been through a period of active bisexuality added to the resources in the group, helping Marian to find a therapeutic home.

The example highlights a further aspect of homosexual development – the need to mourn what is lost or unavailable through the realization of being homosexual. Crespi (1995), in a moving article, describes the sacrifice of conventional family life, children (although that is changing), the sense of biological continuity and so on. A therapy group which is affirmative of gay identity, as in the illustration, may facilitate this mourning more readily than a group in which it is necessary to assert a positive identity and deny any disappointment and regret.

What is homophobia?

Not all psychotherapy groups are as well-functioning as that described above. Tensions of difference of whatever kind are sometimes unresolvable and can lead to escalating and unproductive conflict. Throw in sexual difference and the tensions can intensify. In this example the group was paradoxically both helpful and unhelpful to an individual struggling with conflicts about his sexuality.

In a mixed-sex weekly group run in private practice, Malcolm (29) presented as his main problem a difficult and lonely marriage. He had also lost a male friendship circle since getting married and felt isolated and unsupported. This echoed earlier experiences in his life when, as a child, he had lost an older brother to whom he was close and, as a young man, had lost his father. In the group, he for some time gave no hint of a homosexual side. It was only in response to a gay male group member, who spoke openly about his sexual yearnings and frustrations, that he was able to share with the group a sense that he might be attracted to men. This was presented in very general terms. Members commented on his evasiveness. Was he referring to all men or specific men? What made him think he was attracted?

Eventually, Malcolm revealed that he had been preoccupied for some years with a passive homosexual experience he had had in the first year of his marriage. Hesitantly, and over a period of two or three sessions, he told the story. He had been out for a drink one night with a male work colleague. On realizing that he was well over the alcohol limit and could not drive home, Malcolm accepted his colleague's offer to stay overnight at his flat. He left a message explaining this on his wife's mobile phone. His colleague made a pass at him, saying that he particularly wanted to suck Malcolm's penis. He resisted but the colleague was persuasive and Malcolm allowed him to take off his trousers as he lay back on the bed. He remembered having a rather 'drowsy' erection, as he put it, but his colleague was very active and brought Malcolm to orgasm. Back at work, Malcolm made it clear to this colleague that he did not want to repeat the experience or embark on any other sexual experience with him.

236

However, he remained preoccupied with the incident. He had only slightly enjoyed the experience at the time, having felt a mixture of drunk, tired and anxious, but in his fantasy he began to feel very excited by the experience, repeating it in his mind in a more abandoned and pleasurable way. It became a secret masturbation fantasy and competed with his heterosexual desires.

Malcolm insisted in the group that this was the only homosexual desire he had ever felt and that in his mind he never went beyond this particular fantasy. Members in the group and the therapist interpreted this as a split-off fantasy that might have protected Malcolm from deeper homosexual desires. Malcolm, however, insisted that this was a 'one-off' and that he was essentially heterosexual. Further pressure was at times put on him to accept that he was homosexual or that he had a stronger homosexual side than he cared to acknowledge. But he remained obdurate. At this point a male member he was attached to in the group, Roy, left and this was followed by the entry of a new member, Ruth (34). She was an articulate, assertive lesbian whose antennae were out for any hint of homophobia. She made a strong entry into the group and quickly became an active presence. She was both admired and feared for her directness. Malcolm expressed ambivalence about her arrival and the group noticed that he had recently become quieter and more withdrawn in the group. In the time that he and Ruth overlapped in the group, he had not spoken about his sexual preoccupation but on one occasion relayed a story about how an elderly homosexual relative had died and not left a will, with ensuing chaos about the disposal of his estate. To the group's surprise, Ruth perceived this as a criticism of the deceased gay relative and angrily accused Malcolm of being homophobic. Malcolm flatly denied this but Ruth persisted. The incident distressed Malcolm, who soon afterwards announced his intention of leaving the group. He had planned to leave around this time anyway, he reminded the group, because he felt he had benefited sufficiently from the therapy. Two weeks later he was gone.

There was very little time in which to put Malcolm's leaving in context with Ruth's arrival and her angry accusation. No effort was made to interrogate the use of the term 'homophobic' and its effect on Malcolm. The group intuitively recognized the irony of the accusation, given Malcolm's struggle to come to terms with this aspect of himself, but this was not openly addressed. The group felt, with some regret, that Malcolm had slipped away and that something fundamental had been missed.

This group's paradoxical value to Malcolm consisted on the positive side of enabling him to talk about an encapsulated homosexual experience that was contrary to his view of himself and had yet dominated his fantasies. That he could describe the experience in detail and that members could engage with it reflects the group's capacity both to accommodate the non-normative incident and to grapple fully with sex as a highly specific, embodied act. Malcolm had been plagued by guilt and shame, particularly since the experience was associated with a deterioration in his marriage. The group's open and non-judgemental stance was a marked corrective to this.

At the same time, the group pressed Malcolm to acknowledge and own what they saw as his 'true' homosexuality. Whether in fact Malcolm was homosexual remained unclear. His denial might have been defensive but equally it may have been true that this one homosexual encounter was an exception and that he was predominantly heterosexual or, for that matter, bisexual. The addictive sexual fantasy could be explained in other terms, such as an obsessive-compulsive reaction. Whatever the case, the group adopted a fairly rigid position, reinforcing Malcolm's own rigidity and reversing the more familiar situation in which homosexuals are pressurized into complying with a heterosexual norm. This is why I refer to the group's 'paradoxical value' to Malcolm. It indicates how easily a group can slide from one form of 'oppression' to another; how difficult it is to maintain a balanced view on the fluidity of human sexuality.

There is another aspect of Malcolm's story that bears comment. This concerns the significant loss of male figures of attachment. The first was the loss of his older brother in his boyhood; then came the death of his father when Malcolm was a young man. More recently, he had lost his network of male friends after getting married. All this was echoed in the therapy group when Roy, the male member he was attached to, left the group not long before George joined. When seen in this context, Malcolm's homosexual experience and his subsequent obsession could be interpreted as his longing to be close to a man. This was not necessarily sex for sex's sake but sex as an expression of loss and absence: his passivity in the homosexual fantasy could have symbolized his wish for his brother, father and friends to come back and love him.

The point here is that sexuality is intricately linked to emotional development and that a full understanding of sexual behaviour must take account of the person *as a whole*. What might have mattered more to Malcolm than the question of whether he was gay, straight or bisexual, homophobic or non-homophobic, was his deep longing for a man's love. This ties up with recent reappraisals of a melancholic aspect of heterosexuality as reflecting unmourned homosexual loss (Maguire 2004). This thinking perceives a fragility in heterosexuality – in both individual identity and culture – and links it to unresolved loss. This aspect of loss – the separation from a real or fantasized valued male figure – is also a feature more generally of homosexual development.

'The good doctor'

Homosexuality is not one thing. Both as a lifestyle choice and a set of specific sexual preferences and behaviours, it has wide-ranging and diverse representations – just as heterosexuality does. It may be appropriate therefore to talk about *homosexualities* in the group rather than homosexuality. The next example illustrates the impact on the therapy group of a gay member's promiscuous and risky sexual behaviour.

Sexual promiscuity is often cited as a feature of homosexual life. Differing interpretations are put on it: an expression of the adventure-seeking, risk-taking aspect of male sexuality; a way of achieving sexual satisfaction without commitment; a self-destructive impulse (Socarides 1995). Writers in the queer theory school offer a positive reframing: gay promiscuity strives to evolve a community of friendship, diversity and open-ended non-possessive intimacy (Mohr 1992).

Alan (41) was a successful and popular GP with a busy suburban practice who joined a weekly psychotherapy group. Having considered joining an all-gay group, he opted for a mixed group because he was worried about his increasing immersion in a homosexual underworld. He felt that he needed the balancing influence of a more conventional group. The membership was predominantly heterosexual but with two gay men, Alan himself and a younger man, Paul.

In his preliminary interview with the therapist, before joining the group, Alan described a fraught existence in which, while working practically full-time as a doctor, he made daily and nightly forays into the gay world of active and promiscuous sexuality – cruising spots, cottages (toilets) and the backrooms of bars. He was particularly attracted to group sex, all the more if it was kinky. He was worried about this behaviour being publicly exposed and the damage this could cause to his professional reputation. He was also concerned that he had a developing drink problem. The combination of these problems was placing him under great stress and he feared a destructive effect on his work, although to his own amazement he still functioned competently as a doctor.

Alan was a good-looking man with charm and wit who quickly became accepted as part of the group, liked by both the men and women. Although he was fairly open about his problems, including his potential for self-destructive behaviour, the other members tended to personify him as 'the good GP', one they would all like to go to because of his apparent ability and affability. His communication in the group was often humorous, risqué, even irreverent, and this was enjoyed by all. He also at times took an informal leadership position in the group, offering useful insights to other members.

About a year into the group, Alan appeared to be making progress. His drinking problem improved and he had begun a relationship with another man that had the promise of deepening intimacy and stability. The good doctor was apparently also a good patient. What he did not tell the group at the time was that his compulsive sexual behaviour had continued almost unabated. In fact, his life was even more complex than before because he was now trying to maintain a new relationship at the same time that he was pushing himself on all other fronts.

Things came to a head following an especially intense week in which Alan had a fall-out with his male partner and felt that he was returning to the bottle. He broke down in the group saying that he had reached the end of his tether. The group was shocked to hear about his continuing promiscuity and risk-taking and challenged him for not keeping them in the picture. He complained that he had found it very difficult to talk about these things in the group and that members would feel let down if they knew the full truth of his activities. The group protested that they could and would tolerate hearing it all. But there was also some acknowledgement that they were taken in by his charm and competence as a group member and that perhaps this had added to his difficulty in confiding in them.

For some weeks the group remained alert to his problems and his need for help, but there was a gradual return to the status quo, to his being the good doctor available to everyone else and not fully sharing his own problems. The therapist remembered this as a powerful dynamic in which he got caught up himself. He had been pleased to have as active and facilitating a contributor to the group as Alan. It was potentially a difficult, uncohesive group and Alan's presence had done a lot to strengthen the group. The therapist was aware that there was very little focus on himself as a leader, on possible feelings of disappointment with him – particularly now that things were going wrong with Alan and the value of the group might be in question.

Alan's problems escalated again, culminating in a severe anxiety attack with depressive features that led to admission to a private hospital. He was treated there with a combination of drugs and cognitive therapy and decided to continue with this regime rather than return to the group. However, he accepted the group therapist's invitation to an individual meeting to review what had happened. In this, Alan said that although he had liked the group and found it useful in some respects, he could never talk fully about his sexual activities. He was now feeling an urgent need to do something active about this. He had been offered cognitive-behaviour therapy at the private hospital and intended going ahead.

A feature of this example is the deep split it reveals between an individual's professional role and his sex life: Alan was a respected, hard-working GP, simultaneously living out a highly promiscuous and potentially dangerous sexuality on the fringes of society. Splits of this sort may be more common than is usually recognized, in line with human beings' integration at a psychological level being less complete and consistent than traditional developmental theory would have us believe (Galatzer-Levy 2004). The fact that this was a homosexual lifestyle of an extreme variety is just one example of the sorts of split that may exist.

The extent to which the split was carried over to the therapy group is noteworthy. Through his charm and insight into others, Alan was able to be the good doctor in the group and avoid dealing with the pressing problems concerning his sexuality. The group bought into this, reifying him as 'the good GP' and colluding with the split. It was only when he broke down in the group that more serious notice was taken, but by this time the pattern of his splitting was entrenched and very difficult to reverse.

The example raises questions about how far group members can go in revealing their sexuality in a group, particularly when it reflects a high degree of non-conformity and the sex is transgressive or borders on the transgressive. What is the therapist's responsibility and what is the group's responsibility in instances like this? Should a patient in these circumstances be invited to join such a conventional group in the first place? What is the therapist's role in facilitating the patient's use of the group? Should the therapist have been more active in managing the process, challenging both the patient's splitting and the group's collusion with the split? This therapist appears to have been largely absent, or passive, and not to have attempted to influence the process. The fact that the group did not comment on his role – or challenge him in any way – suggests that this was part of an implicit agreement to keep Alan as the good doctor who, in fantasy, would cure their ills. The implication is that Alan's problem might have been tackled more productively had there been greater attention to the leadership issue in the group. This might have helped Alan to forgo his role as the good doctor.

As is highlighted throughout this book, issues concerning authority are paramount in the unfolding of the sexual subject. Not only was the therapist's authority in question in this example but also the authority of the group as a representation of social mores and values. Could the group have provided a firmer authority, more challenging of Alan's self-destructive behaviour? No doubt it was gratifying for them to see him as the good doctor, but by doing so they reinforced a social construct of caring and decency and denied the shadow side that existed in Alan – and probably themselves – and was played out compulsively in Alan's promiscuity. The shadow side of sexuality is always present in some form in the erotic imagination – even if it does not result in the degree of splitting reflected in this example.

Summary and reflection

This chapter has explored the expression of homosexuality in fairly typical, mixed-sex groups of mainly heterosexual orientation. The examples show how homosexual individuals, and in one case a patient with a confused sexual identity, attempt to communicate their sexuality and how the rest of the group responds. The process corresponds to some degree to the social situation outside the group in which homosexuality is a minority identity, although less concealed than in former times.

Documenting the response of such groups to homosexuality, it may be useful to posit two separate but linked levels or areas of response. One I describe very broadly as social, the other sexual. By social, I refer to attitudes towards homosexuality as an identity or grouping within society that, like most other groups, seeks recognition and legitimization. By sexual, I refer to specific patterns of bodily intimacy between individuals. I suggest that there is a gap between the social and sexual representations of homosexuality in the group setting: an enlightened regard by some groups for homosexuality as a social phenomenon contrasted with continuing difficulty in accepting the bodily aspects of homosexuality. This is not surprising, given our dominant heterosexual culture, but important nonetheless in developing a homosexual discourse that is relevant to groups. The underlying issue is reminiscent of an observation by Altman (1971: 59): 'Most liberal opinion is horrified by persecution of homosexuals and supports abolishing anti-homosexual laws, without really accepting homosexuality as a full and satisfying form of sexual behaviour. Such tolerance of homosexuality can coexist with considerable suspicion of and hostility towards it, and this hostility is reinforced in all sorts of ways within our society'.

The clinical examples presented in this chapter illustrate the complex nature of responses to homosexuality. In the first, a lesbian found considerable support for her struggles concerning identity and relatedness at a social level, particularly regarding her partner and her family, and was able to use the group very profitably. However, the bodily specifics of sexuality were not an aspect of her presentation.

The two other examples (both men) involved greater degrees of openness about sexuality *per se* but also reflect greater degrees of tension in the group's response. The second example was of a married man of avowed heterosexual orientation in conflict about a homosexual experience and fantasies, the third presented a highly promiscuous homosexual whose sexuality veered towards the dangerous and transgressive. In the former case, the group was seemingly open to the communication, in bodily detail, of an incidental but highly charged homosexual experience, but paradoxically closed to perceiving this as anything other than a reflection of an essential homosexuality. In this reification of a sexual category, the group was unable to allow the full stretch of the erotic imagination in a way that could permit a greater sexual inclusiveness. In the third example, the group's difficulty in taking in the full reality of the patient's sexuality reflected a division between the social representation of the individual as a valued citizen and the representation of his sexual behaviour as a denigrated split-off phenomenon. In the two latter cases, shame was an important aspect of the problem and there was some difficulty in both groups in helping to modify the degree of shame.

The examples highlight the impact of group process on the handling of homosexuality. The amplification of attitudes through several group members, a common feature of group functioning, results in the group pressure on Malcolm to accept his 'true' homosexuality. Similarly, the group seems to collude with 'the good doctor' to maintain the split between a respectable social self and a debased homosexual self. Dynamics involving the therapist are of course also crucial. In the first example, the female therapist's own experience of bisexuality may well have helped to facilitate the constructive process that developed in the group. In the third example, the therapist's relying on the patient as a kind of co-therapist, reflecting important leadership difficulties in the group, would have contributed to the collusion with the social-sexual split. The examples illustrate the ongoing interaction between social and individual in the emergence of the sexual discourse.

The three examples are representative of the manifold versions of homosexuality that are brought to groups and illustrate the necessity of maintaining as open a discourse as possible. They indicate the complex potential for the development of the homosexual discourse in therapy groups. Part of the present limitation in taking this forward is the marginalization not only of homosexuality in groups but of sexuality in general. It is likely, however, that the greater inclusion of homosexuals in therapy groups will challenge the status quo. Homosexuals, in spite of (or perhaps because of) a social history of oppression and discrimination, are often more outspoken than their heterosexual counterparts, more explicit about sexuality, more challenging of orthodoxy. Their voices may add strength to the emerging sexual discourse. Their position on the margins of society, as in all cases of marginalization, may enlarge our perspective of what lies at the centre.

This chapter brings to an end Part 3 of this book and the clinical illustrations that form the substance of these chapters. The examples of homosexuality in this chapter alert us to the complex and sometimes difficult representation of sexuality in the group, challenging any easy assumptions about the tolerance of sexual diversity in a mixed group with both genders and different sexual orientations. However, the overall thrust of Part 3 is towards the recognition of sexuality as a vital component of group psychotherapy, one that is present in some form in every group and that has the potential for generating a discourse that is creative and developing.

Part 4

THE LINKED DISCOURSE

15

THE THERAPIST

The importance of the therapist in dealing with sexuality in the group has been noted throughout this book. In this chapter, I draw together some of the foregoing observations with some additional ones, aiming to generate a more comprehensive statement about what may be the most crucial factor in the realization of the sexual discourse in group therapy. This also leads me into the area of training, with which I conclude the chapter.

The degree of openness the therapist shows to the expression of desire and sexuality in their diverse forms, as well as his or her attitudes and theories concerning sexuality, has a major influence on the facilitation or inhibition of the sexual subject. Probably more than in relation to any other discourse, members of the group will look to the therapist for clues concerning the extent to which sexuality can be discussed. This is also not just a one-way process. There is a constant interaction between therapist and group in negotiating the boundaries of sexual exploration, a moment to moment sensitivity about the form and content of the discussion, in which each reinforces or refutes the other in sometimes overt and sometimes subtle ways. All of this makes sense in the light of a social perspective of sexuality which situates individuals' experience of their sexual selves in a cultural context with normative prescriptions and hierarchies of what is socially acceptable and unacceptable, with shame as an important regulating and also restricting factor. This is complicated further by the discussion taking place in the public sphere of a therapy group with its own diverse membership and its developing momentum as a social grouping in its own right – exactly the conditions for a reconstructive view of sexuality but difficult to achieve and a complex task of facilitation and management for the therapist.

Stephen Mitchell (1996), describing the problems of the individual analyst in a contemporary world in which issues of sexuality and gender are of great concern, highlights the confusion of dealing with the striking diversity of theories and beliefs, as well as the complexity of gendered and sexual identities. If this is bewildering in individual psychotherapy, where the focus is on one patient, how much more so is it in group therapy?

The small but promising thread of published literature on sexuality in group psychotherapy has tended to emphasize the significance of the therapist's role. In this chapter I aim to take this observation further. My view of the therapist is as an active presence in the group, active in the sense of real, tangible, involved, in some way constantly interacting with the group, constantly revealing themselves in conscious and unconscious ways, personally affected by all that happens in the group. The therapist, in my view, cannot but have a considerable impact on the process, whether intentionally or unintentionally. This is a view that contrasts with any notion of therapist neutrality or detachment. Even if the therapist says or does very little, this is still a communication. The therapist is irrevocably present in the relational and intersubjective space of the group. I agree with Stacey (2003) who challenges Bion's much-vaunted advice that the therapist should suspend memory and desire. For one thing, I do not believe that this is possible unless the therapist comes from an altogether different and more ascetic discipline. For another, I think that the therapist's lack of desire, if it were possible, is undesirable for the group. The therapist is an embodied, gendered, sexed being and to pretend otherwise is folly. The therapist must be prepared to take their position as both the object and the subject of desire. This is in the spirit of the group as an object of desire, of the embodiment of the sexual subject.

Group and therapist authority

A point on which I depart from Foulkes concerns the way the group therapist represents authority. Foulkes (1964) argues that the therapist, apart perhaps from the beginning phase of the group when patients are usually at their most dependent, should avoid the role of an authority figure. This is in the interest of empowering the group and enabling it to find its own authority. He summed this up in his well-known formulation: 'a crescendo move in the maturity of the group and a decrescendo in the authority of the leader' (1964: 63). While I agree with the principle of empowering the group, I believe that the idea of the therapist relinquishing authority in some absolute way is misguided. The therapist's status and role, in my view, make this practically impossible. In any case, the need for a benign authority is natural and healthy and, further, the group needs to engage, wrestle with and challenge (the therapist's) authority in order to find its own. I have made this point in a previous publication (Nitsun 1996) and it is also backed up in the seminal study by Bennis and Shephard (1956) on group development. The issue of authority, I suggest, takes on a complex meaning in the light of sexuality in group therapy and I wish to elaborate somewhat further on it here.

The social perspective on sexuality makes clear that an individual's sexuality is constructed within a historical and cultural frame. As explored in greater detail in Chapter 7, this involves the influence of a prevailing morality, with its norms and standards, its constraints, its requirements for conformity and its penalties for non-conformity. This is paralleled at an individual level by the development of the super-ego, which various writers (e.g. Elias 1978; Gfaller 1993) see as the internal representation of social restraints. Inevitably, patients coming for psychotherapy, particularly where there are unresolved sexual concerns which may include transgressive wishes, are sensitive to the emergence in therapy of these aspects of themselves, with particular sensitivity to the judgement of the therapist. The therapist is seen, like it or not, as the authority, the representative of social values.

Patients coming for group psychotherapy are in a more exposed position than in individual therapy because of the public nature of the group. Although the group is likely to develop a morality of its own, whether in tandem with or in opposition to current social values, the patient will look to the therapist in some way for authentication of their gender identity or sexual orientation. Therefore, any gross relinquishment of the role of authority seems to me spurious. At the same time, because of the particular complexities and moral ambiguities of sexuality, the therapist can offer only a partial view. This is where the group comes in. By virtue of the diverse nature of the group, it generates a range of opinion in which the patient may find perspectives that are helpful. It also provides a series of checks and balances on the therapist's views, so that the possibility of therapist bias is challenged to a greater extent than in individual therapy. In this sense, the group does become an authority. However, this is different from the relegation of all authority to the group. Both are relevant: the authority of the therapist *and* the authority of the group.

Therapist sexuality

Perhaps the most elusive but important factor in guiding the sexual discourse in group psychotherapy is the therapist's own sexuality. This applies across the board: male, female, heterosexual, homosexual. As Courville and Keeper (1984) point out, the way the therapist deals with sexuality in the group is to a large degree an expression of their awareness and comfort with their own sexuality. This will influence the extent to which their sexuality is known about, sensed or available for comment in the group. This is not meant to imply that self-disclosure on the part of the therapist is necessary or appropriate, but that a degree of latitude is required in order that the group is able to address the subject of the therapist's sexuality. Otherwise, the hiddenness of the sexual discourse arises in the therapist, constraining group members in their attempts to communicate and explore their own sexuality. All of this may influence which aspects of sexuality can be spoken about and which not, which are acceptable and which unacceptable, including sexual feelings towards the therapist and between members themselves. These group processes reflect deep-rooted social constraints, which are embodied by individuals in their relationship to their own and each other's sexuality. The more the therapist is aware of their own position in the sexual matrix, and comfortable with this, the greater the chance that group members can openly express *their* sexuality.

Linked to the therapist's attitude towards their own sexuality is the question of morality. What is the therapist's personal morality regarding sexual behaviour in its diverse forms? This is a question that is seldom asked in any direct way, since, as Warner (2004) highlights, our moral frameworks are usually assumed and so remain obscured. Yet, they influence deeply the messages we transmit to our patients about what is permitted in the group and what is prohibited. Our morality is seldom as private as we may believe, even where it seems obscured, both in the sense of its contingency on social context and in the nature of the attitudes we reveal to others.

Questions of morality are in parallel to questions about prejudice. The therapist is a product, sexually, of a particular time and place, a particular family and society, which together with their own biological proclivities, endows them with a unique sexuality. This includes a gendered self, a sexual identity and a sexual orientation. The 'possession' of an identity – I put this in inverted commas because our current notions of identity are more concerned with fluidity than fixity (Schwartz 1995) – nevertheless renders the therapist able to identify with some more than others and to have similar blind-spots, biases and prejudices to most other people about sexuality. The difference is that in their position of authority, the therapist has greater influence on what is communicated than anyone else in the group

The important requirement here is the capacity for self-reflection. As in all domains of identity and difference, it is impossible to totally exclude prejudice. As Mitchell (1996: 71) says in relation to gender and sexuality, 'The analyst can never be free of personal biases and ought to be constantly searching for them in his or her own experience and in the patient's reactions'. Mitchell goes on to comment that the pursuit or attainment of a bias-free position is futile and disingenuous. The more productive route, and one that serves the patient better, is through 'an openness toward discovering and rediscovering his or her own prejudices, affinities, and fears as an inevitable and interesting feature of analytic inquiry'.

Since the therapy group offers a range of opinion – as noted above – there is in principle less risk than there is in individual therapy of the patients being at the receiving end of sexual bias. But this does not mean relinquishing therapeutic authority, which includes, indeed requires, the responsibility for examining one's own preferences and prejudices.

The paradoxical role

The plot thickens when we consider the therapist's paradoxical role as both conductor and participant in the group. As the conductor, they have the responsibility for what Foulkes (1948) called 'dynamic administration'. This includes the primary management functions: boundary-setting, time-keeping, rule-setting, and so on – crucial functions for the safe conduct of the group, particularly when sexuality with its possibilities of enactment enters the scene. These functions constitute another dimension which imparts authority to the therapist and sets them apart from the rest of the group. At the same time, the therapist is part of the group, constantly acting and interacting in the relational space of the group. This is in line with the group analytic paradigm, as well as the relational approach in psychoanalysis which encourages the therapist's more direct participation as a way of anchoring the therapy in a more real and reciprocal relationship. Arguing the value of this approach, Hoffman (1992, 1994) suggests that the analyst's more active participation does not 'close down potential space' but rather partially shifts the scene of creative reconstruction from the intrapsychic space within the patient's mind to the interpersonal or intersubjective space between them (quoted in Davies 1998b: 818).

The paradoxical nature of the therapist's role as both group administrator and participant comes to the fore in consideration of the sexual subject. Balint (1952) contended that every relation is libidinal and that in analysis it is important to allow the tension of libidinal attraction, holding this tension as far as possible at a near optimum level. Cox (1988: 265), writing specifically about groups, described the 'para-regression' needed of the therapist as they immerse themselves in their patients' perceptual and affective world. When it comes to sexuality, the sensual and impulsive aspects of relationships in the group place an even greater demand for both responsiveness and control on the therapist. Staying firm in their administrative role, protecting boundaries and representing their own authority, while remaining open to the libidinal thrust of the group and the unfolding of the erotic imagination, becomes all the more of a challenge.

Moeller (2002), in one of the very few articles on the subject, gives a very open account of the intensity of his response to the charged atmosphere of the therapy group. With responses ranging from sexual attraction to his patients to falling in love and wanting to 'marry someone on the spot', he highlights the constant potential in the therapist for sexual arousal and longing. His article is valuable because it dares to say what is seldom said. It also highlights the therapist's need to find a way of balancing the twin requirements of administrative conduct of the group and affective connection with the sexual thrust of the group.

This configuration is not taught in group therapy training. Like much of sexuality, it is part of the hidden discourse. It may come up in supervision, but usually in an ad hoc or fleeting way that does not fully prepare the therapist for the conflicting requirements of their role. Further, the intimate nature of some of these feelings is difficult to share in supervision, since supervision has its own restraints, its own parallel version of what is acceptable and unacceptable discourse.

Transference and counter-transference

The challenge to the therapist's involvement in the group, particularly in the context of desire and sexuality, is exacerbated by the occurrence of erotic transference and counter-transference. However, as I suggested in Chapter 13 on the subject, there is a prior question about whether erotic feelings towards the therapist, as well as the therapist's own erotic feelings, are actually transference-based or not. The terms 'transference' and 'counter-transference' are used so loosely in the psychotherapeutic milieu that they can obscure inter-personal responses that have no actual transference component. In some respects, accepting the immediacy of feelings for what they are – rather than viewing them as transference – creates a more difficult situation because we have no recourse to interpretive theorizing. The directness, rawness and pressing nature of sexual feelings in the con-sulting room then have to be confronted in their own right. For the therapist this may mean being both the object of desire and the subject of desire, each of which may be intense and difficult to manage.

There is also the possibility of sexualization, in which therapeutic issues that are not intrinsically sexual assume a sexual character, often for defensive reasons. Here, apparently sexual messages dis-guise problems in the therapeutic relationship such as dependency and anger, potentially reflecting unequal power balances in which the therapist is more powerful than the patient. These situations are ripe for sexualization. It is necessary then to distinguish between responses which are more genuinely sexual and those which are eroticized. A number of writers regard erotic transference as poten-tially growthful but eroti*cized* transference as highly problematic. The distinction, however, is often difficult to make.

Assuming that erotic transference and counter-transference do occur in groups – and the evidence, both in this book and elsewhere, confirms that they do – there are further points of discrimination to be made. I refer particularly to differing views about the regressive and progressive nature of erotic transference (Mann 2003). The 'regressive' view regards erotic transference as dysfunctional, deriving from primitively unresolved aspects of the personality; the 'progres-sive' view regards it as healthy. This again is not an easy distinction, since, as various writers suggest, there are usually both regressive and progressive elements involved. Further, in the therapy group, trans-ference is by definition a group event and, as demonstrated in the examples in Chapter 13, it both influences and is influenced by the group process.

Overall, sexual feelings between patient and therapist, whatever their origin and purpose, transferential or non-transferential, sexual or sexualized, are all the more charged in group therapy because of the openness of the group space, the presence of other members and the greater transparency of the therapist. Group therapists therefore may feel especially anxious about their role and responsibility in dealing with such erotic developments. Decisions about the embodiment of sexuality in psychotherapy and the therapist's function in this are probably among the most difficult in our work. Of the various contemporary psychotherapeutic approaches, the relational analysts seem to me to come closest to identifying both the potentials and risks of encouraging such intimate relationships in therapy. Davies (1998b: 808) highlights this in the following quote: 'As analysts, we steer a narrow and circuitous course between the kind of emotional responsivity that carries the potential to reawaken deadened experiences of hope and desire and the kinds of traumatically overstimulating interactions that become re-enactments of transgressive boundary violations'. Davies recognizes that the emergence of sexual feelings between patient and analyst can represent displaced and regressive enactments but mainly sees these feelings as growing out of the intimacy and mutuality that are at the core of successful analytic work. She also recognizes the possibility of our seductiveness as therapists – the part that wants to be an object of desire – but argues that we protect ourselves and our patients by the responsibility we exercise for constructive reflection and action.

The growing picture is of the group therapist's need to hold in balance the tensions between desire and action, arousal and containment, experience and understanding, in an attempt to safely and constructively realize the sexual subject.

Sexual diversity

We cannot ignore our reaction to sexual diversity because therapy groups tend now to attract people with a wider range of sexual identities and orientations than ever and we need to find ways of integrating this spectrum within our conception of the group. Most psychotherapists probably regard themselves as open and tolerant beings, but changes in the sexual landscape have been so rapid that knowledge of current sexual diversity, and the ability to comprehend and accept it, cannot be assumed. There is in addition the greater visibility of therapists of diverse sexuality themselves and the question of how this is integrated in their work.

In line with the emphasis in the rest of the book, I focus here on homosexuality, considering particularly the implications for the group therapist. Where and how does the therapist position themselves in the increased encounter between heterosexual and homosexual individuals that is current in groups? On the face of it, this might seem like a non-problem – indeed it is an important opportunity for all concerned – because of the greater social acceptance of homosexuality. However, we need to remain sensitive to both underlying prejudice and fears of exposure. At the present time I supervise several therapy groups in which there are gay and lesbian individuals who after many months have not yet divulged their sexual orientation, and another group in which a gay man has eventually revealed his homosexuality, after months of talking about his 'partner' in a way that convinced the group that he was heterosexual. These points are made to alert the therapist to issues concerning homosexuals' anxiety in predominantly heterosexual groups – and not to assume that the greater social acceptance of sexual diversity is such that homosexually-identified individuals will have no problem about revealing their orientation in a therapy group. These points are illustrated further in several clinical examples in Part 3 of this book.

This raises the question of the group therapist's own sexual orientation in dealing with homosexuality. In an earlier section I highlighted the importance of the therapist's sexuality in general. Here I want to look more closely at sexual orientation. I suggest that there are problems on either side, for heterosexual and homosexual therapists. The problem for heterosexual therapists is in empathizing with a form of sexuality that may seem very alien, irrespective of its greater prevalence in society. The straight therapist, male or female, may harbour feelings of bewilderment and disgust at the prospect of intimate sex between two people of the same sex. This is an aspect of homophobia, the culturally inscribed aversion to homosexuality. It may inhibit and constrain therapists in dealing with homosexual patients, and, furthermore, may express itself in rejection, sometimes subtle and sometimes overt, of the patient's sexuality. Rutkin (1995: 183) states his belief that 'the major counter-transference issue for *both* heterosexual and homosexual analysts working with gay and lesbian patients concerns the analyst's own internalized prejudice against homosexuality'.

This leads on to the subject of the gay or lesbian group therapist. There is progress in so far as it is common knowledge that many therapists, individual and group, are gay. However, there are ambiguities here too. Some therapists are openly gay, others selectively so. Some are known professionally to be gay, others not. Many questions arise here about the clinical implications of such knowledge. What do group members know about the therapist's sexual orientation? How much does the therapist divulge? What impact does this knowledge – or uncertainty – have on the group? These questions could go on and on. But the point, rather than raising all possible questions, is to raise awareness of the complex dynamics attendant on the therapist's sexual orientation and how this is handled, in the group, in supervision, in the wider professional setting, all of which are to some degree interrelated.

Having raised these questions concerning the complexities of sexual identification in both patients and therapist, it is important to recognize the very good work that is often done with sexually diverse patients in mixed groups. The fact of being a heterosexual therapist working with homosexual patients, and vice versa, does not debar sensitive and empathic relationships. There may be particular value therapeutically in these mixtures, helping to fill in developmental gaps in people's lives. A straight therapist who is open and sympathetic to homosexuality may be of great help to a homosexual group member. Similarly, a gay therapist who is in tune with heterosexual experience may offer something different and valuable to a straight patient.

The therapist and shame

Shame is another recurring theme in the treatment of sexuality, particularly in groups. I want here to look at two aspects of shame: the group therapist's handling of patients' shame and their handling of their own shame.

Dealing with patient shame

The convergence of cultural norms in both the necessary and unnecessary social restraints that Elias (1978) postulates, and the super-ego, with its individualized constraints, leads to an inevitable affective consequence: shame. In therapy groups, the potential for shaming is exacerbated by the number of people present and the possibility of sudden, unexpected exposure. The problem is compounded further by the discomfort created by personal shame – the shame *about* shame (Mollon 2003) and the invisibility of shame (Gans and Weber 2000) – both of which make it difficult to identify and address. Shame frequently remains hidden, concealed. Lewis (1971) contends that unidentified and unmanaged shame is often the basis of therapeutic impasse and negative reaction.

Particular sensitivity is required to the occurrence of shame and the tendency in groups to avoid disclosing shame. Combined with the secrecy surrounding sexuality, the elusiveness of shame presents a significant challenge to the therapist. Possibly the best that can be done is to show awareness of the potential for shame, to cultivate a climate of trust and to create an attitude of empathic understanding towards the experience of shame. Mollon (2003) suggests that empathy is the main tool we have for combating shame. Since sexual shame is often connected with the experience of trauma, usually trauma concerned with invasion, exposure or humiliation, the possibility of re-shaming in the group is ever-present. This requires vigilance and sensitivity on the part of the therapist – indeed, appropriately active intervention at times when shaming seems to be happening. The example of Belinda in Chapter 11 in Part 3 is such an instance. Here, the rejection of a seemingly affectionate extra-group overture engendered shame that appeared to be gender-, sex- and race-related, a complex amalgam of humiliation that resulted in Belinda dropping out of the group. The group and the therapist, in this example, responded passively to the incident when what was required was active attention to Belinda's shaming.

Dealing with therapist shame

An even more hidden and elusive form of shame, I suggest, is the therapist's shame – 'a much undiscussed topic' (Weber and Gans 2003). It seems to me necessary and important to recognize that therapists are not immune from the same experiences of shame that we more easily identify with patients, including shame about sexuality.

Therapists are usually aware that they struggle with very much the same issues of being human that their patients do. Human nature in our complex and paradoxical western culture is not generally destined to be complete, resolved, content. We are mostly incomplete, partially resolved individuals, struggling with the vicissitudes of life and the sense of ultimate insignificance in the wider universe. We are as prone to confusion, disappointment, despair, loss and envy as most of our patients. Similarly, in the sexual sphere, we may be struggling with a sense of vulnerable incompleteness. Stoller (1968, 1975) comments that much adult sexuality is a compromise, awkward, dissatisfied. While there may of course be moments, indeed extended periods of greater satisfaction, with feelings of pleasure and pride in our sexual selves, at least some of the time we may be struggling with issues of gender identification, with bisexual confusion, with sexual longing and frustration, with guilt about sexual fantasies, with fears of transgression, with incompatibility with our partners or the emptiness of not having a partner. All of these are sources of shame. We may sometimes even feel about our patients: 'If only they knew . . .'

It is the public difference between ourselves and our patients that makes the issue of dealing with our own shame so difficult. As Stacey (2003) suggests, the different categories of therapist and patient create 'I' and 'we' divisions which have clearly differentiated attributes. 'I', the therapist, am (or so it seems) strong, healthy, sane, sexually resolved. 'We', the patients, are weak, unhealthy, disturbed, sexually unresolved. The dichotomy creates in therapists a public self that enacts a social role which, in this case, is generally valued and admired. The fear of shame sets in when there is a danger of being discovered: 'Shame and embarrassment arise in the jarring cracks between the expectation of the other and the actual feelings and behaviour of the self' (Mollon 2003: 17). A form of vigilance is then required which protects us from exposure. The problem is that the vigilance also hardens our defences and so the roots of shame grow deeper. The example of 'the good doctor' in Chapter 14 epitomizes this dilemma.

I am highlighting this problem partly in order to question what effect our shame might have on clinical practice, whether it compounds our problems of dealing with patients' shame or possibly helps us to feel more empathic towards them. It would be problematic if the therapist, through fear of their own shame, were to seek to regulate shame in the group through its concealment rather than its recognition. I also suggest that as therapists we may suffer from a collective shame that both binds us together in our profession and separates us as individuals.

Language and the body

Sexuality is expressed in complex, sometimes direct and sometimes subtle ways, through both verbal and bodily communication. Generally, group therapists are not trained to attune to these nuances, another reason why the sexual discourse in group therapy is so elusive.

Language

I refer here to verbal language, the language of words (Schlapobersky 1994). This is the *métier* of group psychotherapy, the essential therapeutic medium. I believe that a further elaboration of our understanding of language in the group is necessary when dealing with sexuality. Rose (2002) notes how gender is inscribed in language and how this is reflected in verbal communication in the group. She suggests that power differentials between the sexes are expressed in language. But this is equally true of sexuality. Words are highly charged in the expression of sexuality, reflect significant gender differences, can be used to provoke and shock but also contain significant omissions, denials and confusions. Words can also be used to restrict and categorize rather than expand meaning. Lacan (1988a, b) speaks of 'full speech' and 'empty speech'. Derrida (1976) emphasizes the range of meanings and interpretations to which any utterance is subject. I mention these linguistic concerns in order to alert therapists to the complex aspects of verbal communication and the proclivity we all have to foreclose on meaning, particularly in an area as intimate, challenging and potentially disturbing as sexuality. Instead of grand theories and categories, we need to stay with moments of interaction in the group, constructing our understanding of intimacy through the language and co-creation of meaning by individuals in relationship (Weingarten 1991).

The body

I have noted at several points in this book the tendency in group analytic therapy to neglect the body in favour of words. The entire social constructionist ethos underplays material, corporeal reality in ways that leave the theory ungrounded and disembodied (Nightingale and Cromby 1999). But this is unacceptable in the explication of sexuality, which by definition is of the body. There is also the contradiction that the therapy group has such a strong physical presence, that the body is so much in evidence and sexuality so likely to be present in some form – yet this is spoken about with such caution and reserve. The lack of attention to the body, I suggest, may not be entirely innocent: it is the very physicality of the group which creates a chain of excitement, anxiety and defence.

There is a clear need in group psychotherapy to give greater credence to non-verbal communication and greater attention to the body. This includes the facilitation of patients talking about bodily experience as an integral part of sexuality. The body needs to be brought onto centre stage. This is another area in which the therapist can lead by example, encouraging a bodily discourse as part of the sexual discourse.

It is important not to lose sight of the social inscriptions that contribute to the experience of the body. As previously noted, the body is the site of culturally mediated judgements concerning shame and disgust, as well as excitement and pleasure. In the group, there is a rich opportunity to consider the confluence of the bodily and the social in the interest of a deeper understanding of sexuality – including an understanding of why it is so difficult for people to talk openly about the sexed body.

Training

The therapist is to a significant degree a product of their training. In order to discover the therapist's inheritance and influences we need to go to the training institute. We also need to consider the institute with a view to the future and the training of the next generation of therapists.

Psychotherapy training institutes have a major influence on the transmission of cultural norms through their theories of human development, their ideologies concerning training and practice and the social processes of training, with their configurations of power and dependency. Even where they set themselves apart from society, as critics or observers, training institutes generally end up enacting similar norms, values and restraints. This is at least as true of the sexual discourse as any other field of enquiry. Some institutes, particularly psychoanalytic ones, espouse elaborate theories of sexuality that reflect and reinforce conservative norms. They often fail to address openly some of the most glaring problems of sexual identity and orientation, such as those mentioned above, in which therapists and patients may be alike in struggling to integrate their sexual selves within an open and honest relationship with the contemporary world.

Group analytic training in the UK, I suspect like group psychotherapy in general, has to some extent skirted these issues by not developing a sexual discourse of its own. Its assumptions about sexuality have generally come from psychoanalysis, with its orientation towards conventional values, and it is only recently that gender and sexuality in group therapy have begun to be looked at in a more contemporary light. At least this is a beginning, since an enormous and challenging task awaits us in developing a sexual discourse that takes account of both the social construction of sexual identities and individual, subjective representations of sexuality – and hence provides a frame of reference appropriate to the group endeavour. In turn, this should equip therapists with a conceptual understanding, a value system and a set of thinking tools that would make the difference between struggling in the dark and having a torch to light one's journey.

The aims of such a discourse and of training, in my view, should include acknowledgement of all the profound and problematic issues of sexuality in human development generally and the therapeutic frame specifically. This would be the only way of addressing in some coherent form the issues of prejudice, fear and intolerance that constrain the sexual subject and reinforce the propensity for shame and anxiety that mark the sexual discourse. Some writers on sexuality in psychotherapy, particularly critics of conventional analytic approaches to homosexuality, make a point of demanding that psychotherapists deal fully with their prejudice and heterosexist bias before undertaking to work with gay patients (see Domenici and Lesser 1995). This seems to me a tall order for any one psychotherapist as an individual. Prejudice and bias, by definition, are not malleable and open to easy transformation. Rather, change comes slowly at social and institutional levels and this is where psychotherapeutic training, group or otherwise, is critical.

Bias also applies not just to some but to all. The current confrontation with heterosexist bias and homophobia tends to obscure equivalent homosexual bias. Homosexuals may find heterosexuals in some respects as difficult to understand as the other way round and may similarly experience areas of ignorance and prejudice. We do not want to replace one set of prejudices with another. Hence, all constructions of gender and sexuality, and the morality that informs them, should be open to scrutiny.

The structure and process of training

Several writers (Behr 1995; Hearst 1995; Scanlon 2000) have described the tripartite structure of personal group analysis, theoretical study and supervision in the training of group analytic therapists. This is equivalent to training in all analytic psychotherapies with the difference that in group training there is a greater emphasis on plurality and diversity, if only because the trainee is working with several people at any one time. This plurality makes the training challenging and rewarding but potentially more complex and demanding than equivalent individual trainings.

Scanlon (2000) describes the three elements of group training as distinct systems, between which there may be lesser or greater degrees of concordance. Arguing that supervision is the most neglected of the three areas, he goes on to focus specifically on the supervisory group process. However, my view is that these elements cannot be considered in isolation, since the links between them are vital in determining the integrity and coherence of training. This, I suggest, applies especially to the representation of sexuality, in psycho-therapeutic training, which has a particular potential for splitting, given its combination of intensely personal and political investments. There are also generational differences between therapists in their consciousness of current views and debates about sexuality and the extent to which they have been able to absorb these in their own thinking and practice: these too need to be considered when address-ing training as a totality.

Here are some impressions of the three components of training.

The personal group analysis

This is the least visible component of training, necessarily so because of the boundaries of confidentiality that must be preserved. How-ever, its lack of transparency constitutes a problem when we consider the many ways in which sexuality can be marginalized, dissociated and subject to both subtle and obvious group pressures. In so far as the training analysis is the one place where the trainee could and should be able to talk about their sexuality – and its complexities in life and in work – this is a unique opportunity, unlikely to be repeated again in the individual's career. This may apply particularly to trainees from sexual minority groups whose issues of identity and difference may create additional tensions in their training. All of this puts a burden of responsibility onto the training analyst who represents both the group *and* the trainee.

In the training situation in which there are built-in processes of evaluation, the invisibility of the training analysis is a significant factor. The evaluative focus is almost always on the trainee and not the analyst or the group. I am not suggesting any form of policing of the group but am raising the question of how, in the absence of a greater degree of transparency, we may reflect on the inherent invisi-bility of the group. This is one area where continuing professional development for the analyst is important, alongside ongoing super-vision, perhaps with peers, buttressed by institutional awareness and discussion of the particular complexities of the situation.

The trainee's experience of their analytic group influences in important ways not only their personal development but their future practice as a group analyst. Trainees internalize their therapy group in enduring ways, their group analyst often serving as a model – positively or negatively – for their own leadership of groups. Importantly, how therapists' own sexuality has been expressed and interpreted in their analysis or therapy is likely to influence how they respond to their patients' sexuality.

The theoretical syllabus

Until very recently, sexuality appeared to be a minor consideration in the academic syllabus of group analytic training. Generally, it was dealt with not as a subject in its own right but as an aspect of a broader topic. For example, I remember that in my own training – albeit about 20 years ago – the closest we came to looking seriously at sexuality was by reading Freud's 1922 paper 'On Narcissism'. Not only is the paper now approaching a hundred years old but it contains some of Freud's most pejorative categorizations of sexuality. More recently, there has been an increased interest in academic syllabuses in gender and sexuality as specific subjects but still largely within discourses that are outside group analysis.

I suggest that a theoretical programme that gives due weight to the importance of sexuality in the group would need to prioritize it quite differently. To construct such a syllabus merits careful thought as the relevant subjects vary from the social construction of sexuality to sexual development through the lifespan to the passionate and complex nature of desire. It is also important that these topics are owned by students themselves, undertaking their own researches into sexuality in groups, making it the subject of essays, dissertations and papers, taking the initiative in keeping the subject alive in the training community.

Supervision

Supervision is undoubtedly crucial in moulding psychotherapeutic practice and the value systems that support it. As Behr (1995: 4) observes, supervision is 'a way of transmitting an accumulated body of knowledge and expertise from one generation of therapists to the next'. This reflects the process of cultural transmission through supervision, influential but also complex and elusive, making it difficult to identify and evaluate.

There is considerable emphasis in group psychotherapeutic supervision on process, that is, the process of the therapy group, rather than its content. At one level, I agree fully with this emphasis since understanding process is vital to the effective conduct of groups. However, I also believe that the emphasis on process can obscure subjects that are content-specific and that reflect individual bias, such as morality, sexuality and power. A process perspective can be so sweeping and all-encompassing that significant matters of content – personal, moral and clinical – are lost to view.

Supervision can be seen as the integrating point in training: bringing together theoretical understanding and personal, subjective development; helping empathically to identify the trainee's anxieties, projections and blind-spots; and bridging the all-important theory-practice divide. There is sometimes confusion about what should be dealt with in supervision and what in personal therapy and, in my experience, it is only too easy to relegate the really difficult, thorny personal issues to the trainee's therapy. But often there is insufficient space in the therapy group to deal adequately with these issues or the trainee chooses for defensive reasons simply not to address them. The problem then falls between two stools.

I suggest that supervision is the appropriate place to deal with aspects of sexuality such as: the trainee's sexual orientation, acknowledged in a spirit of sensitivity and respect; the trainee's personal circumstances, such as whether partnered or single; their feelings about dealing with sexuality in their training group; their attitude towards the disclosing of sexual concerns in the supervision group; their response to sexual diversity; their perception of erotic transference and counter-transference; and so on. Within this discussion, there would ideally be opportunities to discuss matters concerning personal morality and judgement and how these affect the trainee's role as a conductor, etched against a framework of institutional values and principles. When referring to 'the trainee', I am of course not suggesting that attention be confined to a particular trainee. I am talking about all the trainees in the supervision group, working together, with the supervisor, to develop a spirit of trust and openness in the group.

The training institute

Some recognition is needed of institutional dynamics and the way they contribute to processes of splitting and dissociation. This applies not just to training but to the dynamics of the overall organization, which of course feed into training. We are all aware of how psychotherapy training institutes embody and enact some of the same human dilemmas they set out to understand and help in others. We are aware of how this frequently creates hostile sub-grouping and projection onto individuals who carry unconscious or rejected parts of the organizational psyche. This, I suggest, is linked to the encapsulation of dangerous, exciting and threatening subjects, of which sexuality is most certainly one. When this happens a process of scapegoating sets in and with this an escalation of splitting, in which the institution becomes gripped by conflict and impending chaos, all the while failing to take responsibility for its own contribution. If public exposure and admonition occur, this adds to a sense of collective shame which in turn is concealed by further blame and recrimination.

I mention this, the damaging impact it may have on ourselves as therapists, individually and collectively, as a further reason to recognize the impact of marginalizing the sexual subject – and to encourage an open and unflinching discourse.

Professional support

I am of the view that a greater degree of support and supervision than currently exists should be part of the practice of group psychotherapy. In spite of the current emphasis on continuing professional development, this is still haphazard in some institutes and taken up inconsistently by the membership.

Many therapists work in relative isolation, with minimal contact with peers. This is not necessarily a problem when things go well but when things go wrong, practitioners often do not know to whom to turn. Fear of exposure and criticism makes it difficult to share very real problems with others, compounding the concealment and the sense of isolation. I suspect that problems of dealing with sexuality in groups more frequently come into this category than we would care to admit and that, as we have seen, the intrinsic shame associated with sexuality increases the anxiety about exposure. This is especially true where the therapist's own sexuality is implicated – as it usually is. In all probability, most therapists struggle through difficulties of this kind on their own, or with minimal support, and a greater or lesser degree of resolution is reached. But is this the only way? Is there not more to be gained ultimately from the sharing with others of what are often universal concerns, even though they may be experienced as so intensely personal? The plight of the group therapist in the second example in Chapter 13, caught in the grip of an erotic counter-transference, with no one to turn to, illustrates the dilemma.

Perhaps this highlights the greatest conundrum about the expression of desire and sexuality in group psychotherapy. These subjects unite us in their common humanity and the cultural and moral prescriptions to which we have all been party, yet the individual and subjective experience of sexuality renders us separate and isolated from each other in ways which deeply privatize and conceal the discourse. As group psychotherapists, I suggest we suffer from similar processes of concealment to our patients and the rest of 'civilized' society. But we have within our capability the means to grapple more openly and fully with this problem than we have so far done.

16

OVERVIEW – LINKING THEORY AND PRACTICE

This book began with the intense and potentially explosive nature of desire, particularly sexual desire, and how important and challenging an aspect of all human subjectivity this is. I also challenged the marginalization of sexuality in group psychotherapy, especially as reflected in the overall published literature, and questioned the extent to which the group could constitute an object of desire, in the sense of a meaningful and valued psychotherapeutic approach, if it failed to provide a setting in which the turmoils of desire could be fully expressed and the complexities of sexuality recognized and understood. In this concluding chapter, I set out to consider what this book has taught us and to what extent it alters our perspective of sexuality in the group. I briefly review the findings of the theoretical discourse in Parts 1 and 2 of the book, highlight the main impressions of the clinical illustrations in Part 3 and attempt to draw these together, largely within the framework of the group psychotherapy perspective of sexuality I proposed in Chapter 7. With an eye to the future, I then consider the factors that may facilitate or obstruct the representation of sexuality in the group, concluding that there are ethical considerations which are integral to the debate and which must be addressed.

The theoretical discourse – a reprise

The theoretical discourse in Part 1 began outside of group psychotherapy, coming from a wider perspective in order to examine what sense has been made of sexuality and desire in the fields of philosophy, psychoanalysis and developmental psychology. What the theories explored have in common is their emphasis on desire as a pervasive force in human development and sexuality as a core, if not *the core*, aspect of the self, intimate relationships and the cultural order. The embodiment of sexuality is a major theme, with the detailed elaboration in some theories of the intricate mind-body link. These approaches are usually regarded as adopting an individualized view of human behaviour but often situate the individual in a social context. Psychological accounts of sexual development, for example, very much locate individual development in the family, peer groups and the social milieu more generally. Within psychoanalysis, writers such as Lacan describe desire as the thread of subjectivity that connects the individual and the cultural ethos, mediated through the processes of the imaginary, the symbolic and the real. Marxist thinkers within the early development of psychoanalysis, such as Reich and Marcuse, asserted the revolutionary potential of sexuality to transform society. The criticism that sexual discourses such as these take too little account of the social is, in my view, exaggerated. At the same time, these theories have stopped short of considering the deeper and wider influence of the social, in which sexuality, like all human behaviour, is seen in the light of a more penetrating social construction of our desiring and sexual selves, including the prescription of norms and values which seep through the entire edifice of sexuality. The result is therefore at times a close adherence to conventional values and standards, even where a questioning attitude seems to be implicit in the theory. Psychoanalysis epitomizes this tendency, presenting on the one hand a detailed and complex account of the erotic imagination and yet, in spite of dissenting voices, generally ending up with a conventional rendering of sexuality in which there is a high degree of judgement and pathologization.

I highlight both aspects of these discourses, the radical and the conservative, so as to argue that there is much in these approaches, including psychoanalysis, that is of value to us as group psychotherapists but also much that requires critical evaluation and revision. The shortcomings in some of these theories alert us to particular areas of sensitivity in a social view of sexuality that may guide our own efforts in establishing a sexual discourse. These are facilitated by contemporary political perspectives of sexuality which challenge rigid orthodoxies, particularly from a social perspective.

Moving on to the group discourse in Part 2, we find a diminished emphasis on desire and sexuality. There is a sparse though promising literature on sexuality in group psychotherapy, consisting of a few fairly recent papers (reviewed in Chapter 5) in which the authors raise an insistent question concerning why there has been silence on such an important subject. The marginalization of sexuality appears to exist across the group therapy literature, in the UK and abroad, but I focus my attention specifically on group analysis, the field of my own study. Group analysis has its roots in psychoanalysis, via Foulkes, and hence may be expected to represent sexuality more fully than most, but if anything we find a decreasing emphasis on the subject as the development of group analysis progresses, with one or two not altogether satisfactory exceptions. While this is consistent with the overall situation in group psychotherapy, pointing to a more general problem in the field, in group analysis this coincides to some extent with the movement away from psychoanalysis towards a sociological approach which tends to eschew individual perspectives of human behaviour. Sexuality is virtually absent from the discourse. Although the body is referred to, the discourse is largely de-individualized and disembodied. It could be that these writers have simply not addressed sexuality – there is no obligation in our field to do so – but it is striking that in what are presented as comprehensive accounts of human behaviour, this particular aspect should be so neglected.

The inference in the above is that the more social our approach is, the less place there is for sexuality. But I suggest the reverse: the social perspective is critically important in substantiating a sexual discourse. By looking at sexuality within a cultural and historical frame, we can not only begin to understand more about its marginalization in some discourses, but can begin to construct a framework for representing it more fully in the therapy group. With this in mind, I move on to my proposal for a broad group psychotherapy perspective on sexuality.

A group psychotherapy perspective of sexuality

Within the framework I propose, the marginalization of sexuality in group psychotherapy mirrors the conventional social restraints that influence what can and cannot be revealed in groups. There are unconscious rules about how far we can go in revealing our sexuality, compounded by our own sense of embarrassment and shame, but fundamentally more to do with orthodox norms and standards that exert a pressure for conformity. This is a problem in individual psychotherapy as well, but here the 'confessional' nature of the dyadic patient-therapist relationship is more familiar and may be experienced as a safer bet. The therapy group stirs up additional anxieties by being a social group itself, thereby exacerbating the anxiety about exposure and shaming.

Parallel to the fear of exposure is the interrelated wish and fear of sexual enactment. While the expression of sexual desire implies the wish for enactment, there are social rules that prohibit enactment and influence the settings in which sexuality can take place. The therapy group is by nature a verbal, reflective process that debars sex between group members both inside and outside the group, creating a paradoxical situation in which members are expected to become closer, indeed spend many hours together in a defined physical space, but not to enact their wishes towards each other. This means that sexual attraction and desire may be uncomfortable and risky in the group. The tight boundaries that therapy groups tend to hold around sexuality reflect the anxiety that, without firm controls, things may get out of hand, sexually and otherwise. While this makes sense in terms of the integrity of the group, it means that sexuality may become dissociated, denied, hidden, mirroring conventional social restraints.

While restraints are necessary in any society, indeed any group, in order to ensure the integrity of the group, there is an important question about which restraints are necessary and which unnecessary. Unnecessary restraints usually operate through power and control and compromise individual choice to an unnecessary degree. The individual super ego is, in the view of writers like Elias (1978) and Gfaller (1993), the mirror of social restraints. Both can be cruel, excessive and crushing in their demands of the individual and my view is that the group is there to unravel these demands not to reinforce them.

The psychotherapy group has a choice. Although it is of course not as stark as this, it can choose to go down the road of conformity or it can choose to challenge conformity. This applies not only to actual sexual behaviour but to the morality of the group and whether it deals with issues of restraint in an open, imaginative, facilitating way or succumbs to exactly the same restraints that mirror society. This may mean the difference between being able to talk openly about sexuality in the group and not. Foulkes' Basic Law of Group Dynamics comes in here, a controversial concept which posits the function of the group as leading the members towards the norms of society to which it belongs. There is a benevolent interpretation of this law, namely that the group encourages the ironing out of excessive individual differences into the interest of group cohesion. However, I prefer a conception of the group as representing an alternative social authority, as being able to evolve a fairer, kinder morality that encourages members to bring their individual differences into stark relief, sexual and otherwise, and that provides a tolerant space for considering the articulation of a sexual self. Within this expanded space, there is the potential for transformation, for challenging and reconstructing sexual narratives.

My concern with the marginalization of sexuality in group psychotherapy is that this colludes with the fundamental ambivalence of society towards sexuality and the unwritten requirement that sexuality is kept at bay in 'civilized' groups. Once we establish a more positive frame for sexuality in the group, we can look more seriously at individual differences across a wide spectrum and consider the particular problems of substantiating a sexual self, how this is reflected in the group and how the group impacts on it. I believe that this discourse could be enriched by psychological and psychoanalytic perspectives of sexuality, minus their prejudicial tendencies (in the case of psychoanalysis) and appreciated for their insights about the embodied sexual self. I also suggest that there may be value in considering a notion of the sexual self, not in isolation from the rest of the self but as reflecting individuals' particular ways of construing and performing their sexuality in the complex social universe they inhabit. This includes the erotic imagination, the nature of their actual sexual relationships and the social role they take in the representation of their sexuality.

An important parameter of the self-society link has to do with the tension between the individual's public persona and their private experience of themselves and the world they live in. This is more dichotomous in some individuals than others. But since sexuality is often one of the most secretive parts of the individual, if not the most secretive, the private self is likely to contain all the hidden desires and impulses that are felt to be most at variance with social standards and norms. This is the part of sexuality that is usually most closely guarded and, I believe, one of the reasons people fear joining therapy groups. They fear that this part of themselves will be involuntarily revealed or that they will be under pressure to reveal it. However, the goal of the group is to create a safe setting in which these phenomena can be voluntarily explored and the group can offer an alternative, more generous morality.

The clinical discourse

There are limits to the conclusions that can be drawn from the examples presented in Part 3 because they are in the main relatively isolated examples drawn from different groups. Also, the illustrations are selective in so far as it was necessary to present material in which sexuality featured prominently in the group, whether positively, negatively or ambivalently. These qualifications notwithstanding, the examples combine to confirm that sexuality is a very real and very significant part of the therapy group.

The following are some impressions. The material suggests that in various ways, in spite of anxieties, there are important libidinal or erotic connections in the group. This, when shared, tends to have an energizing, vitalizing, complicating effect on the group and to draw members together in states of surprise, intimacy and often heightened emotionality. The experience is akin to Bion's concept of 'passion', which he linked to three salient emotional states: LHK. L stands for Love, that is, loving and being loved; H for Hate, hating and being hated; and K for coming to Know and being Known (Billow 2002). The loving and hating elements of sexuality are clearly presented in a number of the examples, while knowledge or being known are reflected in several of the conversations reported, usually concerning the nature of sexuality, both as a shared phenomenon and as having very individual variations. Getting to 'know' about each other as sexual beings and 'knowing' about sexuality are both aspects of this. In this way, sexuality is taken outside the zone of privacy and individuality and becomes a 'property' of the group as a whole.

The libidinizing process of the group is seen most clearly, and in unmodified form, in the children's group in Chapter 8. Here, the more adult defences have not yet set in and the children are free to go on a journey of discovery, both literally and metaphorically, with the sea representing the discovery of play, desire and intimacy in the group. That this occurred in a highly traumatized group and was associated with a transformation in the group is a measure of the strength of the libidinal connection. The physical intimacy and active play in this group are inappropriate to adult groups but there are several examples of how in adult groups, as well, the libidinal connection can be achieved in words and symbolic play.

The ways in which sexuality and desire are communicated in the therapy group bear comment since these differ from the process in individual therapy. In group therapy, particularly group analytic therapy, communication takes place through a process of free group discussion, the equivalent of free association in individual analysis. This occurs through resonance and associative response in which group members pursue a theme begun by one of the members: A says something with a sexual theme, B picks up on it, C gives his association, D expands on it and so on, the theme becoming amplified in the process (several illustrations in Part 3 reflect this). The process encourages a loosening of associations and the possibility in conversational form of sharing aspects of sexuality that might otherwise be very difficult to reveal. This can be compared with individual therapy in which the revelation of sex is more likely to be on a confessional basis, one person, the patient, revealing their sexuality to a second, the therapist, in a more vertical, hierarchical fashion in which the therapist is endowed with the authority to interpret or diagnose the patient and the privilege of revealing nothing themselves.

When sexuality becomes a property of the group in the way described, it appears to be possible to discuss aspects of experience that are normally kept hidden because of the shame or hurt associated with them, subjects that reflect social taboos and fears of transgression. This is perhaps most vividly illustrated in the group that was able to share incestuous feelings in childhood and adolescence (Chapter 9). The theme of incest is important here not just because of its historical significance in patients' lives but because of fears that sexual desire and arousal in the immediacy of the group are tantamount to incest. That patients in the aforementioned group could recognize the link enabled them to connect past with present and to move on from there. The constructive exploration of incestuous feelings indicates – at least in this group – that one of the most taboo areas of sexuality can be addressed successfully within the therapy group. There are other examples of individual patients who revealed aspects of their sexuality that they imagined would be impossible to talk about in the group. This included the man who had sexual fantasies about his children (Chapter 11), another who had long-standing repressed homosexual longings (Chapter 11) and a third whose sado-masochistic fantasies inhibited him from having sexual intercourse with women (Chapter 12). In at least some of these cases, there was not only the relief of sharing long-concealed and troubling secrets but a process of working through, often in close interaction with another group member or members.

In most of these cases, even though the outcomes were not necessarily straightforward, the group functioned in the way I have described: as a democratic authority that represents a kinder, more empathic morality than is usually common in these situations. This capacity in groups is reflected particularly in the theme of 'the group as witness' that I introduced in Chapter 11. Here, rather than the whole group sharing in a collective resonance, part of the group functions as observers, watching and reflecting on another part of the group, quite often two people struggling with how to express attraction or affection towards each other or dealing with some other aspect of intimacy. Where the group is able to support the healthy aspects of pairing, adding the perspective of 'the third', there is the possibility of facilitating and supporting the interaction in a way that is usually missing in social groups.

The reconstructive potential of the group can therefore be realized in several ways in relation to the sexual subject: through the overall group discourse, in which all or most members contribute their associations; through the relief of sharing sexual secrets and overcoming the guilt and shame associated with the experience; through the pairing of members in intimate encounter; and through the observational function of the group which represents an alternative social authority, a constructive witness and a forum for change.

I have so far emphasized the positive illustrations of sexuality in the group and the processes whereby this is mediated. It is important, however, to mention the more problematic and less successful attempts to grapple with desire and sexuality. The most negative instance is the male sub-group in Chapter 10 that held sway over the group in a cynical, despairing, anti-libidinal way, managing to eject several female members in close succession. Here, if anything, it was the absence of desire or sexuality that was the problem: a deathly turning away from the libidinal impulse that transfixed the group in a state of impasse. Desire here can be seen as dissociated, linked to traumatic earlier experiences, and harbouring sado-masochistic wishes that were indirectly expressed in the destructive attack on the group. This, however, could be contrasted with another group in the same chapter which was able to confront the dissociation and integrate the splits in the group.

Sexual pairing in several examples in Chapter 12 was very challenging to the therapist and the group. By this I mean the strong attraction that takes place between two people, which is either expressed within the group or enacted outside the group, mainly without the group's knowledge. In the former, where the pairing was openly acknowledged, there were generally constructive developments, the group proving helpful in supporting the relationship in a realistic way. Where sexual enactment occurred outside the group, however, there was considerable fallout. In the one group where this was successfully handled, the therapist intervened strongly, emphatically re-establishing the group boundaries and confronting the meaning of the relationship in the group context.

The expression of erotic transference and counter-transference, reported in Chapter 13, was also problematic. In the first of these examples, a secret transference mediated largely outside of the group was part of the unravelling of the group. In the second example, the patient benefited from a strong emotional involvement with the therapist, which appeared to have an erotic component, but the therapist was left with an unresolved erotic counter-transference. Common to both these examples was the fact that the transference issues were not discussed in the group. Both therapists chose not to bring these issues into the group and the consequence was a problematic intensification of the transference and counter-transference relationship, the therapist feeling increasingly isolated and having to contain turbulent feelings on their own. This raises the question of what difference it would have made had it been possible to discuss the sexual transferences in the group – how it might have affected the transference process and the overall group. The examples here also suggested some important connections between unresolved loss and erotic transference, the longing for the new object representing the wish to replace a lost object. The demanding nature of erotic transference and counter-transference in the group was further taken up (in Chapter 15) in terms of the therapist's need for supervisory input and more general professional support.

There were differential outcomes in the groups in which homosexuality was a prominent feature. In one of these, a lesbian found the group very supportive and helpful in terms of issues of social acceptance and identity. In two different groups (in Chapters 11 and 14), men who regarded themselves as heterosexual but had vivid homosexual longings were able to speak openly about their desires after some time in the group. In one case, this was helpful in overall terms; in the second, the group's insistence on categorizing the man as homosexual led to his withdrawal. In a further example, a man whose compulsive and risky sex life was split off from his professional and social roles, found this split replicated in the group. The group was seemingly open to his homosexuality but at the same time played into the split in a way that was unhelpful to the patient. In this group, there was particular confusion about the leadership of the group. The patient in question, a doctor, took a leadership role, partly in response to the actual group therapist's uncertainty about his role and his tendency to hand over the leadership to the patient. This complicated the issue of authority in the group, leaving the patient floundering due to a lack of a constructive authority to which he could turn. Hence, while I have emphasized the value of a benign morality in the therapy group, I am not advocating the absence of either authority or morality. A fair authority may also have to be a firm authority. Effective group leadership and boundary setting are important components of this.

The contrasting outcomes reported above highlight the complexities arising in the mix of heterosexuals and homosexuals in a group. While we live, ostensibly, in an age of sexual diversity, it is important nonetheless to question assumptions about the ease with which this mix can be realized. We need to be wary of a sharp swing from prejudice to political correctness in a way that obscures underlying anxiety, confusion and hostility. The particular absence of clinical study and publications on this aspect of the group process adds significantly to this problem.

Returning more generally to the examples in which the expression of sexuality was most problematic, it is worth noting some common features. First, the individual patients involved had notably high levels of psychological disturbance. For example, the recalcitrant men in the 'anti-desire' example had severe and long-standing problems, with a large incidence of abuse in their childhoods. Second, in some cases, the therapists were inexperienced and lacked adequate training. Third, the therapists felt unsupported in their work so that when problems arose they had no one to turn to. And fourth, the expression of sexuality occurred prematurely, at too early a stage of the group's development to facilitate the constructive handling of the theme. It is important to note that where these negative developments occurred, the problems were in the group process and not just the individuals.

These examples illustrate the parallel between anti-group developments and the failed representation of desire in the group. I have previously suggested that anti-group manifestations may occur in situations in which sexuality is feared and avoided, generating tensions that undermine group cohesion. The present examples further demonstrate the negative impact of sexuality that cannot be adequately contained, processed or assimilated in the group.

In spite of the difficulties described above, the overriding impression is of the groups' capacity to embrace sexuality and desire, and the value to the group of an open exploration of the subject. That this ran into difficulties in some groups is part of the unpredictable process of the group, particularly in the face of unhelpful contextual factors such as those noted above. This, in my view, does not detract from the considerable potential of the therapy group as representing a group of peers who together can own the possibilities and problems of sexuality, an alternative authority that offers a fairer, kinder morality than is usually encountered and a transformational space in which difficult sexual experiences can be processed and reconstructed.

Through all of this, there is a sense that the group itself evolves as an object of desire. In most of the positive examples presented, the libidinal connection invigorates the group space through play, intimacy and affection. Further, where the deeper and more difficult aspects of sexuality can be countenanced within the group, and where this is dealt with openly and constructively, there is a clear sense of the group's meaning and value to the participants. The most creative and transformational instances described in Part 3 were those in which sexuality was voiced in a group in which there was already a relatively high degree of trust and commitment. In turn, the emergence of a bold and constructive sexual discourse deepened identification with – and appreciation of – the group.

Ethical considerations

There appears to be sufficient evidence to suggest that sexuality is a fundamental part of group life and that its more open representation in the therapy group could strengthen and widen the therapeutic process. However, because this is a highly charged subject with considerable sensitivities, there may be real problems about the extent to which this is realizable. Some of these sensitivities have ethical implications and the way they are managed will depend on the group therapist and the position they take.

The major ethical issue confronting group therapists when considering how actively to encourage a sexual discourse has to do with the safety of the group. There is an inevitable fear that raising the sexual temperature of the group will generate feelings and impulses that cannot be contained within the group boundary and that will lead to acting-out. Another alternative is that group members will be stimulated and aroused in a way that cannot be satisfied because of the prohibition against sexual enactment, creating a tantalizing and frustrating situation. This applies to the therapist as well: they may be afraid of the temptation to transgress sexually in a situation in which they feel particularly aroused. Although enactment may be more difficult in group than in individual therapy, because of the group's greater transparency, the fear of enactment – usually born out of a wish to enact – still exists. Given the professional strictures that currently surround sexual misconduct, many therapists will choose to play safe. Of course, sexual enactment may occur anyway, but this is different from actively pursuing a path that is felt to increase the chances of transgression.

The problem with playing safe is that it leads to what Samuels (1999) calls 'safe analysis', producing a de-sexualization of the therapeutic process. Although the principle of safety is fundamentally important in the clinical situation – in fact it is our primary responsibility – there may be ethical considerations of a different order if this is taken to an extreme. Is it ethical to repress, or at least marginalize, a subject of such importance as sexuality in the sphere of an individual life? And if it needs the therapist to take the lead in legitimizing the subject, is it ethical to hold this back? In any case, as Davies (1998a, b) suggests, not taking up sexuality and not dealing with it directly is *not* necessarily a safer alternative. Several of the examples in Part 3 indicate that sexual enactment took place when sexuality was *not* addressed and that enactment was prevented when sexuality *was* addressed.

There are some linked ethical considerations. One concerns the split between public and private selves and the way sexuality is represented within the split. Much of individual sexuality is hidden, kept separate from others for fear of exposure and embarrassment. Even if people recognize the necessity of talking about it, there are anxieties. How far is it appropriate to push people in this sensitive area? How do we differentiate between the sometimes necessary encouragement to share very personal material and the pressure that can occur in psychotherapy to reveal all? We need to recognize both the overt and subtle exercise of power in psychotherapy and the way in which the group, and not just the therapist, may exert unwanted pressure on the individual.

There are further ethical concerns in relation to sexual identity and diversity. The whole area of identity is charged with social significance. I am aware, for example, that I have not included in the book any appreciable treatment of issues such as race, ethnicity and class. This is essentially because of the limits of space in a single book, but I recognize the complex interplay of identity, of which sexuality is only a part. It would be questionable if one aspect of identity, such as sexuality, were elevated to the detriment of another, but part of the problem of clinical work is holding in mind all the different facets of individual identity. In groups this is often helped by the intelligence of the participants and their sensitivity to difference within each other. Even then, crucial aspects of identity may be overlooked, denied or subverted and, as therapists, we are continually required to monitor our patients' and our own exclusionary processes.

Ethical considerations in group therapy possibly come to the fore more in relation to sexuality than any other subject. This no doubt is a further reason for its marginal status, since avoiding and concealing it is seemingly a way of pre-empting ethical conflicts. These concerns, as with all aspects of sexuality, have been all the more difficult to resolve in the absence of an adequate theoretical and practical discourse.

Social reconstruction

How much do we believe that the psychotherapy group can contribute in some way towards the reconstruction of society in the sense of facilitating more open communication between people, a more challenging attitude to social norms and a more liberal view of the erotic imagination? Throughout this book I have hinted at this possibility. However, therapists are more likely to be concerned with the maintenance and development of their groups in the here-and-now of the clinical setting than with the challenge of making a wider social impact. The idea of influencing society may seem like a distant ideal, an omnipotent fantasy. However, we know that there are limits to change that can be achieved at a clinical level, in the absence of change at a cultural level. Also, as long as we operate within the most orthodox norms of society, we not only mirror social constraints, we reinforce them.

However private and subjective sexuality appears to be, it is always a reflection of the social processes that are inscribed in its formation. Even if the more open representation of sexuality in the therapy group touches and alters one individual, this is a contribution to social change. As the form of psychotherapy that in its structure and process is closest to the social domain, group therapy may have more to offer in this realm than we commonly recognize.

Conclusion

This chapter has attempted to bring together the theoretical and clinical discourses on sexuality in group psychotherapy, using clinical illustrations to substantiate a number of the hypotheses that I have generated and explored in the course of this book. Theoretically, sexuality is at the interface of individual and social models of human behaviour, highlighting the existence of the social in the individual and the individual in the social, and indicating the potential for a more clearly articulated sexual discourse in group psychotherapy. Desire in its passionate subjectivity and culture in its profound sweep both belong here, as contrasting but interlocking elements of the same totality. Yet, sexuality and desire have been singularly absent from the group psychotherapy discourse, reflecting, I believe, a problem that goes to the heart of our models of the group. Clinically, sexuality is a sensitive and complex aspect of group relationships and its increased representation in the therapy group raises a number of concerns, including ethical ones. There may be a choice to be made between a safe analysis/therapy that underplays sexuality and a bolder venture that illuminates sexuality, while acknowledging the risks of exposure and enactment. The overriding impression of this book, however, is that there is considerable value in the more active inclusion of sexuality in the group and that, complexities and difficulties notwithstanding, there is the potential for transformation of sexual selves through the therapy group. It is time for both the theory and practice of group psychotherapy to address sexuality more openly and directly. The increased recognition of sexuality in the group is, I suggest, part of the increased substantiation of group therapy as a form of psychotherapy in its own right, that is, complete, internally consistent and clinically assertive: the group as an object of desire.

REFERENCES

Abel-Hirsch, N. (2001) *Eros*. Cambridge: Icon Books.

Alonso, A. and Rutan, J.S. (1988) The experience of shame and the restoration of self-respect in group therapy, *International Journal of Group Psychotherapy*, 38(1): 3–14.

Altman, D. (1971) *Homosexual Oppression and Liberation*. New York: New York University Press.

Angelides, S. (2001) *A History of Bisexuality*. Chicago: University of Chicago Press.

Armstrong, J. (2003) *Conditions of Love*. London: Penguin.

Balint, M. (1952) *Primary Love and Psychoanalytic Technique*. London: Hogarth Press.

Bataille, G. (1975) *L'Erotisme*. Paris: Minuit.

Behr, H.L. (1995) The integration of theory and practice, in M. Sharpe (ed.) *The Third Eye*. London: Routledge.

Behr, H. and Hearst, L. (2005) *Group-Analytic Psychotherapy*. London: Whurr.

Benjamin, J. (1986) The alienation of desire: women's masochism and ideal love, in J.J. Alpert (ed.) *Psychoanalysis and Women: Contemporary Reappraisals*. Hillsdale, NJ: Analytic Press.

Benjamin, J. (1990) *The Bonds of Love*. London: Virago.

Benjamin, J. (1998) *Shadow of the Other: Intersubjectivity and Gender in Psychoanalysis*. London: Routledge.

Bennis, W.G. and Shephard, H.A. (1956) A theory of group development, *Human Relations*, 9: 415–37.

Bersani, L. (1995) *Homos*. Cambridge, MA: Harvard University Press.

Billow, R.M. (2002) Passion in group: thinking about loving, hating, and knowing, *International Journal of Group Psychotherapy*, 52(3): 355–72.

Bion, W.R. (1961) *Experiences in Groups and Other Papers*. New York: Basic Books.

Bledin, K. (2003) Migration, identity and group analysis, *Group Analysis*, 36: 97–110.

Blum, H.B. (1973) The concept of the eroticized transference, *Journal of the American Association*, 21: 61–76.

Bollas, C. (1987) *The Shadow of the Object: Psychoanalysis of the Unthought Known*. London: Free Association Books.

Bollas, C. (1992) *Being a Character*. London: Routledge.

Bollas, C. (2000) *Hysteria*. London: Routledge.

Boothby, R. (1991) *Death and Desire: Psychoanalytic Theory in Lacan's Return to Freud*. London: Routledge.

Bowden, M. (2002) Anti-group attitudes at assessment for psychotherapy, *Psychoanalytic Psychotherapy*, 16(3): 346–58.

Bowie, M. (1991) *Lacan*. London: Fontana.

Braunschweig, D. and Fain, M. (1971) *Eros et Anteros*. Paris: Petit Bibliotheque Payot.

Breton, A. (1937) L'Amour Fou, in J. Mundy (ed.) (2001) *Surrealism: Desire Unbound*. London: Tate Publishing.

Britton, R. (1989) The missing link: parental sexuality in the Oedipus complex, in R. Britton, M. Feldman and E. O'Shaughnessy, *The Oedipus Complex Today*. London: Karnac.

Britton, R. (2003) *Sex, Death and the Superego*. London: Karnac.

Brown, D. (1994) Self development through subjective interaction, in D. Brown and L. Zinkin (eds) *The Psyche and the Social World*. London: Routledge.

Brown, D. (1998) Foulkes' Basic Law of Group Dynamics 50 years on: abnormality, injustice and the renewal of ethics, *Group Analysis*, 31: 391–419.

Brown, D. (2001) Contribution to the understanding of the social unconscious, *Group Analysis*, 34: 29–38.

Burkitt, I. (1998) *Social Selves*. London: Sage.

Burman, E. (2002) Gender, sexuality and power in groups, *Group Analysis*, 35: 540–59.

Buss, D.M. (1999) *Evolutionary Psychology: The New Science of Mind*. New York: Oxford University Press.

Butler, J. (1990) *Gender Trouble: Feminism and the Subversion of Identity*. New York: Routledge

Butler, J. (1995) Melancholy gender/refused identification, *Psychoanalytic Dialogues*, 5: 165–80.

Carter, D. (2002) Research and survive? A critical question for group analysis, *Group Analysis*, 35: 119–34.

Casement, P. (1985) *On Learning from the Patient*. London: Tavistock.

Chodorow, N. (1992) Heterosexuality as a compromise formation: reflections on the psychoanalytic theory of sexual development, *Psychoanalysis and Contemporary Thought*, 15: 267–304.

Cohen, S.L. (2005) Getting our affairs in order, in L. Motherwell and J. Shay (eds) *Complex Dilemmas in Group Psychotherapy*. New York: Brunner-Routledge.

Cohn, B.R. (2005) Creating the group envelope, in L. Motherwell and J. Shay (eds) *Complex Dilemmas in Group Psychotherapy*. New York: Brunner-Routledge.

Conlon, I. (1991) The effect of gender on the role of the female group conductor, *Group Analysis*, 24: 187–200.

Corbett, K. (1993) The mystery of homosexuality, *Psychoanalytic Psychology*, 10: 345–58.

Courville, T.J. and Keeper, C.S. (1984) The issue of sexuality in group psychotherapy, *Group*, 8(3): 35–42.

Covington, C. (1996) Purposive aspects of the erotic transference, *Journal of Analytical Psychology*, 41: 339–52.

Cox, M. (1988) *Structuring the Therapeutic Process: Compromise with Chaos*. London: Jessica Kingsley.

Cox, M. and Theilgaard, A. (1994) *Shakespeare as Prompter: The Amending Imagination and the Therapeutic Process*. London: Jessica Kingsley.

Craib (2001) Social theory for group therapists, *Group Analysis*, 34(1): 143–52.

Crespi, L. (1995) Some thoughts on the role of mourning in the development of a positive lesbian identity, in T. Domenici and R.C. Lesser (eds) *Disorienting Sexuality*. New York: Routledge.

Cunningham, R. (1991) When is a pervert not a pervert? *British Journal of Psychotherapy*, 8: 48–70.

Dalal, F. (1998) *Taking the Group Seriously*. London: Karnac.

David, C. (1971) *L'Etat Amoureux*. Paris: Petite Bibliotheque Payot.

Davies, D. and Neal, C. (1996) *Pink Therapy*. Buckingham: Open University Press.

Davies, J.M. (1998a) Between the disclosure and foreclosure of erotic transference – countertransference, *Psychoanalytic Dialogues*, 8(6): 747–66.

Davies, J.M. (1998b) Thoughts on the nature of desires: the ambiguous, the transitional, and the poetic, *Psychoanalytic Dialogues*, 8(6): 805–23.

Davies, J.M. and Frawley, M.G. (1991) Dissociative processes and transference-countertransference paradigms in the psychoanalytically oriented treatment of adult survivors of childhood sexual abuse, in S.A. Mitchell and L. Aron (eds) *Relational Psychoanalysis*. Hillsdale, NJ: The Analytic Press.

Denman, C. (2004) *Sexuality: A Biopsychosocial Approach*. London: Palgrave Macmillan.

Derrida, J. (1976) *Of Grammatology*, trans. G.C. Spivak. Baltimore, MA: Johns Hopkins University Press.

Dews, P. (1987) *Logics of Disintegration: Post-Structuralist Thought and the Claims of Critical Theory*. New York: Verso.

Dies, R.R. (1992) Models of group psychotherapy: sifting through confusion, *International Journal of Group Psychotherapy*, 42: 1–17.

Dimen, M. (1995) On 'Our Nature': Prologemenon to a relational theory of sexuality, in T. Domenici and R.C. Lesser (eds) *Disorienting Sexuality*. New York: Routledge.

Dollimore, J. (1999) *Death, Desire and Loss in Western Culture*. London: Penguin.

Domenici, T. (1995) Exploding the myth of sexual psychopathology: a deconstruction of Fairbairn's anti-homosexual theory, in T. Domenici and R.C. Lesser (eds) *Disorienting Sexuality*. New York: Routledge.

Domenici, T. and Lesser, R.C. (eds) (1995) *Disorienting Sexuality*. New York: Routledge.

Einhorn, S. (1999) Commentary on article by Eric Moss, *Group Analysis*, 32: 569–70.

Elias, N. (1978) *The History of Manners: the Civilizing Process*, vol. 1. Oxford: Basil Blackwell.

Elliott, B. (1986) Gender identity in group-analytic psychotherapy, *Group Analysis*, 19: 195–206.

Ellis, M.L. (1994) Lesbians, gay men and psychoanalytic training, *Free Associations*, 4: 501–17.

Fairbairn, W.R.D. (1946) The treatment and rehabilitation of sexual offenders, in W.R.D. Fairbairn (1951) *Psychoanalytic Studies of the Personality*. New York: Routledge.

Fairbairn, W.R.D. (1951) *Psychoanalytic Studies of the Personality*. London: Tavistock.

Fisher, H.E. (1998) Lust, attraction and attachment in mammalian reproduction, *Human Nature*, 9: 23–52.

Fonagy, P., Gergely, G., Jurist, E. and Target, M. (2002) *Affect Regulation, Mentalization and the Development of the Self*. New York: Other Press.

Foucault, M. (1981) *The History of Sexuality*, vol. 1. London: Pelican.

Foulkes, S.H. (1948) *Introduction to Group-Analytic Psychotherapy*. London: Maresfield Reprints.

Foulkes, S.H. (1972) Oedipus conflict and regression, in E. Foulkes (ed.) *Selected Papers of S.H. Foulkes*. London: Karnac.

Foulkes, S.H. (1964a) Concerning leadership in group-analytic psychotherapy, in S.H. Foulkes, *Therapeutic Group Analysis*. London: Maresfield Reprints.

Foulkes, S.H. (1964b) *Therapeutic Group Analysis*. London: Maresfield Reprints.

Foulkes, S.H. and Anthony, E.J. (1965) *Group Psychotherapy: The Psychoanalytic Approach*, 2nd edn. London: Pelican.

Freud, S. (1900) *On Dreams*, in J. Strachey and A. Freud (eds) (1974) *Standard Edition of the Complete Psychological Works of Sigmund Freud*, vol. 5. London: The Hogarth Press.

Freud, S. (1905) *Three Essays on the Theory of Sexuality*, in J. Strachey and A. Freud (eds) (1974) *Standard Edition of the Complete Psychological Works of Sigmund Freud*, vol. 7. London: The Hogarth Press.

Freud, S. (1920) *Beyond the Pleasure Principle*, in J. Strachey and A. Freud (eds) (1974) *Standard Edition of the Complete Psychological Works of Sigmund Freud*, vol. 18. London: The Hogarth Press.

Freud, S. (1921) Group Psychology and the Analysis of the Ego, in J. Strachey and A. Freud (eds) (1974) *Standard Edition of the Complete Psychological Works of Sigmund Freud*, vol. 18. London: The Hogarth Press.

Freud, S. (1922) *The Libido Theory*, in J. Strachey and A. Freud (eds) (1974) *Standard Edition of the Complete Psychological Works of Sigmund Freud*, vol. 18. London: The Hogarth Press.

Freud, S. (1923) *The Ego and the Id*, in J. Strachey and A. Freud (eds) (1974) *Standard Edition of the Complete Psychological Works of Sigmund Freud*, vol. 19. London: The Hogarth Press.

Freud, S. (1935) Letter published in the *American Journal of Psychiatry*, 107: 786.

Friedman, R.C. and Downey, J.I. (2002) *Sexual Orientation and Psychoanalysis*. New York: Columbia Press.

Frommer, M.S. (1995) Countertransference obscurity in the psychoanalytic treatment of homosexual patients, in T. Domenici and R.C. Lesser (eds) *Disorienting Sexuality*. New York: Routledge.

Galatzer-Levy, R.M. (2004) Chaotic possibilities: towards a new model of development, *International Journal of Psychoanalysis*, 85: 419–42.

Gans, J.S. and Weber, R.L. (2000) The detection of shame in group psychotherapy: uncovering the hidden emotion, *International Journal of Group Psychotherapy*, 50: 381–96.

Gay, P. (1988) *Freud – A Life for our Time*. London: Dent.

Gfaller, G.R. (1993) 'Figuration: the contribution of Norbert Elias to group analysis and the contribution of group analysis to the social sciences, *Group Analysis*, 26: 341–56.

Ghent, E. (1990) Masochism, submission, surrender, *Contemporary Psychoanalysis*, 26: 108–36.

Giddens, A. (1991) *Modernity and Self- identity: Self and Society in the Late Modern Age*. Stanford, CA: Stanford University Press.

Giddens, A. (1992) *The Transformation of Intimacy: Sexuality, Love and Eroticism in Modern Societies*. Cambridge: Polity Press.

Giraldo, M. (2001) Chaos and desire: the simple truth of the unconscious in the psychoanalytic group, *Group Analysis*, 34(3): 349–62.

Glasser, M. (1979) Some aspects of the role of aggression in the perversions, in I. Rosen (ed.) *Sexual Deviation*. Oxford: Oxford University Press.

Green, A. (1982) Moral narcissism, *International Journal of Psychoanalytic Psychotherapy*, 7: 243–69.

Green, A. (1986) *On Private Madness*. London: The Hogarth Press.

Greenson, R. (1964) On homosexuality and gender identity, *International Journal of Psychoanalysis*, 45: 217–19.

Hadar, B. (2004) Oedipus in group analysis, unpublished dissertation.

Hahn, W. K. (1994) Resolving shame in group psychotherapy, *International Journal of Group Psychotherapy*, 44: 449–61.

Halberstam, J. (1998) *Female Masculinity*. London: Duke University Press.

Halton, M. (1998) The group and the Oedipal situation, *Psychoanalytic Psychotherapy*, 12(3): 241–58.

Hamer, D. and Copeland, B. (1999) The gay gene, in R. Nye (ed.) *Sexuality – An Oxford Reader*. Oxford: Oxford University Press.

Hearst, L.E. (1995) Simultaneous supervision and personal analysis, part 1: supervisor, in M. Sharpe (ed.) *The Third Eye*. London: Routledge.

Hemmings, C. (2002) *Bisexual Spaces: a Geography of Sexuality and Gender*. London: Routledge.

Hiller. J. (2005) Sex, mind and emotion through the life course: a biopsychosocial perspective, in J. Hiller, H. Wood and W. Bolton (eds) *Sex, Mind and Emotion: Innovation in Psychological Theory and Practice*. London: Karnac.

Hiller, J., Wood, H. and Bolton, W. (eds) (2005) *Sex, Mind and Emotion: Innovation in Psychological Theory and Practice*. London: Karnac.

Hocquenghem, G. (1978) *Homosexual Desire*, trans. D. Dangoor. London: Allison & Busby.

Hodges, I. (2004) Homophobia, disgust and the body: towards a psychosocial approach to sexual prejudice, *Lesbian and Gay Psychology Review*, 5: 82–8.

Hoffman, I.Z. (1992) Expressive participation and psychoanalytic discipline, *Contemporary Psychoanalysis*, 28: 1–15.

Hoffman, I.Z. (1994) Dialectic thinking and therapeutic action in the psychoanalytic process, *Psychoanalytic Quarterly*, 63: 187–218.

Hopper, E. (1991) Encapsulation as a defence against the fear of annihilation, *International Journal of Psychoanalysis*, 72: 607–24.

Hopper, E. (1995) A psychoanalytical theory of 'drug addiction', *International Journal of Psychoanalysis*, 76: 1121–42.

Hopper, E. (1998) Introduction, in M. Pines, *Circular Reflections*. London: Jessica Kingsley.

Hopper, E. (2003a) *The Social Unconscious: Selected Papers*. London: Jessica Kingsley.

Hopper, E. (2003b) *Traumatic Experience in the Unconscious Life of Groups*. London: Jessica Kingsley.

Hopper, E. (2005) Getting our affairs in order, in L. Motherwell and J. Shay (eds) *Complex Dilemmas in Group Psychotherapy*. New York: Brunner-Routledge.

Hyde, K.R. (1991) Idealization and omnipotence within the group matrix, *Group Analysis*, 24: 279–97.

Irigaray, L. (1985) *This Sex Which is Not One*, trans. C. Porter. New York: Cornell University Press.

Irigaray, L. (1991) Women – mothers, the silent substratum of the social order, The bodily encounter with the mother, The limits of the transference, in M. Whitford (ed.) *The Irigaray Reader*. Oxford: Basil Blackwell.

Isay, R. (1991) The homosexual analyst, *Psychoanalytic Study of the Child*, 46: 199–216.

Kennedy, R. (2001) *Libido*. Cambridge: Icon Books.

Kernberg, O.F. (1995) *Love Relations*. New Haven, CT: Yale University Press.

Kinsey, A.C. and Pomeroy, W.B. (1949) *Concepts of Normality and Abnormality in Sexual Behaviour*.

Kreeger, L.C. (1992) Envy pre-emption in small and large groups, *Group Analysis*, 25: 391–412.

Kristeva, J. (1983) *Tales of Love*. New York: Columbia University Press.

Kumin, I. (1985) Erotic horror: desire and resistance in the psychoanalytic setting, *International Journal of Psychoanalytic Psychotherapy*, 11: 3–20.

Lacan, J. (1988a) *The Seminar of Jacques Lacan*, Book 1, trans. J.A. Miller and J. Forrester. Cambridge: Cambridge University Press.

Lacan, J. (1988b) *The Seminar of Jacques Lacan*, Book 2, trans. J.A. Miller and J. Forrester. Cambridge: Cambridge University Press.

Laplanche, J. (1970) *Life and Death in Psychoanalysis*, trans. J. Mehlman. Baltimore, MD: Johns Hopkins University Press.

Lasch, C. (1979) *The Culture of Narcissism*. New York: Warner.

Le Brun, A. (2001) Desire – a surrealist invention, in J. Mundy (ed.) *Surrealism: Desire Unbound*. London: Tate Publishing.

Lewis, H. (1971) *Shame and Guilt in Neurosis*. New York: International Universities Press.

Lichtman, R. (1982) *The Production of Desire: the Integration of Psychoanalysis into Marxist Theory*. New York: Free Press.

Limentani, A. (1989) Clinical types of homosexuality, in *Between Freud and Klein: The Psychoanalytic Quest for Knowledge and Truth*. London: Free Association Books.

Lomas, D. (2001) The omnipotence of desire: surrealism, psychoanalysis and hysteria, in J. Mundy (ed.) *Surrealism: Desire Unbound*. London: Tate Publishing.

Maccoby, E.E. (1998) *The Two Sexes: Growing Apart, Coming Together*. Cambridge, MA: Harvard University Press.

Magee, M. and Miller, D.C. (1995) Psychoanalysis and women's experience of 'coming out': the necessity of becoming a 'bee- charmer, in T. Domenici and C.L. Lesser (eds) *Disorienting Sexuality*. New York: Routledge.

Maguire, M. (2004) *Men, Women, Passion and Power*. London: Routledge.

Mann, D. (ed.) (2003) *Erotic Transference and Counter-Transference*. Hove: Brunner-Routledge.

Masson, J.M. (1984) *The Assault on Truth: Freud's Suppression of the Seduction Theory*. New York: Farrar Straus & Giroux.

Maturana, H. (1988) Reality: the search for objectivity or the quest for a compelling argument, *Irish Journal of Psychology*, 9: 25–82.

May, R. (1995) Re-reading Freud on homosexuality, in T. Domenici and R.C. Lesser (eds) *Disorienting Sexuality*. New York: Routledge.

McDougall, J. (1979) The homosexual dilemma: a clinical and theoretical study of female homosexuality, in I. Rosen (ed.) *Sexual Deviation*. Oxford: Oxford University Press.

McDougall, J. (1989) *Theatres of the Body*. London: Free Association Books.

Mead, G.H. (1934) *Mind, Self and Society, from the Standpoint of a Social Behaviourist*. Chicago: Chicago University Press.

Meltzer, D. (1973) *Sexual States of Mind*. Perthshire: Clunie Press.

Mitchell, J. (1982) Introduction 1, in J. Mitchell and J. Rose (eds) *Feminine Sexuality: Jacques Lacan and the Ecole Freudienne*. London: Macmillan.

Mitchell, S. (1996) Gender and sexual orientation in the age of postmodernism: the plight of the perplexed clinician, *Gender and Psychoanalysis*, 1: 45–74.

Moeller, M.L. (2002) Love in the group, *Group Analysis*, 35: 484–98.

Mohr, R. (1992) *Gay Ideas: Outing and Other Controversies*. Boston, MA: Beacon Press.

Mollon, P. (2003) *Shame and Jealousy*. London: Karnac.

Money, J. (1986) *Lovemaps: Clinical Concepts of Sexual/Erotic Health and Pathology, Paraphilia, and Gender Transposition in Childhood, Adolescence and Maturity*. New York: Irvington.

Moss, E. (1999) The hysterical group and the hysterical analyst, *Group Analysis*, 32: 559–68.

Motherwell, L. and Shay, J.J. (eds) (2005) *Complex Dilemmas in Group Psychotherapy*. New York: Brunner-Routledge.

Nicolosi, J. (1991) *Reparative Therapy of Male Homosexuality: A New Clinical Approach*. Northvale: Jason Aronson.

Nightingale, D.J. and Cromby, J. (1999) *Social Constructionist Psychology: a Critical Analysis of Theory and Practice*. Buckingham: Open University Press.

Nitsun, M. (1990) Sexual abuse as a theme in group-analytic psychotherapy, *Psychoanalytic Psychotherapy*, 5: 21–35.

Nitsun, M. (1991) The anti-group: destructive forces in the group and their therapeutic potential, *Group Analysis*, 24(1): 7–20.

Nitsun, M. (1994) The primal scene in group analysis, in D. Brown D. and L. Zinkin (eds) *The Psyche and the Social World*. London: Routledge.

Nitsun, M. (1996) *The Anti-group: Destructive Forces in the Group and their Creative Potential*. London: Routledge.

Nitsun, M. (1998) The organizational mirror: a group-analytic approach to organizational consultancy, part 1 – theory, *Group Analysis*, 31: 245–67.

Nitsun, M. (1999) Debating the anti-group, *Group Analysis*, 32: 418–26.

Nitsun, M. (2000a) The future of the group, *International Journal of Group Psychotherapy*, 50: 455–72.

Nitsun, M. (2002) The application of group work in the NHS, *Healthcare Counselling and Psychotherapy Journal*, 2: 30–3.

Nitsun, M. (2005) Destructive forces, in L. Motherwell and J. Shay (eds) *Complex Dilemmas in Group Psychotherapy*. New York: Brunner-Routledge.

Nitzgen, D. (1999) From demand to desire: what do we offer when we offer group-analytic training? *Group Analysis*, 32: 227–39.

O'Connor, N. (1995) Passionate differences: lesbianism, post-modernism, and psychoanalysis, in T. Domenici and R.C. Lesser (eds) *Disorienting Sexuality*. New York: Routledge.

O'Connor, N. and Ryan, J. (1993) *Wild Desires and Mistaken Identities*. London: Virago.

Panksepp, J. (1998) *Affective Neuroscience: the Foundations of Human and Animal Emotions*. New York: Oxford Universities Press.

Parin, P. and Morgenthaler, F. (1963) *Die Weiben denken zuviel*. Zurich: Atlantis.

Perls, F. (1972) *Gestalt Therapy Verbatim*. New York: Bantam.

Phillips, A. (1998) *The Beast in the Nursery*. London: Faber & Faber.

Pines, M. (1982) Reflections on mirroring, *Group Analysis*, 15 (supplement): 1–32.

Pines, M. (1987) Change and Innovation, decay and renewal in psychotherapy, *British Journal of Psychotherapy*, 4: 76–85.

Pines, M. (1995) The universality of shame: a psychoanalytic approach, *British Journal of Psychotherapy*, 11: 346–57.

Pines, M. (1998a) Psychic development and the group-analytic situation, in M. Pines, *Circular Reflections*. London: Jessica Kingsley.

Pines, M. (1998b) *Circular Reflections*. London: Jessica Kingsley.

Riggs, D.W. (2004) The politics of scientific knowledge: constructions of sexuality and ethics in the conversion therapy literature, *Lesbian and Gay Psychology Review*, 5: 6–14.

Roback, H.B., Ochoa, E., Bloch, F. and Purdon, S. (1992) Guarding confidentiality in clinical groups: the therapist's dilemma, *International Journal of Group Psychotherapy*, 42(1): 81–103.

Roberts, J. (1983) Foulkes concept of the matrix, *Group Analysis*, 15: 111–26.

Rose, C. (2002) Talking gender in the group, *Group Analysis*, 35: 525–39.

Rosenfeld, H. (1971) A clinical approach to the psycho-analytic theory of the life and death instincts: an investigation into the aggressive aspects of narcissism, *International Journal of Psychoanalysis*, 52: 169–77.

Ross, J.M. (1982) Oedipus revisited: Laius and the Laius complex, in *Psychoanalytic Study of the Child*, vol. 37. New Haven, CT: Yale University Press.

Ruszczynski, S. (1993) Thinking about and working with couples, in S. Ruszczynski (ed.) *Psychotherapy with Couples*. London: Karnac.

Rutkin, R. (1995) Psychoanalysis with gay and lesbian people, in T. Domenici and R.C. Lesser (eds) *Disorienting Sexuality*. New York: Routledge.

Ryan, M., Nitsun, M., Gilbert, L. and Mason, H. (2005) A prospective study of the effectiveness of group and individual psychotherapy for women

CSA survivors, *Psychology and Psychotherapy: Theory, Research and Practice*, 78(4): 465–79.

Samuels, A. (1985) Symbolic dimensions of Eros in transference-countertransference: some clinical uses of Jung's alchemical metaphor, *International Review of Psychoanalysis*, 12: 199–214.

Samuels, A. (1999) From sexual misconduct to social justice, in D. Mann (ed.) (2003) *Erotic Transference and Countertransference*. Hove: Brunner-Routledge.

Samuels, A. (2001) *Politics on the Couch: Citizenship and the Internal Life*. London: Profile Books.

Sandler, J. *et al.* (1970) Basic psychoanalytic concepts: eight special forms of transference, *British Journal of Psychiatry*, 117: 561–8.

Scanlon, C. (2000) The place of clinical supervision in the training of group-analytic psychotherapists, *Group Analysis*, 33: 394–415.

Scharff, D. (1982) *The Sexual Relationship: An Object Relations View of Sex and the Family*. London: Routledge & Kegan Paul.

Scharff, D. and Scharff, J.S. (1991) *Object Relations Couple Therapy*. New York: Jason Aronson.

Schaverien, J. (1995) *Desire and the Female Therapist: Engendered Gazes in Psychotherapy and Art Therapy*. London: Routledge.

Schlapobersky, J. (1994) The language of the group: monologue, dialogue and discourse in group analysis, in D. Brown and L. Zinkin (eds) *The Psyche and the Social World*. London: Routledge.

Schlapobersky, J. (1996) The group-analytic approach in forensic psychotherapy, in C. Cordess and M. Cox (eds) *Forensic Psychotherapy*. London: Jessica Kingsley.

Schwartz, D. (1995) Current psychoanalytic discourses on sexuality, in T. Domenici and R.C. Lesser (eds) *Disorienting Sexuality*. New York: Routledge.

Segal, H. (1993) On the clinical usefulness of the concept of the death instinct, *International Journal of Psychoanalysis*, 74: 55–62.

Seidler, G.H. (2000) *In Others' Eyes: An Analysis of Shame*. Madison, CT: International Universities Press.

Shilling, C. (1993) *The Body and Social Theory*. London: Sage.

Sklar, J. (1989) Gender identity – fifty years on from Freud, *British Journal of Psychotherapy*, 5: 370–80.

Socarides, C. (1968) *The Overt Homosexual*. New York: Grune & Stratton.

Socarides, C. (1995) *Homosexuality: A Freedom too Far*. Phoenix, AZ: Adam Margrave Books.

Spitzer, R.L. (2003) Can some gay men and lesbians change their sexual orientation? *Archives of Sexual Behaviour*, 32: 403–17.

Stacey, R.D. (2003) *Complexity and Group Processes*. Hove: Brunner-Routledge.

Stein, A. and Plummer, K. (1996) I can't even think straight: queer theory and the missing sexual revolution in sociology, in S. Seidman (ed.) *Queer Theory/Sociology*. Cambridge, MA: Blackwell.

Stern, D. (1985) *The Interpersonal World of the Infant*. New York: Basic Books.

Stoller, R.J. (1968) *Sex and Gender*. New York: Jason Aronson.

Stoller, R.J. (1975) *Perversion: the Erotic Form of Hatred*. New York: Delta.

Stoller, R.J. (1979) *Sexual Excitement: Dynamics of Erotic Life*. London: Maresfield Library.

Stoller, R.J. (1985) *Observing the Erotic Imagination*. New Haven, CT: Yale University Press.

Stone, E.G. (2001) Culture, politics and group therapy: identification and voyeurism, *Group Analysis*, 34(4): 501–14.

Thompson, A.E. (1991) Freud's pessimism, the death instinct, and the theme of disintegration, in Analysis terminable and interminable, *International Review of Psychoanalysis*, 28: 165–80.

Thomson, J. (1999) Eros: the connecting principle (or the complexities of love and sexuality), in D. Mann (ed.) (2003) *Erotic Transference and Countertransference*. Hove: Brunner-Routledge.

Throckmorton, W. (1998) Efforts to modify sexual orientation: a review of outcome literature and ethical issues, *Journal of Mental Health Counselling*, 20: 283–304.

Turner, B. (1996) *The Body and Society: Explorations in Social Theory*. London: Sage.

Tylim, I. (2003) Eroticism in group psychotherapy: psychoanalytic reflections on desire, agony, and ecstasy, *International Journal of Group Psychotherapy*, 53(4): 443–57.

Verhaeghe, P. (1999) *Love in a Time of Loneliness*. London: Rebus.

Volkan, D.V. and Ast, G. (1997) *Siblings in the Unconscious and Psychopathology*. Madison, CT: International Universities Press.

Waddell, M. and Williams, G. (1991) Reflections on perverse states of mind, *Free Associations*, 22: 203–13.

Warner, S. (2004) Contingent morality and psychotherapy research: developing applicable frameworks for ethical processes of inquiry, *BPS Psychotherapy Section Newsletter*, 36: 11–22.

Weber, R.L. and Gans, J.S. (2003) The group therapist's shame: a much undiscussed topic, *International Journal of Group Psychotherapy*, 53, 395–416.

Webster, R. (1995) *Why Freud was Wrong: Sin, Science and Psychoanalysis*. London: Fontana.

Weegmann, M. (forthcoming) Group analysis and homosexuality: difference, indifference and homophobia.

Weingarten, K. (1991) The discourses of intimacy: adding a social constructionist and feminist view, *Family Process*, 30: 285–305.

Weinstein, R. (1988) Should analysts love their patients? The resolution of transference resistance through transferential explorations, in J. Lasky and H. Silverman (eds) *Love: Psychoanalytic Perspectives*. New York: New York Universities Press.

Whitaker, D.S. (1985) *Using Groups to Help People*. London: Routledge & Kegan Paul.

Winnicott, D.W. (1963) The development of the capacity for concern, in D.W. Winnicott (1965) *The Maturational Processes and the Facilitating Environment*. New York: International Universities Press.

Wodak, R. (1986) *Language Behaviour in Therapy Groups*. Berkeley, CA: University of California Press.

Wouters, C. (1997) In-formalization and the civilizing process, in P.R. Gleichmann, J. Goudsblom, and H. Korte (eds) *Human Figurations: Essays for Norbert Elias*. Amsterdam: Sociologisch Tijdschrift.

Wouters, C. (1986) Formalization and informalization: changing tension balances in civilizing processes, *Theory, Culture and Society*, 3: 1–18.

Wrye, H.K. and Welles, J.K. (1994) *The Narration of Desire: Erotic Transferences and Counter-transferences*. Hillsdale, NJ: Analytic Press.

Yalom, I. (1985) *The Theory and Practice of Group Psychotherapy*. New York: Basic Books.

Zinkin, L. (1983) Malignant mirroring, *Group Analysis*, 16: 113–26.

INDEX